10/6

PHILOSOPHY OF RELIGION

THE TEACH YOURSELF BOOKS

PHILOSOPHY
OF RELIGION

by

H. D. LEWIS
M.A., B.Litt., D.D.

*Head of the Department of the History and Philosophy
of Religion in the University of London and
Dean of the Faculty of Divinity
Fellow of King's College, London*

THE ENGLISH UNIVERSITIES PRESS LTD
ST. PAUL'S HOUSE   WARWICK LANE
LONDON E.C.4

First printed 1965

PRINTED IN GREAT BRITAIN
FOR THE ENGLISH UNIVERSITIES PRESS LTD,
BY COX & WYMAN LTD, LONDON, READING AND FAKENHAM

TO

Major and Mrs. John Mostyn

PREFACE

This book sets out to be just what its title says. It is addressed mainly to those who are not very familiar with philosophy, and the chief purpose has been to help such persons to make their own way into the subject. To this end there is provided an indication of how philosophical problems about religion arise and of the main ways in which they are handled today. But it is not enough for the student to learn about the subject, he must be more actively engaged and think about the problems for himself as they present themselves. In this he will be helped, I trust, by the reading lists appended to each chapter. These are not of course exhaustive. Nor is it claimed that all the suggested reading should be done before proceeding to the next chapter. Some of the books mentioned will be already familiar to some of my readers. Others are books for extending one's knowledge and understanding later. But the fuller the use that is made of further reading, like that suggested as we proceed, the more is the student likely to become keenly aware of the import and significance of the questions he is invited to consider. He should then be able, having reached the point to which this book tries to take him, to proceed with profit on the way on his own and discover for himself what the next stage should be, bearing in mind the view of Plato that the true philosopher, once launched into his subject, is committed to it for the rest of his life.

At one or two points I have drawn upon material already published, and I am grateful for permission to reproduce passages already printed in *The London Quarterly and Holborn Review* and in my contribution to *The Saviour God* edited by S. G. F. Brandon. In the second half of the book I have also made considerable use of material which I prepared for my Cadbury Lectures given in the University of Birmingham in the winter of 1962.

Much of this book was written in the home of my very kind cousins, Miss H. M. Davies and Miss Margaret Davies, at Llandudno. Alas, since these words were penned one of these remarkable ladies, Miss H. M. Davies, has died. She had a profound sense of humour and great common sense, and she had an interest in other people that was spontaneous and easy. I do not believe she knew what malice meant. It is a great privilege to have known her and to pay her tribute.

I was also greatly helped, in the difficult times through which I passed when writing this book, by the unfailing kindness and resourcefulness of my friends Major and Mrs. John Mostyn of Guildford. It is with both pride and pleasure that this book is dedicated to them.

The whole of my book was read in typescript by my distinguished and learned colleague, Professor E. L. Mascall; and my friend Dr. D. A. Rees of Jesus College, Oxford subjected the entire work to a typically close and careful scrutiny before it went to the printer. The proofs were read for me by The Reverend Huw Parri Owen, also of King's College, and by Miss Ann Pinkerton, secretary to my department. Mr. Owen also made the Index. I am very grateful for this help and I also wish to express my warmest gratitude to Mr. Leonard Cutts of the English Universities Press for his patience and kindness during the long interval between my undertaking to write this book and the fulfilment of my promise.

H. D. LEWIS

CONTENTS

ix

CONTENTS

CHAPTER ONE

PHILOSOPHICAL QUESTIONS

Almost everyone asks philosophical questions — sooner or later. This does not mean that everyone is able to formulate these questions in a satisfactory way. That calls for much skill and experience. But it is none the less true that certain situations force upon us all the questions to which philosophers give close and systematic attention and whose status, as problems, occupies the minds of philosophers a great deal at present.

This may not be very plain in respect to the sort of questions which philosophers raise, in the subject usually known as Perception, about the nature of the physical or external world and its relation to ourselves. We are of course, all of us, curious about 'the world around us' and at times especially concerned about the constitution of the physical world. This interest comes in part from the desire to control our natural environment and exploit it for the provision of better amenities. The advances made in these ways in our time are astonishing, and there are few, if any, who can be indifferent to them. We all enjoy the products of modern invention, labour saving devices, cars, aeroplanes, television and so forth; and not even the most austere person can live any kind of normal life in the world of today without these. We have also a further, less agreeable, interest in modern inventiveness. For we also know well how these can be turned to our destruction, and at the moment one views with profound alarm the possibility of the total destruction of life as we know it in sudden atomic warfare. Even if the sense of helplessness, in the face of enormous perils, should make us for a time indifferent, that reaction itself discloses more than it disguises our initial concern.

I need not labour the obvious here. In more ordinary matters it is also a great advantage to be able to know how things work, to be able to repair a puncture or mend the car or the wireless set. There are many who still lack these accomplishments, but they would be the last to deny the importance for someone to have these skills. Nor is the interest in question merely utilitarian. It is agreeable in itself, and often exciting, to understand how things work, and this leads to a sense of power in manipulating things, driving a car, an aeroplane and so on. The generalized knowledge which lies behind the technological skills appeals strongly also to those who can appreciate it; and even those who cannot rise to strictly scientific understanding will usually be much interested in the general findings or tentative suggestions of scientists about the origin of life and its development on this earth, about the formation of the world, about the constitution of the solar system and of other systems of stars and planets in remoter regions of space, and about kindred matters near or remote.

About this sort of interest, then, there can be little doubt— it is widely enjoyed by the layman as well as the professional scholar. But this is also the interest which it is the business of science, rather than philosophy, to satisfy. It is a very different sort of question which the philosopher asks about the external world. His curiosity begins with features of the world which are common to all times and places, not with specific matters established by close observation and experiment. The main facts for him were as much within the reach of Greek or Indian philosophers of long ago as they are today. We observe, for example, that objects seem to vary much, in the way they present themselves to us at least, according to the conditions in which we observe them. The pillar-box looks small in the distance, and the dim blue mountains we view from the plains look green and rugged to those who climb their slopes. The round tower looks square against the sky-line, and the railway lines seem to taper in the distance. We all know that the rails are in fact parallel—there would soon be an accident if they were not. But how then do they seem so plainly to taper? The answer to this question is, at one level, a scientific one to be given in terms of the way light travels and the structure of our eyes and nervous system. But when all this has been noted, or, if you prefer, quite independently of its being noted, there remains the question of what we *seem* to see in these conditions. Can we be said to see the real rails when we seem to see something quite different from what we know the rails to be? Some have said we only see 'an appearance' of the rails. But we have also an equally firm impression that we are looking at 'the real thing'. If I look down on the rails from a bridge I feel sure that I see the real rails along which the train will go, and yet the train cannot go along the narrow lines I seem to see in the distance. Nor can I restrict this to what I see in the far distance, although that is what brings the problem out most sharply. There is a continuity of what I see below me and the more obviously converging lines far away. Even when the variation is in suspense or reversed (as it is within a few inches of our eyes) this does not reduce our perplexity. There are in any case other obvious variations which cut across those of size. The colours of things vary with the light, with the structures of our eyes, with the sort of spectacles we have on and so forth. Sounds vary in similar ways. A puff of smoke in a quarry is followed some time later by the sound of an explosion. But those who set off the fuse in the quarry will have heard the explosion almost at once. The sound they heard seems over and done with by the time we hear a sound. Do we hear the real sound or some duplicate of it, and when exactly, in the latter case, is the real sound heard? Some have maintained that we never strictly see or hear the real thing, but only a private copy or impression. But how in that case do we know what the real thing is like or how far our impressions of it are reliable clues? Others, like Berkeley, have sought to come to terms with common-sense by maintaining that what we seem to see is always the real world but that this world is dependent on being perceived and only seems to have more permanence than that because of the invariable and coherent way in which things occur in it.

This only touches the fringes of one of the most fascinating problems in the whole history of philosophy, and the student who is new to the subject would benefit much by acquiring the feel of a philosophical problem through study of some of the main views that have been held about a subject like

Perception. Suggestions for this purpose are appended to this chapter.

The ordinary person does not however trouble himself much about the problems of perception as they are raised by philosophers. He finds that the world is 'there' in a way that completely satisfies his purposes, and he is usually content to think no more about it. Many live their lives without ever being aware of there being the philosophers' problem; and when it is brought to their attention they treat it with little more than faint amusement. This is partly due to failure to grasp what it is that philosophers say, and the subject of perception is notoriously susceptible to entertaining tales and limericks which gently attempt to put the philosopher in his place. Everyone knows that the world 'is there', so why pretend; we should come to a sudden and sticky end if we went about assuming that nothing is real outside our own minds. This was in fact the last thing that Berkeley, for example, wished us to do. But misunderstanding is easy and it is also easy to get on with the work of the world without bothering much about problems that can have no direct bearing on the way we live and manage the world around us.

But even these problems of perception, divorced as they seem to be from any question of practice, are not altogether irrelevant to practical attitudes. Their ramification beyond their immediate context is indeed subtle, but it is not negligible. It makes a substantial difference to our general outlook to realize how much stranger the world is than we take it to be at first, whatever theory about it we finally adopt, and when we do take up some particular position it is likely to colour our views on other questions in many ways, even if this is not immediately perceptible. One could not easily agree with Berkeley without feeling somewhat differently about the world of nature, especially if we should find in Berkeley's arguments, as he did, reasons for supposing that God is very closely involved in the existence of natural things. For those who are more reflective, our views of other persons, and the sort of respect we owe one another, could also be affected in similar ways, as I shall hint a little more fully later.

The same thing happens more obviously when we turn to

other familiar features of the world—for example its being in space and time. Here again there seem to be quite simple matters which no one finds it hard to understand. We all know in one way what is meant by space and time. We can tell the time, and we are not in the least at a loss if we are informed that something happened half an hour ago, or this morning or long ago. Even idiots understand this, and anyone who could not understand it could not take his place at all as a responsible human being. Without the notions of 'sooner' and 'later' we could not make sense of any undertaking. In the same way we all understand 'above' and 'below', 'to the right', 'near and far', 'big and small', 'fat', 'round' and so on. And even if we forget the words we would have to use these notions in some elementary way to move about at all. There seems thus to be nothing more simple or more obviously a matter of common experience than space and time. In one sense they present no problem to anyone.

And yet, suppose you were asked, 'Just what then is this space (or time) which we all understand so well?' what would you say? You might say that space is that in which things have these relations of above and below, to the right, and so on. A number of objects, we might say, can be laid out in space. But what sort of thing is the space in which things are laid out, or in which they are adjacent to one another? It cannot be itself like some part of space. That is, things are not laid out *in* space in the same way as they might be laid out *in* a field. A field is just another part of space, bigger than any of the things we might deposit in it, and thus containing them, but much less than the neighbourhood in which it is located. Nor could we remedy this by supposing that space itself is some quite enormous container; for however big we make that it is still itself some part of space, and it could in turn be enclosed in a bigger area. But if things are *in* space in some quite different way from the way they are in a field, and a field in a county, just what sort of idea have we here? What is the space itself of which particular spaces are parts and in which things stand in spacial relations? Some are inclined to say that it is nothing, and that we should only think of particular things as being in certain relations to one another. But then they are distinctive relations, quite different from temporal ones. There seems to be some sense in which we must say that things are *in* space, the particular relations are conditioned in some way, they are what they are because of what space itself is. But if space is something over and above a particular thing 'in space', then it is certainly a most elusive something.

And so is time. For time itself is not a particular stretch of time. Today is a part of this year, and this year of this century. We might have some different method of counting, and on a different planet and or in a different solar system a day would be different. But all such relations or counting seem to be made possible by the fact of time. Time itself is not any method of telling time. We should not need such a method were it not for the fact of time itself with which we try to cope in this way. We can alter what we mean by 'a minute' or 'a second' but we cannot extend or reduce any stretch of time as such. We measure something which in some sense is there, and with which we have to cope very carefully. If we decide to pay no heed to time we shall soon know it. Time is real and not some convention with which we might dispense, but time is not just what happens now and what happened yesterday and so on. Now and yesterday are what they are because of time. These are events in time and stretches of time. But none of these, not even very long stretches of time, are time itself. There seems certainly to be more than the events which 'take time'. The events could be different, but the time the same. But then what is this time which seems to be more than the things which happen? If it is not itself something which happens, then what sort of thing could it be? It seems to be so elusive as to be nothing at all, but that goes altogether against the plainest and most inescapable experience of everyone.

There are other problems which arise here too, although we need to be a little more sophisticated to think of them. Thus: we all know what it means to say that something happened half an hour ago. That event and all like it are not 'over and done with'. They affect what happens now and will affect things in future. Their consequences, as we say, go on; and the past is real enough in this sense now; if it were not we

6

could make little sense of any situation. All the same what is over is over. The breakfast I had this morning is sustaining me now, but I am not now eating my breakfast—that was finished long ago and is only real now in a highly metaphorical sense. The memory of some pain I may have had may be very vivid to me now, but if I have had some injection to stop it, it is not a pain I am suffering now, indeed no pain I have now, however like and continuous with a past pain, is the pain I had before. Likewise, the future *will* be real, and I know there is no escaping this. Coming events cast their shadows, as we say, and I may be much elated or depressed by impending events. If I am told that I am to have a painful operation tomorrow I may be worried and dismayed today, but the mental pain I suffer now (or the induced physical pain) is not the suffering I shall undergo tomorrow. That has still to happen, and perhaps it will not happen, however 'real' to me now 'in anticipation'. In short, the future, however much it (or the thought of it) may in some sense affect us now, is not yet real, it is still 'to come'. But this holds of what will happen in a minute as well as tomorrow, and *mutatis mutandis*, the events of a few seconds ago are as much over as the death of Julius Caesar. They may matter more to me now and be very vivid in my thoughts, but they are not real any more. When the clock strikes twelve, the stroke of one (and indeed of eleven), is over. But where do we stop in this business? The past is not real, the future is not yet real; only the present is real. But just what is the present? If we exclude what happened a minute ago, we must say the same of a second ago, and of a split second and of the very slightest instant. But in this way we seem in danger of shutting out the present altogether, it becomes just a point, or a line of division between past and future. What seemed most real is least real, and we seem in danger of saying that nothing at all is real —which seems plainly absurd.

Some philosophers have tried to cope with this in terms of what they call 'a specious present',[1] that is a present which

1. There is a well-known statement of this doctrine in the *Principles of Psychology* by William James, and a brief discussion in the *Idea of God* by Pringle-Pattison, Chapter XVIII. The topic is discussed by C. D. Broad in

contains some past and future within itself, in very minute stretches. Its relation to the past has sometimes been compared to a boat moving ahead of its wake. But this is an exceptionally difficult notion to present, and although it has been much discussed from time to time, it involves very great difficulties of which its advocates have been acutely aware. But if we do not accept some solution of this kind, what are we to say? The problem is plainly not just some trivial conundrum. Some very great minds have been exercised over it, and some have been seriously led to the conclusion that time is not real. There are of course other reasons which have induced some philosophers to hold that view, and we cannot pause to consider them here. But what I want to show is that you do not have to be an out-and-out mystery-monger, or a crank or a person who lays claim to some quite extraordinary 'out of this world' experience, to be led to such a curious and apparently preposterous conclusion as that time is not real. You can be led to this position by just thinking about our common experience or the phenomena we usually describe by 'the passage of time'.

My aim here is not to persuade anyone that time is not real—I am far from thinking that myself, and it is evident that no one (even the contemplative who seems most detached from ordinary human affairs) can go about his business in the world without taking account of time. But there seems to be all the same a very real and most perplexing problem, and it is worth our noting that some of the thinkers who have been led to hold surprising views about it are those who, far from being dreamy obscurantists, have, as in the case especially of Spinoza, had the greatest confidence in reason—just as it was the clear-headed and fine stylist Berkeley who did so much to stir up doubts about the way we normally think of the world around us. We begin to be philosophers when we find ourselves puzzled in the ways I have outlined, and in passing moments at least I suspect that most persons find themselves caught up in these perplexities in some way. The problems,

The Mind and its Place in Nature, p. 267, etc.; and in a very comprehensive way by J. D. Mabbott in 'Our Direct Experience of Time' in _Mind_, Vol. LX.

in short, appear to be genuine problems, they seem to come directly at us out of what our common experience is like; and the more we are mentally alert the more unavoidable such problems appear to be. They are not due to some oddity or quirk of our thoughts to be shrugged aside with a smile. The more we think about them the more perplexing they become, and we ourselves become properly philosophical when such questions get a real hold on our minds so that we feel we must go on doing something about them if only understand better just what sort of questions they are.

In passing moments, I suspect, most persons feel something of this kind of philosophical perplexity. They may wonder about their own identity or memory or the insides of things. We know roughly what a piece of wood or a stone would look like if we cut it open, but it is very hard to think that it could be like that through and through all the time. But then what is the solid bulk of an object inside, and what sort of answer can we really expect to this kind of question? Most persons however manage to pass these awkward questions by lightly when they do arise, and in this they follow the precept given in one place at least by one of the most famous of all philosophers, David Hume. When his problems, and the sceptical conclusions to which he felt he had to come, overwhelmed him he would turn to backgammon or some kindred familiar pursuit and forget about it all. There is shrewd sense in this. No one should attempt to be sharply philosophical all the time. The world is certainly a very odd place, much more so than we normally suppose. But it does not do to have this in mind all the time, for the world is also such that it imposes itself upon us in certain ways which it is best to take at their face value for ordinary purposes. To get about our normal purposes it is best to take things as they usually seem to be.

This is also a help to the philosophical pursuit itself. Good work in philosophy does indeed require sustained and very trying concentration, and great philosophers have been very dedicated people. But it is also wise to stand away from the problems at times and get the feel of the facts from which they arise and see things in the right perspective and proportions. We may otherwise find ourselves spinning rather fanciful webs of our own out of relation to the situation in which the problems arise. This is the strength of the plea often made, and made very forcibly of late as we shall see, that we should be down to earth and matter of fact. This plea can also become onesided and inhibiting. For as we have seen there are very peculiar features which the world and our experience of it seem to present. We may miss them if we are too determined to be commonplace. There seems to be needed a balance between the point of view of common experience, the starting point and anchor of sound philosophy, and the complexities of more sophisticated reflection.

It is in the latter however that philosophy is found and it becomes important for us when we find ourselves provoked and challenged by features of the world which induce us to revise our day-to-day impressions of it and consider the sort of perplexities of which I have been giving some examples. One of the great advances made in philosophy happened when Socrates (and Plato[1] after him) gained a particularly clear picture of the sort of question the philosopher asks and of ways of making other people see how important and fascinating such questions could be. This is part at least of what Socrates meant in the celebrated statement that the life that is not examined is not worth living; and this is why we find today that there are few, if any, better introductions to what philosophy is really like than those parts of the dialogues of Plato in which he sets out to make his contemporaries conscious of the sort of perplexities in which philosophy begins and the questions it asks. Some suggestions are given at the end of Chapter V about ways in which the student may sample such writings. He will find it a great advantage to do so at an early stage if he is new to the subject.

FURTHER READING

The following books provide excellent general introductions to philosophy:

An Introduction to Philosophy. W. A. Sinclair (Oxford).

1. See the books suggested for further reading at the end of Chapter V.

The Problems of Philosophy. Bertrand Russell (Williams and Norgate).

Philosopher's Quest. Irwin Edman (The Viking Press).

The Fundamental Problems of Philosophy. A. C. Ewing (Kegan Paul).

A somewhat more difficult book, but one which the reader will find it exceptionally rewarding to study carefully is:

Some Main Problems of Philosophy. G. E. Moore (Allen and Unwin).

This book, like *The Problems of Philosophy*, by Russell, is a philosophical work of outstanding importance as well as a fine introduction to the subject.

Those who wish to make a more thorough study of the problems of perception should go on to a work of established importance by H. H. Price, namely *Perception* (Methuen), and then proceed to a more recent book which both reviews the state of the subject today and makes important contributions to it, namely *The Problems of Perception*, by R. J. Hirst (Allen and Unwin). An earlier book which the student is likely to find particularly helpful, although parts of it are difficult for the beginner, is *A Prolegomena to an Idealist Theory of Knowledge*, by N. Kemp Smith (Macmillan).

CHAPTER TWO

SOME LIMIT PROBLEMS AND ETHICS

I have already instanced some peculiarities of space and time
which induce philosophical wonderment about them. But
both of these present further perplexing features which bring
us a little closer to our special concerns in the philosophy of
religion. Some note of these may be taken now. They concern
questions of beginning and end. It is a straightforward matter
to think of a beginning and end of some particular stretch of
time or expanse of space, however vast. But it is very hard to
put any limit to time itself. It seems to be unlimited or
infinite. But this is also an extremely difficult notion to handle.
The Greek philosophers disliked it intensely. They were apt
to say that 'evil is of the infinite'. We know where we are with
something that has form and limit, we can at least hope to
understand it. But that which has no form or structure goes
beyond the grasp of reason altogether, it is at odds with the
harmony and shape on which the significance and worth of
things depend so much. We do not feel at home with things
which seem to bedevil our reason itself. On the other hand it is
hard to avoid something of this kind when we let our thoughts
stray to the very edges of the sort of experience we have, and
this comes out sharply in thought about space or time. We
may cover up the problem by using words like 'for ever' or
'always' or 'without end'. But what do these words mean here?
What sense is there in saying that time has always been going
on or will go on for ever? These are themselves terms which
seem to presuppose time, and it is a moot point whether it
makes sense at all to think of time as having always been or
never having had a beginning. But time seems all the same
real enough. It is not something we impose on things, a convention we could set aside, it belongs to the real world and
we have to cope with it. On the other hand how can we set
any limit to time or think as we would have to in that case, of

a first moment? Must there not have been a time before that and so on *ad infinitum* again? There seems to be no end to perplexity, we seem equally bewildered however we view the problem; and the problem is not a manufactured one to be set aside with a smile. It seems to come at us again directly from what we find to be a quite basic and unavoidable feature of all our experience.

This is not the place to pursue this particular question further. We shall return to it or at least to the sort of general puzzlement which it involves. But it will be a very good exercise for the student of the philosophy of religion to set himself asking at this stage just what he is to make of the sort of problem which has just been set before him. Perhaps he could discuss it with his friends and discover whether it strikes them as a genuine problem at all. Is there any prospect of solving this kind of problem? What do we gain by asking it? The peculiarity of it is that it does not seem to admit of even provisional or tentative answers, as seems to be the case when we ask questions about perspectival distortions or what sort of thing time is in distinction from particular occurrences. We might agree with Berkeley about perception—or sharply disagree. There is here some solution proffered, and it is only one of many. We may ask which is the most plausible, or devise a new one, or some refinement of old ones, ourselves. But the oddity of questions about the first moment of time and so on is that it does not seem possible to start setting out an answer. We seem to have a genuine problem posed by what the world is like, but a problem which also seems to stun our reason or go altogether beyond its grasp. For this the name 'limit problem' has sometimes been used, although that term has also been used in other ways. The more real such problems become for us the more dizzy we feel, we seem to be caught up in utter perplexity with no way out; and this is the sort of dizziness which the philosopher, as Plato was fond of stressing, must be prepared to endure at times if he is to meet the challenge of his problems in a wholehearted way.

With these limit problems we also come very close to religion, as will be stressed again in due course. And that is why I urge the student to be turning them over in his mind at this stage and considering what he is to make of them. But in the meantime it will be well to drop down from these rather dizzy heights and seemingly distant problems to some matters which again appear to be close at hand and to be part and parcel of our lives from day to day. These are the distinctions of good or bad, right or wrong, which in some way we seem to be making all the time, although not always explicitly.

Nothing appears simpler than the words 'good' and 'bad'. We use them all the time, the least reflective as well as the most sophisticated person. They have many synonyms like 'worth' or 'value' and the less literary or more slangy terms we use often, 'the goods', 'it', 'all right', 'O.K.', 'something' wrong un', 'square', to say nothing of the many signs or gestures we use in the same way, applause, the hearty handshake, boos and gestures of contempt, the light in the eye, the nod of approval and the well-nigh infinite variety of these. We are most unlikely to agree with all that is conveyed in these ways. But we are not usually puzzled in the least as to what is meant. Children and idiots seem to know quite well what is meant by 'good' and 'bad' and their equivalents. Our friends would be most perturbed if we seemed not to understand what such simple words meant, they would doubt our sanity. Good and bad are distinctions which in some way meet us at every turn, there is nothing we can do without in some way implying them.

But even here nothing is quite as simple as it seems. On the contrary perplexities abound, and he must be a very dull person who is not made aware of them in some fashion sooner or later. They have caused very sharp and sometimes even bitter and impassioned controversy. Take one of the more serious uses of the word 'good', as when we say that X is a very good man or has done some very fine deed. What do we mean when we say these things? You might reply that we are saying that X is a most considerate person, that he has regard for other people's feelings and makes himself helpful, that his word can be trusted and that he will not be daunted by danger and so on; or we may say of X's deed that it showed courage and willingness to sacrifice himself for others. But is this strictly what we mean by the use of 'good'? Have I not rather been listing the sort of things we have in mind as entitling a person to be deemed good, the sort of things *because* of which a person is good? If so we mean something further by the word 'good' itself, we imply that considerate action and regard for others are things to which goodness belongs or by which it is earned.[1] But what is this goodness which considerate action or dauntlessness seem to have, and what is the badness of ruthless self-seeking? Is there anything to which we can point beyond the characteristics of conduct or character by which we describe these? When we have said that the action was considerate and kindred things what more is there which the word good conveys? Do we strictly need such a word?

It seems hard to say that we can dispense with a word which is in such common use. Nor does it seem enough to say that it is a helpful way of holding together such qualities as thoughtfulness for others or disregard of danger. For why should we want to hold these together unless there is something which characterizes them all? But what could this be? What sort of thing can we ascribe to an action which is not part of the description of the action? This familiar attribute of goodness begins in this way to be very elusive indeed and appears to be in danger of slipping from our grasp altogether and becoming 'aery nothing'.

One common way of dealing with this situation has been to think of goodness, not as a quality strictly belonging to actions or persons, but as interpretable in terms of the reactions of other people to them. But who are the people whose reactions are to count? Any person whatsoever? But surely some persons may be wrong and their reactions not appropriate. A body of experts? But are they not fallible? Society? But who speaks for society, and do not its standards change? Are they not notoriously fluid today? And do we not in any case find ourselves persisting in thinking that goodness must somehow belong expressly to the good deed or person, irrespective of our recognizing it or applauding the deed or person and even when we or our society are averse to doing so? Is not goodness

1. Plato brought out this point early in a discussion of goodness in the *Meno* and made a similar point about the definition of knowledge in the *Theaetetus*.

something more than we ourselves make it, by our attitudes or in any other fashion, does it not shine in the actions which have it? But 'shine' is a metaphor, and for what?

Nor is this a difficulty which just affects our meditative attitudes, as will be largely the case for the problems of perception for example. It may greatly affect our practice and our attitudes to one another. This is why such problems have a particular urgency at times, especially when standards of worth are uncertain or menaced in some way. For may we not be led to suppose that good and bad are distinctions which have no ultimate status and need not be taken very seriously after all?

This tendency is sharply accentuated when we turn from the general nature or meaning of goodness, which could be taken to be mainly at least the problem of very sophisticated persons, to the practical perplexities which sooner or later confront us all, especially today. There have indeed been thinkers who have denied that there are moral perplexities. Even Kant, the most famous and influential thinker of the centuries we know as the 'Modern Period',[1] seemed to think this. It was affirmed in so many words by T. H. Green[2] in the nineteenth century, although he was not unaware of the difficulties. But it is astounding to me that anyone should have been as confident as this about the possibility of always knowing what we ought to do. The nineteenth century was a period of great confidence and optimism. But there were very grave practical and social problems in those days as now, slavery, the poverty exposed by Dickens, educational reform and so on; and as was shown in a novel which stirred people up a great deal in its day, tame though it may seem to us, namely *Robert Elesmere*, there was far from general agreement about the way to deal with them. We are certainly not unaware of problems today, sex, the colour bar, capital punishment, censorship, the very grave issues of war and peace and the use of atomic power. It is by no means plain what should be done about these, and it is not surprising that they should provoke very sharp differences of opinion. These are brought vividly to light by events like the

1. From about A.D. 1500 to the present day.
2. *Prolegomena to Ethics*, Book IV.

Suez crisis, and it will certainly not do in a case of this sort to invoke T. H. Green's principle that if we are honest and mean well the way forward will define itself clearly for us. We certainly need to do more than mean well.

This holds also of more personal problems, like the famous dilemmas of doctors or the problems of persons in occupied countries. Nor is anyone, even in fairly normal circumstances, likely to avoid such dilemmas altogether. We are all caught up sometimes in matters of moment where it is very unclear what we ought to do. Our friends, or others whose advice we may seek, may be equally uncertain. What then shall we say of these situations and of the many discordant voices which assail our ears? It is not surprising that some should wonder whether there is such a thing as a right course of action beyond our own preferences or the shifting rules and conventions of our society; and that can have repercussions, in my view serious ones, in practice.

Another very important aspect of these problems of practice presents itself when we consider the praise or blame we bestow on one another and the remorse we may feel on our own account if we do wrong. We feel that we are to blame for some things, and we denounce certain actions for their meanness, spitefulness, cowardice and so on. We praise others. But we are also told, especially by some psychologists today, that what we do at any time depends on the way we have been 'conditioned' in the past, perhaps in our infancy. We do not blame people if it seems that they cannot help what they do—if you tread on my toe because you have been pushed unexpectedly in a crowd it would be boorish of me not to accept your explanation, and if the bank clerk was held up at gun point we could hardly blame him for not stopping the burglars. But where does this extenuation stop? If what I do depends on the sort of person I am, and if this is determined by heredity, conditioning and environment and so on, should we continue to praise or blame one another and deem ourselves responsible? We certainly do count on one another to act 'in character', we anticipate what people will do. In religious contexts we sometimes say 'There but for the grace of God go I', or we speak of divine providence as shaping our

17

destinies. But in that case it is hard to see how our actions can also be free; but if we are not free how can we be responsible? Are we to say that praise and blame are merely social devices to ensure conformity with agreed standards and conventions, and that the allegedly guilty person only needs treatment, not condemnation or punishment in the strict sense? Many certainly do say this today. Others of us feel that something very vital is in jeopardy here. We should hate to feel that we are not free and accountable creatures.

This is not the point at which to go further into these very old problems of freedom, guilt, predestination and so forth. We shall meet them all again. My concern now, as earlier in the chapter, is simply to show how inevitably, in a way that we do not have to contrive at all, such questions as freedom and responsibility arise from what we normally feel and think. It is very hard for anyone not to feel the pressures of those problems at times, however easy it may be also to turn aside from them or seek escape in facile and muddled solutions. The sort of things we say from day to day throws these problems sharply into the front of our own lives—'you must remember the poor home he had', 'what can you expect when religion is in such a decline?', 'I blame the teachers', 'something came over me', 'I am liable to these fits of temper', 'I had not slept very well', 'that is the sort of little girl I am, Mummy' (said by a precocious child to her parents recently). We also say: that was 'detestable', 'vile', 'wicked', he is 'a scoundrel', 'a dreadful blighter', 'a bounder', and so on. We have surely to make some sense of this. But how?

These questions may be driven underground, perhaps with more serious effects than we realize. But those who are not willing to chain their minds or to immerse and lose themselves wholly in the daily round (and can anyone do that all the time?) will find these problems returning to trouble their peace—and also to fascinate them. Once the barb of a philosophical problem has struck us we find that it is hard to be rid of it, like the poor beast in Virgil's *Aeneid*:

> So when the watchful shepherd, from the blind,
> Wounds with a random shaft the careless hind;
> Distracted with her pain she flies the woods,

18

Bounds o're the lawn, and seeks the silent floods
With fruitless care; for still the fatal dart
Sticks in her side, and ranckles in her heart.[1]

Some of us are more fortunate in being able to give more of
our time to these problems than others, to study in more
detail what others have thought of them and follow their
more intricate courses. But in doing so they are only carrying
out in a more recondite and sophisticated manner what most
people are apt to do from time to time in more rudimentary
ways; and without the interests which make them do so life
would lose much of its point and savour. Even when we falter
most and remain most uncertain what solution, if any, we
prefer, there is much satisfaction and enrichment of experience in seeing more clearly what the issues involve. But this
does not mean that it is a matter of indifference whether we
arrive at the truth or not—quite the reverse. Without love
of the truth the enterprise is not worth beginning.

The issues to which I have just been alluding are usually
denoted by the term 'ethics', and it is in a book on ethics that
they can be properly and closely discussed. I much urge readers
who are new to the subject to consult some helpful introductory book on ethics at this stage, for example the excellent
Teach Yourself Ethics, by Dr. A. C. Ewing. This will help us
greatly later, for while we cannot discuss ethical questions in
detail we shall have to take account of them in due course.
For questions concerning the good life and moral obligations lie very close to the heart of religion. This will be plain
to all and is evident in what has already been said.

FURTHER READING

The student who is prepared to tackle a somewhat difficult work,
but one which is also very clearly written, will find a very suggestive
treatment of the type of question raised in the first part of this
chapter in Chapters I–III of C. A. Campbell's *Sceptism and Construction* (Allen and Unwin). The notion of 'limit problems' is given
much prominence in the work of a well-known philosopher of
today, namely Karl Jaspers. One of his best books, and certainly

1. *Aeneid*, Book IV. Dryden's translation.

the one to be recommended most confidently at this stage, appeared in an English translation under the title *Man in the Modern Age* (Routledge). This stimulating work is very relevant to the problems of today. There is an admirable short guide to the work of Jaspers, entitled *Guide to the Thought of Karl Jaspers*, by E. L. Allen (Hodder and Stoughton).

The ethical questions mentioned in this chapter are discussed at various levels in the books listed next. They will prepare the student also for the topics considered in Chapters Seventeen, Twenty-one, Twenty-two and Twenty-three, and the list is rather long for that reason. An excellent general introduction to ethical problems is another volume in the present series, namely *Teach Yourself Ethics* by A. C. Ewing. The Penguin *Ethics*, by P. A. Nowell-Smith, approaches these problems from a different standpoint and provides an admirable complementary work to that by Ewing. A student who has paid close attention to these two books should have a good notion of the different ways in which ethical problems are treated today. The objectivist position favoured by Ewing is defended also in fairly simple terms in *The Theory of Morals*, by E. F. Carritt (Oxford) and in Ewing's *The Definition of Good*—see especially Chapters I and II (Macmillan). The more ambitious student may then go on to more difficult, but outstanding books, namely G. E. Moore's *Ethics* (Home University Library) and his *Principia Ethica* (Cambridge) and W. D. Ross' *The Foundations of Ethics* (Oxford). *Principia Ethica* is already a classic in the subject and C. D. Broad said of Ross' *Foundations of Ethics* that it was 'much the most important contribution to ethical theory made in England for a generation'. Broad's *Five Types of Ethical Theory* (Routledge) will provide some of the historical background to the works already mentioned, and in A. N. Prior's *Logic and the Basis of Ethics* (Oxford) will be found a very careful assessment of how some of the main arguments in *Principia Ethica* stand in the light of subsequent comment, including that of Moore himself. A very different approach to ethical questions, and one more in the fashion at the moment than the type of objectivist ethics favoured by Ewing and, as it happens, myself, is represented in Chapter VI of A. J. Ayer's *Language, Truth and Logic* (Gollancz) and in *Ethics and Language*, by Charles Stevenson (Yale University Press). A position to which many are drawn today—it may be roughly described as a 'commitment theory of ethics'—is set out in a well-known book by R. M. Hare, *The Language of Morals* (Oxford). A highly selective survey of recent ethics, but very illuminating on the particular writers treated, is Mary Warnock's *Ethics Since 1900* (Oxford). A very notable critical survey of the course of recent and contemporary ethical thought, centred on the question of objectivity on which sharply opposed views are advanced in the books I have listed, is to be found in Brand Blanshard's *Reason and Goodness* (Allen and Unwin), a very solid work as remarkable for its penetration as for its lucidity.

The question of moral responsibility is the theme of the following works: *Ethics*, edited by Milton K. Munitz (Free Press), is a selection of readings in ethics and section V of it is devoted to the problem of freedom and responsibility; it has papers presenting very different views of the subject. A similar work is *Readings in Ethical Theory*, by Sellars and Hospers (Appleton Century Crofts). A good general discussion of responsibility, in a religious as well as an ethical and legal context is that of Walter Moberly in his Riddell Lectures *Responsibility* (Oxford). A modified form of determinism, the position known as self-determination, had a classical presentation in F. H. Bradley's *Ethical Studies*, Chapter I (Harry King and Co.) and is defended also in Ross' *Foundations of Ethics*, Chapter X. The libertarian position had a notable exponent in Nicolai Hartmann's *Ethics*, Volume III, but its best known defender today is C. A. Campbell in his *Scepticism and Construction*, Chapters IV and V (Allen and Unwin), his *In Defence of Free Will*, his *Selfhood and Godhood* (Allen and Unwin) and other writings. A very different view of the question is taken by Nowell-Smith in Chapter XIX of his *Ethics* and this takes us a long way towards the views of sociologists who tend to question the soundness of the very notion of responsibility. Barbara Wootton inclines to the latter position in her gifted *Social Science and Social Pathology*, Part II (Allen and Unwin). A sharp reaction to this type of position is found in 'Freewill and Punishment', by J. D. Mabbott printed in *Contemporary British Philosophy*, Series III, Edited by H. D. Lewis (Allen and Unwin).

The more the reader can study the sort of book listed above the more prepared will he be for the discussions which come later in this volume. But the reading suggested here is not strictly presupposed at any stage.

CHAPTER THREE

METAPHYSICS

Closely allied to the ethical questions we have been noting, but more wide-ranging and somewhat less precise, is a further type of question which most people feel impelled to ask at times, questions about the worth or point of our lives as a whole. We may find ourselves asking, for example, 'what are we in the world *for*?' 'has life any meaning?' or, a little more crudely perhaps in moments of despondency, 'what is the good of it all?' People protest against their ill fortunes: 'Why has this to happen to me?'; and in extreme despair they may say things like 'I did not ask to be born' or 'why must this always be happening?' This presupposes that we can look for some justification for the way things are or that there is someone (or something) with whom the protest may be lodged. We are apt also to offer answers to these questions, ranging from superstitions and 'old sayings' to more considered reflections. After a fine summer we say 'We shall pay for this', or the soldier may say of his fallen mate that the bullet 'had his number on it'. The optimist will say 'Every cloud has a silver lining', or 'it is all for the best'. We may also be more precise and say that 'we are in the world to help one another' or, with Keats and some celebrated thinkers after him, that life is 'a vale of soulmaking'. In these ways we seem to be trying to make sense of things in general.

The attempt to do this may reflect subtle, if not very systematic or deliberate, observation of the way things happen. This appears true of much that we say about the weather, unreliable though it is. In other cases the explanation may be much deeper or hidden in the mists of times and habits far removed from our own. The anthropologist will have much light to throw on them. But behind much that we ask and say in these somewhat unco-ordinated ponderings there lies some expectation that we can make sense of things, not over a passing phase, but as a whole, that there is some clue to what the world and the lot of men in it are like, some main principle or overriding purpose perhaps.

There are some occasions which induce us more than others to wonder in these ways, in particular perhaps some grave misfortune, disappointment or bereavement. When brought sharply face to face with death, in the loss of a close relative or friend, we are apt to ask 'Can this life be all?', 'Is there anything after this?', or we may say that such a fine life 'can never be lost' or 'lived in vain'. It is hard for anyone to avoid wondering about such things altogether.

When such wondering takes a sustained and deliberate form, and is carried out with skill and understanding, it becomes the branch of philosophy we have mainly in mind when we use the word 'metaphysics'. There are other uses of this word. In its broader use it may extend to questions about any matters which seem to go beyond what we directly encounter in experience of the world around us, questions like the ones listed above about the way time is more than particular events in time or about some material world which may lie beyond what we actually see or observe. The question whether there is some principle of goodness or duty not accounted for wholly by events in nature and our own reactions would be metaphysical in this sense, and thus we find a philosopher like G. E. Moore, who could be very vigorously opposed to much of the more speculative kind of metaphysics, propounding, in his ethical theories, a view which is boldly metaphysical (and denounced as such by many today) in the broader sense.

It is in speculative thinking, in the attempt to form worldviews, to consider whether the world as we find it is related to anything beyond that and in what way, to consider whether there is some unity which holds all things together and what its nature may be and how it may be known, if it can be—this is where we find metaphysics of the fullblown kind, metaphysics *par excellence*. The conclusions of such metaphysics may sometimes be negative or sceptical, at other times very bold claims are made. There is in other ways a great variety of speculative metaphysics, some offering elaborate, colourful, and sometimes most exciting, suggestions about what the universe as it extends beyond our normal ken is like. Others put forward some one main notion, like 'a Life Force' or some principle of inevitable change or evolution, and some turn more than others to expressly religious ideas. It is evident that religion is never very far from speculative metaphysics, and we shall have to ask some metaphysical questions of this sort in this book before long.

It should be evident also that metaphysics presents many traps for the unwary and the over-bold. Once we pass beyond the range of ordinary disciplines and look beyond the normal tests of experience, fantasy may easily take charge. It needs a good deal of skill and experience to distinguish genuine metaphysics from bogus; the charlatan and the impostor can easily have their way with us if we are not careful in this field. So much so that many have come to the conclusion today, as others have done in the past, that there is something bogus or improper about the metaphysical enterprise as such, most of all in its speculative form. Some maintain that the questions raised in metaphysics are not genuine questions at all, that the answers are not just beyond us but essentially unobtainable, that we are somehow bemusing ourselves in supposing that the questions make any sense. This is in fact a natural reaction against some of the extravagant and sometimes muddled and obscurantist things which have been said in the name of metaphysics and the irritating tendency of some metaphysical thinkers to set themselves beyond the range of critical discussion or to exploit the obvious difficulties of their subject, and the need of some adventurousness, and thus proceed in disregard of the sort of discipline which the subject does allow. There has certainly been some extreme abuse of metaphysical privilege, and it is hard to persist in trying to make sense of some abstruse notion if we have the thought at the back of our minds that we are perhaps being imposed upon after all. But grave misuse is no justification for abandoning a subject, it is only a reason for exceptional care and caution, and there are in fact other reasons advanced for considering the whole metaphysical enterprise ill-judged. We shall have to take account of them shortly.

In addition explanations are offered for the lure of metaphysics and the fact that thinkers of exceptional power have indulged in it and thought they were talking genuine, if also very difficult, sense. The main consideration here has been that we may be deceived by the words we use, and by the general forms of our language, into supposing that our thoughts make sense in some cases where they do not begin to do so, we delude ourselves in this way; and as this contention has had a very prominent part in recent philosophy the student will need to understand fairly closely what it involves. I shall try to help him to do so later. But a provisional mention of the matter must suffice here.

When questions are raised about the nature of the universe and man's lot or destiny in it, especial importance is ascribed to the question of the nature of human personality. What is it to be a person, and how are the mental and physical sides of our natures related? We normally consider ourselves to be distinct beings, but we also speak at times of being 'members of one another'. Which is the ultimate concept, man or society? Could minds be merged in one greater mind, or is mind an irreducible entity? Could the mind function and persist without the body? If so, what kind of reality is it, and how do we refer to anything as elusive as a quite intangible non-material reality? How do we account for the continued identity of persons in the light of split personalities and loss of memory and so on? These are all questions which bear closely on religion. But they have central importance in philosophy on their own account, and the main controversies and divisions of allegiances in recent philosophy tend to converge sharply upon them.

In thinking of identity in the context of personal existence we have also to consider the general nature of identity, and this is also a basic philosophical question. It was one of the main preoccupations of the early Greek philosophers with whom the subject began in the Western world. We are all accustomed to think of there being several entities in the world around us, the tables, chairs, books in this room, for example. But the table has legs and a top which could be detached, and it is itself a part of the room. Which unit, if any, is ultimate, and how are the properties of a particular entity related to the thing itself? When I have thought of the colour, shape, weight, size of the table and so on, what further is there to consider? What is the table which, as we say, has these properties? Is it more than the union of the properties in some fashion, and if so what sort of thing could it be? Is the problem of thinghood or identity the same in the case of persons and in that of material realities? These may seem to be remote and artificial questions, since we all pick out particular things and recognize persons without difficulty. But we cannot in fact think deeply about any of the major questions with which our existence in the world presents us without coming firmly to grips with these questions of 'thinghood', unity and identity; and involved in this is the question of the relation of different things to one another and the way they affect one another, the problem of cause and effect. The latter is also something we all appear to understand well and which we imply, even when not specifically mentioned, at almost every turn of our thoughts— 'what accounts for this?', 'how will I accomplish that?', 'what made me do this?' Nothing seems simpler, and yet few things are harder to handle in thought than the nature of causation—what guarantees it and what, if anything, does it involve beyond the fact that things do happen as a rule in a specific way? We often imply that there is more, but what is it? On the answer to such questions as these will depend much of our approach to the question of the ultimate nature of the world and the way in which it may be said to be one or many in the final analysis, or of any meaning we may find in our experience as a whole and in whatever we suppose to extend beyond that. Disagreement about seemingly remote and detached issues like the principles of identity and causation has led philosophers to widely divergent views about what the world, in its concrete reality, is like and about issues which have much more the quality and urgency of life and death about them.

In the present short book it will not be possible to go in a close and systematic way into all these questions in the vital bearing they have on religious issues. Some of them will loom up more sharply than others and all of them will find their way into the discussion in some form, perhaps not always overtly. To consider them separately on their own account would be to divert our attention to the general study of philosophy, and that is not the task we have set ourselves here. But it is well for the student to understand the way philosophical problems in general arise, and to give as much preliminary thought to them as he can.

We have had a glimpse of the sort of general perplexities which arise when we try to get a clear picture of what our experience is like in some specific regards, such as awareness of the natural world or our moral life. Aesthetic experience, in painting or music or literature, likewise presents certain problems peculiar to itself in which some of the major general questions of philosophy are also involved in various ways and measures. So do science and history, and we have thus the special branches of philosophy known as aesthetics (or the philosophy of beauty), the philosophy of science and the philosophy of history. In this book attention must now be turned to what we find religion to be like and to the major questions which present themselves when we try to understand it. As religions appear at least to make certain claims which must be assessed for their truth or falsity, a central place will be given to a basic philosophical question which I have not specifically mentioned yet, but which is prominent in most philosophical undertakings, namely the question of the nature of knowledge itself and its range. How, if at all, is certainty attained, and what are its limits? I shall not say more at the moment about this question, as I shall be taking it up again very shortly. But now the reader has been reasonably apprised of the general nature of a philosophical venture and the way it relates to our own experience and major concerns. It is time therefore to advance to the special topic of this book. I believe it will be found that, in dealing with religion, as elsewhere in philosophy, the problems are not of merely academic interest, in our rather odd use of this term. They are part of the life of religion itself, most of all in mature and progressive communities, although they must also of course be viewed with detachment and an open mind.

FURTHER READING

An outline of general metaphysical questions is found in *An Introduction to Metaphysics*, by C. H. Whiteley (Methuen), *Metaphysics*, by W. H. Walsh (Hutchinsons) and *Metaphysics*, by Richard Taylor (Prentice Hall).

An older book, but still of much value, is *The Elements of Metaphysics*, by A. E. Taylor (London). It reviews some of the main metaphysical problems in turn.

Three books already mentioned are also relevant here, namely Moore's *Some Main Problems of Philosophy*, Ewing's *The Fundamental Problems of Philosophy*, and Ayer's *Language, Truth and Logic*. The latter contains a formidable attack on metaphysics on the grounds mainly that the basic contentions of metaphysical writers are meaningless. This has been a common theme in a spate of other books, of which *The Revolution in Philosophy*, edited by Gilbert Ryle (Macmillan) is a good example. This book consists of a series of broadcast talks and is largely aimed at the layman. The view of metaphysics as consisting of suggestive verbal innovations is also the theme of Morris Lazerowitz's *The Structure of Metaphysics* (Routledge). The defence of metaphysics against these attacks was taken up in a cautious way by Dorothy Emmet in *The Nature of Metaphysical Thinking* (Macmillan) and by Winston H. F. Barnes in *The Philosophical Predicament* (Black). A bolder defence of metaphysics, including a chapter on the 'linguistic veto' on metaphysical speculation, is *The Modern Predicament*, by H. J. Paton (Allen and Unwin). A defence of metaphysics with a more strictly religious orientation is that of Illtyd Trethowan in *An Essay in Christian Philosophy* (Longmans) and we find an exceptionally impressive defence of some basic metaphysical notions in Brand Blanshard's *Reason and Analysis* (Allen and Unwin). In *Prospect for Metaphysics*, edited by Ian Ramsey (Allen and Unwin) we have essays by various writers indicating their view of some aspect of metaphysics in the light of recent controversy.

CHAPTER FOUR

THE STUDY OF RELIGIONS

It is not difficult to anticipate what the word 'religion' would first call to mind for readers of this book. They would probably associate it, in the first place, with certain kinds of buildings, called churches or temples, and the performances called 'acts of worship' that go on there. Closely allied to this is the role of persons specially appointed and instructed to take a leading part in these performances, priests and preachers. These are known to wear special kinds of clothes, sometimes because that is involved in the part they play in acts of worship and sometimes as a general indication of their office and the way it is thought of by themselves and other members of the community. In the first case we have vestments of various kinds and in the second the round collar and the rather sombre cloth of the clergy. These have their well-known equivalents in religions other than the Christian one.

In these more visible and obvious manifestations of religion a prominent place is also accorded as a rule to special books, like the Bible or the Koran or the sacred prayer scrolls of the Buddhist monk. These will include books of songs like the Christian hymn-book which share in varying measures in the holy or sacred character of the other special books or scriptures. As we think further there will come to mind also various articles used in public or private devotions, a communion cup or christening bowl or praying wheel; and of these 'instruments of worship', as they are sometimes called, it is well known that there is a very wide variety as we take in our survey the vast range of religions practised at different times and places.

With these practices there is associated also, in many cases, the role that is played in the life of the religion as a whole by one or a few persons of outstanding importance. In the most obvious examples these will be the founders of the religion and persons specially connected with the founder, Christ and his apostles, Muhammad and the first caliphs, Buddha and his first converts. But the status and functions of the pre-eminent person in this sense vary a great deal from one case to another. There will also be veneration of those who have played some outstanding part in the development of the religion, Moses and the prophets in the Hebrew-Christian tradition and King Asoka in the Buddhist religion and Rama and Ramakrishna in Hindu religion. Veneration of notable persons in various ways is thus also a fairly unmistakable feature of religion.

The role of the founder and kindred persons gives prominence also to a body of teaching, most of all the teaching of the founder himself. In reflecting upon this we remember also that in all its forms, including the more overt and explicit acts of worship, religion is associated in a fairly continuous way with the manner in which we conduct our lives as a whole, and it is generally taken to have a great deal to do with leading a good life. For many this tends to become the most prominent feature of religion. This is reflected in the importance accorded to ceremonies that have to do with certain outstanding occasions like being married or being initiated into membership of some society. But there are also other reasons for the importance of the rites that are practised at birth, in marriage, or at death.

If we think further we shall find that religion brings to mind for us many other things. But it is plain that the ordinary person thinks of religion, in the first instance, in terms of practices and attitudes such as I have instanced; and some will think of them in fairly precise ways, according to their own familiarity with religious practices, while others, especially perhaps today, will have much vaguer notions of what exactly is involved. But few, at least among those who are likely to use this book, will find any difficulty in recognizing in a rough and ready way what the term 'religion' betokens. It is a most familiar word, and no one finds any difficulty at this level in understanding what religion is like. We all know roughly what sort of things religious people do and what goes on in churches and temples, even though we may be extremely ignorant about the details of any religion other than the one practised in our own community. If, in travels abroad perhaps, we witness some unusual and puzzling performance and are then told, 'It is a religious rite that is being carried out', then we find this a perfectly intelligible explanation. One would need to be an exceptionally ignorant person to be puzzled by the word 'religion' at this level.

The same is true in art. Everyone knows that when we speak of art we are thinking of pictures, sculpture, music, poetry and so on. Works of art are what we hope to view at an art gallery. No one other than a foreigner is puzzled by the word 'art' in the sense that he does not understand to what sort of thing we allude when we use the word. If he were, the dictionary would be the proper book to consult. And yet Tolstoi wrote a very famous book with the title 'What is art?' He was clearly not exercising his outstanding gifts to tell people what they could learn quite easily in the dictionary. His concern in this very controversial book is to ascertain what is involved in painting pictures and looking at them and, in particular in this case, the composing of works of literature. Why do we do these things, are the aims we set ourselves the best ones, could we do better if we worked on some new principle? Similar questions can be raised about religion, and while we all know, in a rough and ready way, what religion is, we cannot probe deeper without raising some unusually difficult and complicated questions.

We know in a fashion what people do in religion, but why do they do it? Do they do it for the same reasons at different times and places? What is the point of elaborate performances and sustained personal observances? What do we hope to gain by them? It might be thought that the answers to these questions were simple. But we have only to consider the very great variety of the definitions of religion offered from time to time[1] to realize that the answers to our questions are by no means as evident as some might suppose at first; and it would be an admirable exercise at this stage if the reader should consider what sort of answers he and his friends (or his mates in a class if he belongs to one) would give to such questions as 'Why do people go to Church?', 'Why do we

1. Forty eight are listed by Leuba in his *A Psychological Study of Religion*. For comment on this see *Selfhood and Godhood* by C. A. Campbell, p. 234.

pray?' 'What is the point of being religious?' It will be strange if the exercise does not produce some lively debate which can be continued with profit.

The questions I have just posed could be regarded, in part at least, as historical questions. They would lead us on to ask how religion began, whether people practise it today in the same way, or with the same expectations, as in the past. What progress has been made in religion, and can we now discard certain elements which were prominent in early times? What are the main differences between religions? How much have they in common? These are extremely important questions and the pursuit of them in detail can be one of the most fascinating and colourful of studies. But it is not quite the study we have to undertake in this book. It is the subject which used to be named 'Comparative Religion', but for which the name 'History of Religions', or 'The Study of Religions' is more common today. In this latter subject we try to indicate what has in fact been the course taken by various religions in the past and what they are like today; and to some extent at least this must be regarded as a different undertaking from that of the philosopher.

Ideally the Study of Religions and the Philosophy of Religion should be very closely related. We cannot get far with the examination of what religions in fact are like without passing from bare description to questions that border at least on philosophy; and in some religions, like Hinduism, where philosophical reflection has had a prominent place, it is obviously an advantage, if not an indispensable requirement, to be familiar with philosophical issues and the way to approach them. On the other hand, it is well for the philosopher to have the fullest knowledge possible for him of the phenomena about which he proposes to raise philosophical questions. The situation is paralleled again in the case of art. The connoisseur of art, or the art critic, does not have to be a philosopher, but he is apt, without always being aware of the fact, to make philosophical pronouncements which he is not always competent to handle and which yet may have much to do with his discharge of his own specific task. In the philosophy of art it is obviously necessary to have first-hand acquaintance with art and skill in appreciating it and treating it critically and historically.

On the whole the linkage between the study of religions and philosophy seems to me closer than that between art criticism and aesthetics or the philosophy of art. But this is itself a matter much in debate at the moment. There is a tendency among those who are engaged in the study of religions today to treat the subject as much in a factual way as possible and to bring it into line with scientific study. The attractiveness of this course is evident. Science brings precision and exactness into matters which are otherwise vague and allusive, and its prestige is deservedly high. There are, moreover, certain things in the study of religions which can be conclusively settled by the use of scientific techniques, for example the age of the soil in which relics of various kinds have been deposited. The date of manuscripts may be settled in similar ways, and there are other matters which, even where a strictly scientific technique is not used, can be settled with reasonable certitude and precision, for example how people built their temples, how they buried their dead and performed kindred ceremonies. Some scholars, in the interest of reliable scientific study, would confine the subject of the history of religions to matters which admit of being handled in these very dependable ways.[1] But others hold that this is a very narrow view of the subject and omits some of the most important and intriguing issues; and when we proceed to speculation about the reasons men have had for the practices which we can ascribe to them, when we pass from external fact to motives and beliefs, we move to questions which easily pass over to the philosophical questions presented by religion; and it would thus appear to be a great advantage for the historian of religion to know his way about in philosophy.

The controversy between those who would confine the study of religion to strictly scientific matters and those who wish to give it wider scope and bring it close to philosophy is a very lively one at present. It takes a particularly sharp form when certain philologists and other linguistic experts

1. See the Proceedings of the Tenth Conference of the International Association for the History of Religions held at Marburg in 1960, p. 229.

question the right of those who do not share their own specialized knowledge to approach the study of religion at all. One understands well the scholar's suspicion of the charlatan and the dabbler apt to make bold assertions on partial and very slender evidence.[1] But I myself take my stand firmly on the side of those who wish to give the subject a broader scope and I think that the study of religions and disciplines cognate to it suffer much impoverishment from a rigid restriction of the scope of the history of religions and its isolation from philosophy. The issue can not be helpfully pursued further at this point, but much that we shall consider later will bear closely upon it.

This holds specially of questions about the origins of religion. It would be plausible to treat this as a purely historical question, but I hope to make it clear in due course how much our understanding of this matter is affected by philosophical considerations. In the meantime the reader must be warned not to expect in this book the close examination of the history and varieties of religion appropriate to a work on comparative religion or the history of religions. He will find today admirable introductions to that subject, both in its general scope and in the study of particular religions, and he will be much aided, in his properly philosophical studies, if he has also managed to familiarize himself with some of the main features of various religions and the way they have developed.

In philosophy, however, the probing must be deeper, if also more general. We wish to know not merely the proximate aims of certain practices and the beliefs which seem most obviously associated with them, but also whether these have some deeper motivation and have aspects other than those which present themselves to the more superficial view. The facts, including religious beliefs, may not be in doubt at a certain level. We may be able to say with confidence what sort of things Christians or Muslims do and believe. But are these beliefs and practices quite what they seem to be at first? When the worshipper falls on his knees and utters words of

1. Criticisms of extreme forms of this suspicion may be found in the Hayter Report on Oriental, Slavonic, East European and African Studies.

prayer is he intending to address some being who, although invisible to him or to 'the naked eye', is none the less a being not altogether unlike himself? We should hesitate in most cases, today especially, to say that he was. Outwardly his procedure is not unlike our speech to one another and prayer has often been described as talking to God. But it is obviously an unusual sort of talking, and in private devotion it often happens that no sound is uttered. The activity of prayer is not therefore quite what it seems to be, it is not even like transmitting a message to a distant continent or to another planet, although this would be a happy metaphor for certain purposes. But in that case how different is it? This is what I mean by probing and asking how far the performances we examine are properly described in terms of what they appear at first glance to be. It is in this sense especially that we ask in philosophy why people indulge in certain practices and what their beliefs involve. We have to go beyond the answer which might be quite adequate for at least the more limited forms of the scholarly history of religion. We might be told, for example, in reliable detail how certain peoples worship a thunder god Shango, but this may still leave us wondering in certain ways why people believe in such a being and adopt certain attitudes towards him—and what it is to have such a belief.

The point of such wondering will be plainer if we note the sharp diversity of the answers to it that have been given from time to time. It has been held, for example, that the true explanation of religious practices lies in deep and unspecified fears which do not reveal themselves overtly in the practices they prompt. Some thinkers have found the clue to religion in sex. Others regard our religious habits and expressions as convenient ways of summing up for ourselves the main impressions we have of our present life as a whole or providing 'overarching symbols', as they have been called, for our main aspirations. For others the purpose of religion is to evoke or express certain emotions, and the element of affirmation or of religious propositions is not to be taken at its face value at all. Yet others find the clue to religious practice in the stimulus it gives to conduct of a certain kind and tend thus to take the moral factor as the essential and decisive one. Those whose approach is not quite so novel or subversive of what we normally take religion to be like are nevertheless apt to stress the peculiarity of the propositional or belief element in religion. We say that we believe in God and declare this God to be invisible and at the same time present everywhere, we say that He is one God and also three persons, that He is a God of love and also a God of wrath; we say that God is a Father but he is not anyone's parent in the normal sense; we say that God answers prayer but seem very evasive when challenged to bring unmistakable evidence of this; we say that we hope to have eternal life but that this is not at all the same as going on for ever; we speak of sin which is not the commission of particular wrongful acts and go on to tell of sacrifice and redemption in ways that go far beyond the initial and superficial meaning of these terms. We affirm that we are 'bought', not with gold but with blood, and we are obviously falling back on metaphor when we speak of healing and cleansing, however much practices like ritual washing may come into the matter. In all these ways we seem to travel far from what we might be superficially thought to be doing or saying; and the question thus becomes insistent of what goes on in religion, of what we really mean and do.

And since much that we do takes the form at least of expressing directly or indirectly certain beliefs or convictions, the question arises also of the soundness of these beliefs. Granted that we understand what is meant by saying 'I believe in one God', 'God is love', 'Allah is merciful', 'our prayers will not go unanswered', how far are these beliefs justified? How are our beliefs and expectations to be assessed in these matters? We may agree that it is important to believe in God or we may like to be assured that we shall live hereafter. But how is such assurance obtained? May not our expectations be wishful thinking? If they are not, on what is our confidence based, can religious claims be subjected to any tests like those we would expect in science or day-to-day affairs. If not, if we are told, as we sometimes are, that we must believe through faith, what sort of thing is faith and how is it related to ordinary certitude?

It is plain that questions of this kind are bound to have a very central place in sustained reflection on religion or the probing to which I have referred. There are indeed hardly any religious practices which do not appear at least to involve beliefs or affirmations of some kind. It may be an important advance in the scholarly investigation of religion to learn exactly how certain people buried their dead, just what sort of temples they built, what they did or said in marriage or initiation ceremonies, and it may be possible to conduct such inquiries in detachment from any further curiosity we may have — that may even be the best course, although I myself much doubt it. But it is also evident that these activities had some meaning, as we put it, beyond the overt performance. The dead were buried in certain ways because of certain expectations, the temple was a place where a god (or gods) dwelt or where he might be approached, the wedding was conducted in certain ways because this was supposed to be propitious and so on. Such beliefs might not always be explicitly formulated and they may not always be as simple as they seem. Nor need we suppose for a moment that such beliefs were carefully thought out or assessed for their truth. Habit and custom would have more to do at certain times with overt ceremonial than direct reflection. But belief or expectation of some sort could hardly have been altogether absent, and in some of the higher religions, as they are sometimes called, in Hinduism or Christianity for example, it is evident that what seems to be formally at least a belief or expectation has a very central place. Without the factor of belief, it would seem, to the 'first look' at least, impossible to make any sense of the overt practices. Indeed 'a religious person' and 'a believer' have sometimes become nearly synonymous terms.

The beliefs need not always be expressed in firm doctrinal terms as they have been, for the most part, in Christianity. There is not much place for doctrine in this sense in Hinduism, for example. Hinduism is an extremely tolerant religion and the varieties of it are unusually great. But there are certain things, the doctrine of rebirth for instance, which all Hindus believe. The beliefs of some forms of Buddhism may be exceptionally hard to specify, but at no point do we seem to dispense altogether with everything in the form of belief. If we did we should still have on our hands the fact that in most religions, at any rate, the factor of belief, or what seems at least to be belief, is central and indispensable for the understanding of everything else the religion involves.

It is not surprising, therefore, that questions about the nature and status of belief have been given a prominent place in the philosophy of religion. This conforms with the main concern which most people have when they think seriously about religion. They wish to know what the religion 'says' and whether this can be known to be true. The questions of meaning and truth seem thus to be crucial, and there can hardly be a better point at which to begin the wondering and probing in which the philosophy of religion consists than that of the significance and status of religious affirmations. By considering these we may now therefore make our way deeper into the subject.

FURTHER READING

Some of the themes of this chapter are taken up again in Chapter Twenty-seven and a number of books are mentioned in that chapter and a list of others appended to it. For the present therefore it may suffice to mention three books which the student will find it helpful to consult at this stage. They are:

Comparative Religion. Geoffrey Parrinder (Allen and Unwin).

Revelation and Reason. H. H. Farmer (Nisbet).

Varieties of Religious Experience. William James (Longmans).

The first of these is a general review of the subject known as Comparative Religion as we find it today, in the second various deviations of aim in religion are examined and considered in relation to what the author takes to be the norm in religion. The third book is a classic in which the author examines various types of religious attitudes.

CHAPTER FIVE

EMPIRICISM AND RATIONALISM

Suppose someone were asked to indicate the sort of things of which he feels most certain or to answer the general question 'Can we know anything for certain?', how would he respond? If he were very sophisticated he might complain, with some philosophers and notably the late H. A. Prichard, that the question is not well formulated, since knowledge implies certainty. If we really know something can there be a doubt about it? But we can leave this kind of sophistication aside at the moment and just concern ourselves with the question, however it should be stated more precisely, of where we feel that most certainty is found. Of what sort of things can we be sure?

This is not, it must be stressed, a question of what we consider to be most important, what some might be inclined to call the 'basic certainties', the things in the light of which we lead our lives. If that were the question some might be disposed to give a religious answer or to instance certain moral convictions. But the question now is not what matters most but simply where, in our experience of either trivial or important matters, we would be most likely to find some bedrock of certainty.

When this question is raised I think it will be found to be a common tendency to react in one of two ways, and the reader will perhaps experiment with himself to find how far this is the case. On the one hand we shall be disposed to say that we find certainty when there is something we can see, feel or handle and so on. I know for certain, one might say, that there is a pen in my hand now; I feel it between my fingers, I see it and I see the marks it makes on the paper. There seems to be no room at all for doubt here, and in the same way I am quite certain that the sun is shining outside and that the gardener is mowing the lawn. The sun may not shine for long and the gardener may be called away. But I am quite certain about both at the moment. I see the bright sunny lawn and I both see and hear the gardener. I can hardly doubt the direct evidence of my eyes. For such reasons the evidence of an eye-witness has particular value in a court of law.

This is also why we attach such force to scientific proof. For although an enormous amount of calculation is involved in science, the ultimate test is what we observe, what we find in the test-tube or the pointer reading. There is no gainsaying 'the facts' as it is sometimes put; and when scientists tell us some astonishing things, or make astounding claims, we generally give them credence, for we know that it is their habit to go by the facts as they see or observe them by the techniques they have developed to supplement the report of the 'naked eye' or extend its range.

When we consider immediate experience we feel that our certainty is at its height. If the gardener is working round the corner I may be wrong in supposing that he is mowing the lawn. Perhaps, after all, it is my neighbour that has started upon his. But in the main we are tolerably certain about such matters, even when they pass beyond what we immediately observe. I am as certain as I would wish to be for ordinary purposes that the man who comes to give me a morning in the garden is about now, even though I do not see him, and I confidently take him his cup of tea at eleven o'clock. We base our activities on certainties of this kind resting, in the last resort, on what we have found, through one or more of our senses, to be the case.

Starting from this basis some philosophers have proceeded to formulate theories about the nature of knowledge and its range in terms of the certainties we find in sense-experience. The test of truth, they maintain, is experience, and by experience here must be understood, in the main at least, what we find in the report of our senses, more simply what we see and touch and so on. The name for this approach to the problems of knowledge is empiricism, and of this there are many varieties, some much more rigid than others. The basic factor is the appeal to sense experience.

Empiricism is not of recent origin. It is about as old as

philosophy, and some of its shrewdest advocates were found among the early Greek philosophers, such as Protagoras and, in a qualified way, Heraclitus. It is to Protagoras that we owe the famous words 'Man is the measure of all things'. This has been understood in various ways from time to time, but Protagoras meant by it that whatever appears to any individual to be the case, including the report of his senses, must be so. From Heraclitus come the well-known words 'all things are in flux', and by this he meant that nothing can be real besides the changing scene as it presents itself to us from moment to moment.[1] In later European thought we find many outstanding empiricists, including the classical British empiricists, Locke, Berkeley and Hume to whom I shall allude again in a moment.

But even in these very tenuous allusions it will perhaps be apparent that everything is not plain sailing for the empiricist. We seem to be on a very safe course when we say that we trust our senses. What could be more certain? But what we sense at the moment may need to be corrected by what we sense at the next. If I am drunk, like Malvolio, I may see two candles instead of one. When I look through distorting panes the cows in the field take odd shapes. To be quite certain that my gardener, and not my neighbour, is mowing the lawn I have to look out of the windows as well as listen; and do we not sometimes say, 'My eyes deceived me'? Is it not a well-known fact that eye-witnesses of obvious integrity have sworn in courts of law to things which, it was afterwards proved, they could not possibly have seen? If we put absolute trust in the report of our senses we may find ourselves believing some very strange things and committed, as Protagoras and Heraclitus seem to have been, to accepting whatever appears to our senses at the time and taking nothing else to be real in the world around us. We seem to need at least some way of testing the report of one sense against another.

There arises here also the question broached earlier of the status of the world as it presents itself directly to our senses.

1. But Heraclitus did also have a doctrine about *logos* and the way changes took place. He cannot thus be thought of as an out and out empiricist.

Is this the real world or some image of it? That is not a question we need to pursue closely now. But it will be evident that, even in the field where we would expect it to be strongest, if not foolproof, the appeal to sense experience raises some difficulties which may call at least for some modification. And there are other areas of experience, such as art or ethics where our judgements seem to compel us to go beyond the report of our senses.

Some philosophers have felt these difficulties very sharply and have taken a course that is much in line with another way we may react to the question 'what do we know for certain?'. Some would be disposed to say: 'We cannot be very sure about the reports of our senses, our eyes do deceive us, and even when we do have all the certainty that matters, there is yet a theoretical possibility of being wrong. Perhaps at no point is there quite fool-proof certainty, I may not have noticed that someone has substituted another pen for the one I thought I was using, perhaps even the table on which I lean my elbows is an illusion which some practical joker has cleverly contrived and which will collapse in a moment. Perhaps I am dreaming or have been put into a trance or some other hypnotic state. But whatever the possibilities of error and delusion here, there seems to be one province where the possibility of error is strictly excluded; and that is where I have carefully reasoned my way to a conclusion in matters which do not rest on the uncertain report of my senses. One thus proves that the sum of the angles of a triangle is 180 degrees or more simply, perhaps in one rational insight, sees that twice two is four. There seems to be some initial unavoidable necessity here. We cannot conceive of the truth being other than it seems. In no universe could twice two make five; this is not a matter of experience, of what we in fact find the world to be like but which could conceivably be otherwise, as that grass is usually green and fire hot. There seems to be no possibility, now or at any other time, here or elsewhere, of two and two making five or of any of the other matters which are set out before us step by lucid step in an abstract or purely rational argument being other than we find them. This may not cover all that interests us. But here we do find at least some irrefutable certainty, and the body of mathematical proof appears to be an ideal instance of it. Would we could find the same certainty elsewhere!'

So someone might speak, and if he did he would be reflecting a strain in philosophy which is as old as empiricism and which has often been the sharp rival of it. It is usually called rationalism. In the work of one of the two main philosophers of the ancient world, namely Plato, the rationalist element is very pronounced, although it does not cover the whole of his thought. Plato was much taken with the thought of Protagoras and Heraclitus and he himself developed their arguments in a very subtle and thorough way in the dialogue I have already commended to the student, the *Theaetetus*. But Plato hoped also to find a reality other than the passing show of the world as disclosed to our senses and this he believed (like Parmenides to whom he also owed a great deal) became evident to us in what our thought found that it had to be, as we learn what must be true in mathematics to which Plato, like other rationalists of later times, attached great importance. This allowed of much variety in the real world, the leading idea being that of a system in which unity and variety involved one another, although in some ways the ultimate principle of things went beyond this. Parmenides had tended to take up everything there is in one undifferentiated whole. Plato did not follow him there, and he also believed that the world around us and the events of our lives had reality of some kind conferred upon them by the world discovered by thought. But how far he was prepared to go, at times at least, as a rationalist may be seen in passages in the *Republic* where he claims that even in a study like astronomy we must disregard facts of the natural world, crude as they are on his view, and proceed by thought alone.

Among the most remarkable rationalists of the Modern period were Descartes, Spinoza and Leibniz, and the student who wishes to understand the background of recent philosophy should try to learn as much as he can about those celebrated European thinkers as well as about the British empiricists. These two sets of thinkers provide the main figures around whom courses on the early part of modern philosophy are usually arranged. I shall refer to some of them later but they should be studied more closely in their own works and in books about them.

The two streams of thought to which I have referred are conflated in the philosophy of Kant. He thought the rationalists had been too ambitious in trying to settle all major questions by thought alone—or by 'pure reason' as he called it; and he was also much perturbed by the scepticism which Hume had so skilfully shown to be the proper end of rigorous empiricism. How could we avoid the perils of those two procedures? If thought by itself is inadequate and if the reports of our senses are uncertain, what avenue of escape have we? Kant thought he could provide the answer in terms of certain principles which are objective and certain at least in the sense that they are essentially involved, and thus indispensable, in the sort of experience of the world which we in fact have. They are not private to any person as an individual but conditions of our experience as such. But the world so experienced is not the world of things as they truly are—or 'things in themselves' in the famous Kantian term. The latter are beyond the range of our knowledge and experience, and we thus tend to have a system of two worlds, called by Kant the world of phenomena and the world of noumena. The relation between these two is never quite as clear in Kant's philosophy as we could wish, and this provides fertile ground for much scholarly debate. To the world of noumena belong God and also the soul as a subject of experience more abiding than its fleeting contents. But we cannot have knowledge of these noumenal realities which transcend experience, although Kant believed that something different, to which he gave the name 'faith', could give us all the assurance we need here. In this system we tend to have a dualism or dichotomy of the world as it appears to us and some further world, and this affected almost everything of importance which Kant had to say about the many problems of human existence with which he dealt, notably in ethics.

A great deal of the philosophy which followed Kant and was inspired by him centred on the problem of the two worlds in his philosophy and the way the gulf between them might be bridged. Clues were sought within the world as we find it to what the other more complete reality must be like, and in many cases the world as it ultimately is, or as it is 'in itself', was thought to be some extension or completion of the world as it appears to us. The dichotomy would thus be lessened, and some maintain that this was the intention of Kant himself. There came to be inspired in this way many ambitious systems, of which that of Hegel was the most outstanding and influential, in which the nature of the universe, in its ultimate structure or principle, was disclosed in some significant features of experience, such as reason (in the case of Hegel) or will (in the case of Schopenhauer). The details of these systems are often very complicated and intriguing, and from the major systems there tended to proliferate a host of subsidiary ones offering refinements or modifications of the original suggestion. Much of the philosophy known as nineteenth-century idealism consisted of such modifications of the philosophy of Hegel; and even when this was least successful in its ultimate aim it provided much incidental illumination of the course and nature of human experience.

It is also unhappily true, as we might well expect, that, when speculative thought of this kind became the fashion, it should run riot and afford much scope for the portentous charlatan. When we speculate about what the world must be like beyond the sphere of our own experience, and indeed at all times when we seek to establish some over-all principle about the way things are, it is not evident what are the tests to which we must submit or what conditions must be observed. We are in a somewhat shadowy realm where ingenious speculation is not easily distinguished from bogus and pretentious play. It seems evident that many gave themselves license to speculate in a very random fashion and manufactured notions, sometimes put forward in very obscurantist terms, for which it was not easy to provide any good test of either meaning or soundness. This tended to bring the whole enterprise into ill-repute, although it is certainly not proper, as we ought to remember well today, to condemn any enterprise, in its aims or method, simply because its difficulties make it exceptionally open to abuse, intentional or naïvely innocent. What we have, on the contrary, is the need for exceptional care and awareness of the pitfalls with which the course is strewn.

In our own times we have seen an exceptionally sharp reaction against the bold speculations of nineteenth-century philosophy, some of which is amply justified and some of which is due to impatience and failure of sympathy. Many factors have contributed to this reaction besides the expressly philosophical ones; and these include especially the climate of the age in which we live. We have passed, and are still passing, through a period of almost unprecedented change—especially in the external conditions of existence. Inventions which have revolutionized our mode of living have come about altogether within the memory of people not yet very old—motor-cars, aeroplanes, telephones, cinema, radio in sound and vision, and various electrical devices; and latterly we have fantastic developments in the use of atomic power, in the exploration of outer space and in the understanding, in biochemistry, of the molecular structure of living things. Many of the amenities provided in these ways are almost already deemed to be necessities, although they were barely thought of at the turn of the century. Add to this the carnage and upheavals of two world wars and the uprooting of peoples and the disrupting of societies. The extent of these swift and far-reaching changes, the disturbance of normal social existence, may well be greater and sharper in their impact upon us than we realize who are still in the midst of them. But they are sufficiently evident to everyone not to need detailed comment and exemplification, and it is not strange that, in these upheavals and whirls of change, men should feel able to cope with little beyond the demands of each situation as it arises.

There are parallels to this in times of change and upheaval in the past. In the classical period of ancient Greece, for example, there were extensive social and political changes, wars, new contacts with other people and colonization; and this contributed much to the uncertainty, the ferment of inquiry and debate, the impatience with ambitious and seemingly remote speculation, the demand for attention to practical issues which held promise of being handled with success and some profit, which defined the situation within which the greatest of the Greek thinkers, Socrates, Plato and Aristotle, set to work. Some of my readers may at least find comfort in the thought that the finest, and most ambitious, constructive and metaphysical work of the Greek philosophers came after, one could perhaps say out of, a deep uncertainty and much arrogant scepticism.

How close a parallel is afforded here with the state of the world of thought today may not be easy to determine, and it is always risky to run historical parallels closely. But it is certain, at any rate, that among philosophers of today, in English-speaking countries especially, there has been a very sharp reaction against ambitious speculation and, in some quarters, a total rejection of all forms of metaphysics. The plea has been for a return to the more manageable matters of the world around us, to come down to earth as it were and confine attention to questions to which a clear answer may be offered in terms of what seem to be the hard facts of experience, to return to common sense, to be 'tough-minded' and perhaps even commonplace as a safeguard against the perilous delusions and obscurities of vague system-building and the making of unnecessary mystery. Tell us, so it might be said, in the plainest terms what you mean and how exactly your contention is established, do not try to bemuse us with wordy fantasies. In this situation one is not surprised to see empiricism come into its own again and the wheel come full circle round to the philosophy of David Hume as the proper point of departure for further advance in the subject.

It will be evident that the return to empiricism in philosophy is closely allied to the progress of science and its enormous and deserved prestige. In science, as has already been noted, we bring our theories, even the most pure and speculative, to the test of fact or observation. This is what set science, in the modern world, on such a steady course of progress, and while there are not many philosophers who would wish to treat philosophy itself as a part of science, there are many today who turn to science for the model of what truth and knowledge are like and thus for the answer to one of the most basic of all philosophical questions. Nothing, so it is claimed, can be known or even properly believed unless it can be established by methods not different in substance from the procedures which are followed in science; and whatever we finally think of this view, it is certainly not a surprising line for thinkers to take at a time when science is making such impressive strides, to the great advantage, if also in some ways to the peril, of us all.

But there are other ways in which the extensive advance of science has affected our attitude towards the main questions of religion, and before taking up, as we must in a moment, the impact of modern empiricism and its offshoots on religion, it will be well to pause, and perhaps even deviate a little, to consider some of the more direct ways in which science has affected religious beliefs and attitudes. This will give us a fuller background for our examination of the shape which religious problems are apt to take in philosophy today.

FURTHER READING

The student who is not familiar with the general history of thought should try to fill out as much as possible at this stage the outline of the development of modern thought provided in the preceding chapter. He could begin by reading the relevant parts of some good book on the history of philosophy. Some teachers are a little contemptuous of 'histories of philosophy', and they are certainly justified if the 'histories' are made to do duty for sampling the work of various philosophers at first hand. But 'histories of philosophy' can provide very useful guides and outlines which help us to read other works with more profit. Among the books which can be recommended are:

A Student's History of Philosophy. A. K. Rogers (Macmillan).

A History of Philosophy. C. C. J. Webb (Williams and Norgate).

Neither of these are recent but they still serve their purpose admirably. A more recent work is Bertrand Russell's well-known *History of Western Philosophy* (Allen and Unwin). This is a delightfully written work, but allowance must be made for bias which the distinguished author has not always been able to suppress.

The development of fairly recent philosophy is very ably sketched by John Passmore in *The Development of Recent Philosophy* (Duckworth).

I would also strongly urge the student at this stage to read good biographical studies of the great philosophers. This will much help to put the student in the picture, and the best of such biographies are excellent reading on their own account. I recommend the following:

John Locke. Maurice Cranston (Longmans).

The Life of George Berkeley. A. A. Luce (Nelson).

David Hume. J. Y. T. Greig (Jonathan Cape).

The Life of David Hume. E. C. Mossner (Nelson).

The Life of René Descartes. Elizabeth Haldane (John Murray).

The last book is not very recent but it is informative and readable. I also find that students gain much from an outline of the main ideas of some of the first modern philosophers in *The Dawn of Modern Thought,* by S. H. Mellone (Oxford). *Idealism,* by R. F. Hoernlé (Hodder and Stoughton) also covers much of the same period and is a remarkably helpful book for the beginner. It also continues the discussion into the work of Hegel and his followers to whom reference is made in this chapter and elsewhere. A good introductory book about Hegel by a writer much in sympathy with him is Edward Caird's *Hegel* in the Blackwood series — well-known at one time. A more contemporary approach to Hegel is found in a more elaborate work *Hegel: a Re-examination,* by J. N. Findlay (Allen and Unwin). A good introduction to the philosophy of Kant is provided by A. C. Ewing in *A Short Commentary on Kant's Critique of Pure Reason* (Methuen). Most students will also be familiar with the Penguin series of books about the great philosophers. These are perhaps a little more difficult than they should be for their purpose. But they can almost all be warmly recommended in every other way.

A typical Idealist position will be found in Chapter XXI of Ninian Smart's *Historical Selections in the Philosophy of Religion* ('Royce on Reason and Religion'). This book will be found useful at many other stages in the study of the present work.

The student who wishes to follow up the references made here and elsewhere to Plato would profit by study of G. C. Field's *The Philosophy of Plato* in the Home Universities Library and he could then go on to the relevant parts of Plato in F. M. Cornford's translations (with admirable running commentary) of the *Theaetetus* and the *Sophist* in his *Plato's Theory of Knowledge* (Routledge). There is also a very helpful analysis of these (and other) dialogues in

A. E. Taylor's *Plato*. In his very famous dialogue, the *Republic*, Plato deals with problems in the theory of knowledge and with other basic philosophical problems. This work provides in itself an admirable general introduction to philosophy.

CHAPTER SIX

RELIGION AND SCIENCE

A great deal has been written, from time to time, about the alleged conflict of science and religion. It might be possible, in some sense, to trace this back a very long way, to civilizations like that of the Greeks for example. But in the form in which we think of it as a serious issue today it began when the so-called 'dawn of modern science' confronted men with a new intellectual and cultural situation in the sixteenth and seventeenth centuries. The reasons for regarding science as in some way the rival or opponent of religion were not however very grave or obvious in those days. There was not a great deal in what scientists claimed to have discovered at that time which was sharply inconsistent with the religious beliefs of their contemporaries in Christian countries. It was of course disturbing to have to alter one's conception of the relation of our earth to other known heavenly bodies and so on. But one wonders how far this was a truly religious issue and not just a matter of a general reluctance to make sharp and unsettling changes of outlook, a natural conservativism. Many of the early scientists, including Newton, regarded their work as something to be undertaken for the glory of God and had not the least intention of undermining religious faith. All the same in some ways 'the little rift' can be seen from the start.

This was more evident in the methods than in the early findings of science, and that in the method of science which was apt to cause offence was the appeal to independent rational judgement. The tendency had been, but more a partial one than is sometimes thought, to rest, in the last resort, on some established authority in matters of belief and culture. This would include parts of the teaching of Aristotle and the settled canons of the Church. The ultimate test of truth was conformity with such accepted standards. But the scientists owed their success to the direct examination of questions on their merit and by careful observation and experiment; and once this method was begun it could not easily be confined to study of the natural world. Free inquiry extended itself to other fields as well. Freedom is not easily restricted to special spheres, and it has been for this reason that despotic rulers of our own day have realized that if they are to control opinions in political matters they must eventually do so in art and science and religion as well. It was as a challenge to tradition and established authority, more than for the content of what they taught, that the early scientists began to fall under suspicion, and many of them little thought they were upsetting the religious world.

In due course, however, there developed certain attempts to probe more deeply into the principles of science and to form new philosophical theories about the world on the basis of the developing sciences. This is a not unfamiliar reaction. When men are impressed by some new achievement, especially in science, there is a proneness to regard it as a master clue to all other questions. Witness the exploitation of the idea of evolution in the nineteenth century. So, at a much earlier date, science began to be regarded as the key to all other questions.

In one regard at least this had advantages. For it encouraged people to think for themselves in religion and politics. This was itself a source of strain which was felt both by those who were jealous of the prestige of established authority and by the champions of open inquiry. This is very evident, for example, in the writings of the philosopher Thomas Hobbes. Among his many interests were questions of government, and he set a new fashion by insisting that these questions should be considered directly on their own account divorced from religious doctrines such as the divine right of kings. This did not lead him to favour democracy in our sense. He desired a strong, unified, authoritarian government to ensure peace and security at all costs, although this would require for its maintenance the support of the people as a whole; and Hobbes thought that all would see the wisdom of such a regime, as a strictly rational device, if only their minds were cleared of muddled and obscurantist notions which were often perpetuated by traditional authorities. In

his spirit he often inveighed, with wit and a crispness of
style that has rarely been excelled, against the universities and
the Church. To those who would set up as the norm and
ustification of government anything other than 'the preserva-
tion of man's life on earth', Hobbes says that they are relying
on a 'beliefe grounded upon other mens saying, that they
know it supernaturally, or that they know those, that knew
them, that knew others, that knew it supernaturally'.[1] 'The
Divines', he complains, 'and such others as make shew of
Learning, derive their knowledge from the Universities, and
from the Schooles of Law, or from the Books, which by men
eminent in those Schooles, and Universities have been published ... and that the doctrines maintained by so many
Preachers, against the Sovereign Power of the King, and by
so many Lawyers, and others, that had their education there,
is a sufficient argument, that though the Universities were
not the authors of these false doctrines, they knew not how
to plant the true.'[2] But it was not merely in the appeal to
reason and to severely secular considerations in politics and
morals that the break was made. It appeared also in the
extension of allegedly scientific principles to the understanding
of the whole of our lives.

An excellent instance of this is the mechanistic explanation
that came to be offered of human aims and experience. It was
thought that the world of nature could be regarded as one
vast machine in which the distinct operation of one factor on
another was invariable and could in principle always be discovered, and this highly questionable model for natural
occurrences was thought by Hobbes himself and others to
apply to human conduct as well. Spinoza shared this view,
although there were other very different sides to Spinoza's
thought. Descartes held it in general but made a partial
exception of human action. Closely allied to this were various
forms of materialism by which our desires and decisions,
usually thought to be determined in the first instance by
expectations of our own pleasure and pain, were ultimately
held to be determined by the mechanistic changes that

1. Leviathan, Chapter xv.
2. op. cit., Chapter xxx.

occurred in the physical world. Theories of this sort were not part of the findings of science, they were propounded by philosophers who were impressed by the science of their day and in fairly close contact with it; and it is plain that teaching of this kind would find itself in sharp opposition to the usual religious view of existence and of man as a spiritual being.

In due course, however, we find, not merely certain extensions of scientific notions beyond the sphere where these properly apply—and at that exceptionally questionable extensions of questionable notions; but also that substantial elements in the actual teaching of science itself, including discoveries whose essentials no one would question, were found to be sharply at odds with opinions thought to be required by religion or a part of it. This is the point at which the conflict became really acute, and the most striking and historic form of it came about in the nineteenth century with the clear formulation of the doctrine of evolution. Man, it appeared, had not been brought into being by one act of creation which conferred upon him at once his present aptitudes and understanding. He had ancestors among much more lowly creatures, and the ascent even from the creatures nearest to men, to say nothing of the slow emergence from the amoeba or other primeval forms of animate existence, had taken, not a few thousand years, but millions of years far beyond the reach of our imagination to compass. The earth itself in turn was proved, on the basis of rock formations, fossil remains, and other strictly scientific evidence, to be of an age fantastic by contrast with the few millennia awarded it in Christian tradition and taken, though by no means by all theologians of earlier times, to be the possibility that alone accorded with the Bible.

Religious people were forced in these ways into what was for them at the time a much more serious dilemma than we can easily appreciate today. The idea of evolution and kindred notions have become accepted and indeed commonplace by now, although of course there can still be sharp debates about the mode of the changes in question.[1] There may even be a case for saying that we have become too familiar with some

1. See *The Ascent of Life*, T. A. Goudge.

remarkable scientific discoveries about the world to be taking the full impact of them. But there are certainly very few educated people today who are not well acquainted, so far as the layman can be so, with matters like the tremendous age of our own planet and the vast distances of other known nebulae. The closer understanding of these matters, although many secrets remain to be unravelled, is one of the many triumphs of our age, and the discoveries made in what we usually call 'cosmological' studies of the world around us are staggering when we ponder them closely. But these ideas which almost everyone accepts in principle without demur today were a source of considerable shock and bewilderment in the nineteenth century and, indeed, until quite recent years in some quarters. You do not have to be very old to remember people who were actually scandalized by the idea that we were descended from brutes, and there are perhaps moods in which most of us secretly find this a little disturbing; many thought that religious truth and the dignity of human existence depended on retaining the notion of the creation of the world, and of human life in substantially the form in which we find it, within a few days a few thousand years ago.

To the shock which such people suffered in the encounter with novel cosmological theories was added the necessity of adjusting one's ideas about the Bible in a host of other ways. How far in past times men really took the Bible to be literally inspired and inerrant in every regard is not perhaps as clear as we think. But the general tendency had been to take most that we read in the Bible at its face value, even the stories of which there were different and contradictory versions in the Bible itself. How the difficulty of reconciling some parts of the scriptures with others failed to trouble people more than it seems to have done is a perplexing matter; we have, it appears, an amazing facility for departmentalizing our thought and putting our critical faculties to sleep in matters where we are averse to being deeply disturbed. But the results of scholarly investigation could not long be held back, and scientists, historians and leading theological scholars themselves began to make it plain beyond doubt that the Bible could not be taken to be strictly correct in all points of historical fact and that the books of the Bible were not all composed in the order (or by the persons) commonly accepted in the past. This is a very familiar tale by now and it is not for me here to provide further detail about the achievements of Biblical scholarship and the many matters now in debate among Biblical scholars. In some respects recent scholarship, in the form of archaeology for example, has provided striking confirmation of matters mentioned or described in the Bible. But it is also evident that we cannot take Biblical narratives as strictly dependable history, and this applies, moreover, not merely to parts of the Bible that refer to the remotest Biblical times but elsewhere, and to the New Testament as well as the Old. It is well known that some scholars of today take an extremely sceptical view of New Testament narratives. But if the dependability of the Scriptures is impugned in this way where is the matter to end? On what is man's faith to rest?

The dilemma was further aggravated by the development of more systematic study of society in sciences like anthropology and social psychology, and by the scholarly study of religions other than the Christian. It was learnt, for example, that there were striking parallels between the contents of the Bible and customs and beliefs of communities of pagan antiquity. In the light of this, Biblical matters appeared a little less sacrosanct and distinctive than had been the case before. And we are thus not surprised to find that some alarmed religious leaders, supported by many of lower place in religious communities, set themselves firmly in opposition to these new studies and refused to countenance their claims at all. The suspicion and dogmatism of religious people was, moreover, little assuaged by the jaunty self-confidence with which many scientists set out to debunk religion and reject it *in toto* as nothing more than superstition bred of ignorance and credulity and bound to obstruct the advance of science and enlightenment. The battle thus joined raged much more fiercely than we can easily appreciate today when many of the fires it kindled are smouldering only very feebly indeed; and I much doubt whether it is properly appreciated today how much the issue of science and religion, in the form of the incompatibility of traditional orthodoxy and the new discoveries of science, proved to be one of the dominant themes of late nineteenth-century history; students of the period ignore it at their peril. Echoes of the conflict went on swelling long into the present century.

One remarkable reaction to this conflict was to take refuge in a dualism whereby there could be a 'truth of the heart' side by side with an incompatible 'truth of the mind'. But this was certainly an impossible position, and one wonders how men of great intelligence were able to rest in it at all. Confused our thought may often be and in this way we may affirm contradictory notions. But if we feel impelled, in a clear-sighted way, to believe one thing, whether on scientific grounds or on any other, it does not seem possible, much less proper, to go on believing what we know is the exact opposite of it. Paradoxes are sometimes useful and illuminating, and there may be some truths which, at some stage at least, can only be expressed paradoxically. But downright contradiction on matters which present no particular difficulty of comprehension is another thing; we may find it hard to understand science at certain points, but if we are in fact persuaded that the world is many million years old then we can hardly fail to see that it is preposterous to believe also that the world was created a few thousand years ago. In matters as plain as this, to believe one thing on Sunday or in church and another on week-days and in the laboratory, was to lapse into the sort of intellectual and spiritual schizophrenia which, if persisted in, could only have the most devastating effect on the mental balance of individuals and societies.

This soon became evident; serious belief could not be upheld in a wholly equivocal way, and leaders of thought were found urging others to abandon so desperate an expedient. They contended that unqualified concessions should be made to science in the matters where the sway of science had to be undisputed. But they also held that what was really important for religion was unaffected by those modifications of traditional beliefs which a better understanding of our natural environment required. Let it be admitted, they said, that the earth and other heavenly bodies have existed for a time beyond the power of our imaginations to grasp, but it can still be held that God is the author and sustainer of all there is; let us admit our own humble animal origin, but that does not affect what we are now; let us sacrifice the literal inerrancy of the Bible, but we may yet regard the Bible as presenting in its substance the truth about God and our relation to Him. This was surely the unavoidable step to take, so much so that there can hardly be serious writers on religion now who would not readily accept it. Our difficulties may be sharpened thereby in other ways and we may need a subtler understanding of the authority of the Scriptures and of the dependence of faith upon them. But we clearly cannot go back to crude literalism or any other form of fundamentalism.

Once embarked on our course of reconciling science and religion in the way suggested, it is not however always easy to determine where we are to stop. Concessions may be made which are not required by the legitimate claims of science, and some of the first appeasers became so intoxicated with their own open-mindedness and the exciting business of re-fashioning religion in terms appropriate to an age of scientific advance and enlightenment, that they went to the length of seeking to interpret even the most vital religious principles exhaustively in terms of the latest scientific knowledge. The enthusiasm and recklessness with which some religious apologists carried out this suicidal policy is remarkable. Nothing seemed to be left of the mystery of religion. All was to be comprehended, and that in terms of what we understand about our present lot and the world around us. Miracle, prayer, and even God himself came to be interpreted thus as features solely of activities or processes in the 'here and now' of which an exhaustive rational explanation was in principle at least possible and by now brought well within our reach by the advance of science. The religious apologists may not have seen well how they were building in this matter, but many shrewd opponents of religion understood that the game was being played into their own hands and welcomed the new religious moves as the best way of speeding on the dawn of an entirely secular age. If there is nothing left that is distinctive of religion, if every feature of it can be exhaustively described in scientific terms, what need is there of religion? Must we not regard it as at best only a useful illusion which we can set aside with other childish things as the race passes from infancy and adolescence into proper maturity?

In extenuation of the excesses of 'modernism' and what came to be known for a period as the New Theology,[1] it must be added that it did much to bring about an enlightened view of religion and also to give prominence to certain ethical elements in religion which some forms of traditionalist doctrine were apt to obscure. We have also to remember that the prevailing philosophical fashion of the time was the post-Hegelian idealism of which mention was made earlier and which set the possibilities of an exhaustive rational explanation of things very high. An account will moreover be given later of some of our contemporaries who, in desperation and a great eagerness to win over a secular age, adopt subtle forms of the same expedients as appealed to the modernists of the early years of this century. In both cases, it seems to me, the price being paid is disastrous.

It is, however, in the spread of recent empiricism, and of the attitudes and procedures associated with it, that we most clearly see the impact on our thought and culture of the achievements and prestige of science, and it will be well for us now to return from our short deviation to our main course in the philosophy of religion by considering more closely the impact of empiricism today on our thought about religion. This will in turn provide an instructive mode of entry into further questions.

FURTHER READING

Religion and the Modern Mind. W. T. Stace (Lippincot).

Chapter IV on 'The Rise of Modern Science' will be very relevant to the theme of the foregoing chapter.

Christian Theology and Natural Science. E. L. Mascall (Longmans).

This is not mainly a historical survey but it deals in an impressive way with the general problem of science and religion. The author

1. This term subsequently came to be applied to Barthian theology which is at the opposite extreme to modernism.

is one of the few accomplished theologians who have more than a layman's knowledge of science.

Makers of Modern Thought. Gwilym O. Griffith (Lutterworth).
This book consists of light studies of formative modern thinkers.

The Ascent of Life. T. A. Goudge (University of Toronto Press).
This is a recent study of the way we should think of the notion of evolution and associated ideas today.

Natural Religion and Christian Theology, by C. E. Raven (Cambridge).

A substantial and well-known work which provides an excellent example of the more restrained sort of modernism. The more extreme type of modernism is found in another well-known and much discussed book, *Scientific Theory and Religion*, by W. E. Barnes (Cambridge). The modernist position is very ably discussed in *Types of Religious Philosophy*, by Edwin A. Burtt — Chapter VIII. Chapter V of this book (on 'the Religion of Science') and Chapter IX (on 'Humanism') can also be much recommended.

The New Theology (Chapman and Hall), sets out the main ideas of R. J. Campbell who created the sort of stir at the beginning of this century which has been created recently by the thinkers discussed in Chapter VII of this book. Consult also *What about the New Theology?* by W. L. Walker (T. & T. Clark).

Nature, Mind and Modern Science, by Errol E. Harris takes a broader sweep and includes much critical discussion of modern empiricism. It is a lucid but elaborate book by a writer very little in sympathy with recent trends in philosophy.

CHAPTER SEVEN

RECENT EMPIRICISM AND LINGUISTIC PHILOSOPHY

Some account has already been given of what the word 'empiricism' means. It stands for the view that nothing can be known, or even that no proposition can be meaningful, unless it can be established through the facts that become known to us in the reports of our senses. Sense experience is the sole test of truth and significance. Not all the famous empiricists adhered to this principle with the same rigour. John Locke, who was the father of British empiricism, had to admit into his theories many elements which went beyond the limits of the empiricism he set out to defend. Consider, for example, his account of substance. Locke held that we do not know the material world directly, we have to learn about it through sense impressions which mirror or represent the real physical world. Some of these impressions strictly resemble the qualities of the objects which produce them. This is true of size and shape and other so-called 'primary qualities'. It is not true of 'secondary' qualities like colour. But all the qualities of an object inhere, or belong together, in the object. What then is this thing or substance in which the qualities inhere?

In reply Locke tells the story of an Indian 'who saying that the world was supported by a great elephant, was asked, what the elephant rested on; to which his answer was, a great tortoise: but being again pressed to know what gave support to the broad-backed tortoise, replied, something, he knew not what'. Substance is likewise something we know not what. This notion has more interest than many would accord it today, as I have maintained elsewhere.[1] But it obviously involves something more elusive and mysterious than sense impressions, and when asked how we know that qualities inhere in substances Locke can only answer that this is

1. 'God and Mystery' in *Prospect for Metaphysics* Ed. I. T. Ramsey.

something we have to suppose. We have thus a physical world altogether beyond the world of the senses, the mystery of substance, and some necessity for thought which is not derived from experience at all, but *a priori*. Locke also finds it hard to keep to 'the way of ideas' in his account of the way we build up our more complex notions by the operations we perform on the simple impressions of our senses.

His successor, Berkeley, tried to be more consistent and to prune the philosophy of Locke of its non-empirical elements. He saw no necessity to postulate any material reality other than the world as it directly comes before us in experience. But even he maintained that we have a very different knowledge of ourselves as the subjects of experience. 'We comprehend our own existence by inward feeling or reflection.' We have 'a notion' of the 'active indivisible' mind or spirit, and so here, as also in perceiving the relations between things, the term 'idea' which, in Berkeley's use stands for what is derived directly from sense impressions, 'would be improperly extended to signify *everything* we know or have any notion of'.

The third member of the famous trio, namely David Hume, carried his empiricism through with much greater ruthlessness. He made a very clean sweep of some of the most cherished conceptions of other philosophers. Not only substance but causation also, as involving a rational necessity, went by the board. The association of ideas was invoked to support an account in psychological terms of our normal expectations about the way things happen. The self was dissolved into the fleeting impressions and ideas we have from moment to moment, there is no soul or inner reality which may outlast the flow of passing events, immortality is impossible in principle, and of an eternal spiritual being like God we can have no knowledge or even a proper conception. Hume was quite undaunted by these conclusions and showed great equanimity and humour when his friend Boswell found it irresistible to tax him about them on his death-bed. Hume's scepticism is well summed up in words that have often been quoted:

When we run over our libraries, persuaded of these principles, what havoc must we make? If we take in our hand any volume, of divinity or school metaphysics, for instance; let us ask, Does it contain any abstract reasoning concerning quantity or number? No. Does it contain any experimental reasoning concerning matter of fact and existence? No. Commit it then to the flames: for it can contain nothing but sophistry and illusion.

These words provide an admirable text for a great deal of the philosophy of our time. The sceptical philosophy of David Hume seemed to meet the mood of our day and it has been taken up afresh and developed with exceptional vigour and ingenuity. Among those who prepared the way for this movement were G. E. Moore[1] and Bertrand Russell, although neither of them, least of all Russell, was altogether happy with the turn which events subsequently took. Both of them were very clear-minded thinkers and masters of clear and graceful English prose, and both of them came to disapprove thoroughly of the speculative idealism which prevailed in their youth, they detested intellectual pretentiousness and obscurantism wherever they thought they found it. Moore set up common-sense as the touchstone of philosophy and thought that his main task at least ought to be just to analyse the obvious propositions or truisms of common-sense which, unlike Russell in this respect, he never wished to doubt; on the contrary he stated that 'every one of them I know to be true', he was puzzled and sceptical only about the correct analysis. But this could involve, as it certainly did in Moore's ethics, the recognition of some non-empirical matters. In course of time Moore also came to have a marked respect for the ordinary use of words, 'the meaning we all understand'.

It is here that we find the link between G. E. Moore and another influential body of thinkers who have been responsible for much that is distinctive in recent philosophy. These are known as the Vienna Circle, a group organized around Professor Moritz Schlick[2] in Vienna and much influenced also by Ludwig Wittgenstein[3] who did not strictly belong to the

---

1. But Moore was also very critical of some of Hume's ideas (see his destructive essay on Hume reprinted in Feigl and Sellars' *Readings in Philosophical Analysis*) and there is a distinctly metaphysical element in Moore's ethical views as may be seen especially in his well-known *Principia Ethica*.

2. and 3. See the books listed at the end of the chapter.

group. Wittgenstein moved to England and settled in Cambridge from where he exercised considerable influence on the course of philosophy in English-speaking countries. The first significance of this movement for our purpose is this. If we are to hold, as Hume did, that nothing can be significant unless it can somehow be reduced to what in fact we observe or discover in sense experience, there remains still the oddity, from this point of view, that we seem to say and believe many things which go beyond sense experience and physical fact, however conceived. We may, or we may not, wish to speak of some world 'beyond' the world of the senses, but most of us are apt to speak of the self or the soul as some inner reality which we cannot strictly witness or observe, we speak of responsibility and freedom of choice which can not be proved from the mere outward course of our activities, we refer to rights or duties which are not reducible to what we actually do or feel, we think of time as more than events in time, we have expectations of after life in some 'bourne from which no traveller returns' or of having a 'spiritual body' or existing perhaps with no body at all, we speak of eternity and of being united to a Being who is altogether beyond the world as we know it, a spiritual Being who is the author and sustainer of everything else, an invisible Being who is perfect or absolute but who is also held to be intimately present to men. Can this even appear to be intelligible talk if we never get beyond what we find in sense experience? Why have men persisted, and seem to do so still, in thinking and talking in these ways?

The reply is that we are misled by the words we use and the forms and structures of language. We delude ourselves in this way and come to believe that we are saying meaningful things when in fact we are not saying anything at all but only giving formally correct expression to rubbish or meaningless nonsense. Literary jesting turns very often on the deliberate exploitation of this possibility, and nowhere is there such a mine of entertaining examples as in the writings of Lewis Carroll. 'We mostly' (said The Red Queen) 'have days and nights two or three at a time, and sometimes in the winter we take as many as five nights together – for warmth you know.' A little later she declares that part of the roof came off, and ever so much thunder got in—and it went rolling round the room in great lumps. Perhaps the most celebrated instance is the King's reference to Nobody. The messenger is asked whom he passed on the road and replies 'Nobody'. 'Quite right,' said the King, 'this young lady saw him too. So of course Nobody walks slower than you.' The Messenger protests that 'nobody walks faster than I do'. 'He can't do that,' said the King, 'or else he'd have been here first.' Now we all know that this is a quibble or playing with words, the King is assuming that 'nobody' can be treated like a proper noun; but no one would be seriously taken in by such verbal juggling. In philosophy, however, we do have to draw some very subtle distinctions and view things in unusual ways that make it all too easy to pass from careful analysis to aimless hair-splitting and the manufacturing of notions and problems which owe their existence to some kind of prevarication in which the confusion of forms of speech has an important part.

The discovery that this is a kind of occupational disease of philosophers is by no means new. Socrates and Plato were fully aware of it, and a great deal of Socrates' famous technique or method depended on skilfully exploiting this situation to reduce his pupils to the state of bewilderment in which they could be brought to realize the difficulty of the subject and the need to proceed very cautiously by making the relevant distinctions clear. The reader will find an excellent example in Socrates' handling of his young friend Polemarchus in Book 1 of Plato's *Republic*. Socrates gets his friend to conclude that justice is useless and the just man a thief, although this was the last thing Polemarchus wanted to say. Socrates, moreover, made himself extremely unpopular by showing that many of the pretentious utterances of some of his contemporaries came to no more than impressive-sounding verbiage which could bear no close examination. And in line with this, his equally famous follower Plato is found all the time warning us about 'the charm of words' and their power of making us suppose we were profound when in fact we were hardly saying anything at all. His distrust (in theory at least)[1] of poetry was

1. See my 'On Poetic Truth' in *Morals and Revelation*.

due to this; he thought poets, and even more those who, quoted them, were easily bemused by words in this way. He warns us that philosophers are apt to be blinded by the light of philosophy itself, and he vividly compares those who are making progress in philosophy to a prisoner escaping from a dark cave and stumbling about uncertainly in the dazzle of the sunlight. Many thinkers after Plato, including Hobbes to whom reference was made above, have realized how easily the philosopher may bemuse himself and how prone we all are to be led astray by words.

This danger is intensified by the fact that we have sometimes, in some studies especially, to use ordinary words in a modified and somewhat unusual sense, 'infinity' and 'dimension', for example, in mathematics, 'waves' in physics. It is very easy even for the expert to forget his rather strained use of the ordinary terms he sometimes borrows or adapts for a technical purpose and thus to arrive at strange conclusions by mixing the two levels of discourse. The amateur, especially when he philosophizes about the specialized investigations in question, is even more apt to do so. Some extraordinary theories about time or an alleged fourth dimension have been propounded in this way, the arguments having a great deal in common with those of the Red Queen; and once we have begun on this course there is no end to the glorification of confusion in the elaborate structures we may fabricate.

How much of this has in fact happened in serious philosophy is a moot point. It may be that even our more obscure and provokingly allusive thinkers have more method in their madness then some suppose today. But I think we can all allow the danger of being bemused by words and confusing different types or levels of discourse. Perhaps no one would be taken in by the frivolous example invented, I believe, by Professor Antony Flew and now very familiar in our classrooms, namely the question 'Does gravity run faster than virtue?' But we do use words like 'value' in a very special sense in mathematics, and it might be supposed on this basis that our question is meaningful in some similar way. Apart from that it is obviously not a question, and we would only be led to suppose that it was because it goes easily into the proper grammatical form. But the danger of taking nonsense to be intelligible when it has the structure of normal discourse is obviously a serious one.

A well-known form of such confusion is that known as hypostatizing an abstraction, that is treating some general or abstract notion as if it were an entity of some kind, some concrete reality. It has been thought that many theories about 'universals' have suffered in this way—when questions are asked for example about a 'realm' or place in which properties like redness or goodness exist. We forget that 'the world of values' is at best a metaphor. Similar confusions arise in the treatment of memory—'where', it is sometimes asked, 'are our thoughts when we are not thinking them?', the suggestion being that there is some subterranean place or, something not unlike a place, 'the unconscious' perhaps, in which our memories are stored. We are apt to err in the same way in politics. It is natural to speak of England as being at war with France, well disposed towards Spain, making a treaty with Russia and so on. This is perfectly proper, but we could easily pass from this into supposing that England and France, etc., were individuals, not quite unlike the individual members of these states. There is strictly no such thing as England, whatever the song may say. There are only individuals living together and organized in certain ways. We must not allow our convenient metaphors to suggest anything different. Much that has been said about corporate personality may be traced to the present confusion, and not so long ago it was not uncommon for philosophers in Europe to treat the state as some curious superstructure over and above the lives of its individual members. This can have serious repercussions in practice, and it has been held that the rise and persistence of offensive political regimes in our time may be traced in part to that source. That was one of the themes of L. T. Hobhouse in his celebrated *The Metaphysical Theory of the State* published during the First World War.

An example that bears more closely on the themes of this book is the proneness to think of man, in the general sense, as if there were some entity other than particular men and women who is also in some way all of us together. It is proper, and hardly avoidable in some contexts, to speak of 'the destiny of man', 'the perils confronting man today', and in a more theological context of 'the Fall of Man' (if we believe in it) and of his confrontation by God and his redemption and so on. Or we might say that man is a gregarious animal. No one should be misled by this. Our talk would become hopelessly complicated if we did not have recourse to metaphors and similar devices in these matters. But such devices are treacherous too, and some forms of traditional Christian teaching about the Fall and the sinful state of man have owed not a little, in my view, to confusions engendered by allowing our metaphors to impose too readily upon us here. There are other reasons for so-called collectivist notions of society, guilt and accountability, but the deceptiveness of words has I suspect been much at its mischievous work here to deepen confusion. And this in turn has much to do with erroneous, indeed sinister, views about matters of morality, law and politics — as I have tried to show in Chapters VII, VIII and IX of my *Morals and the New Theology*.

In other fields we have the confusion engendered by misuse of terms like 'instinct' or 'telepathy'. We ascribe the behaviour of birds, when they migrate, to an instinct that guides them, and when people seem able to communicate or to affect one another's thought without the usual media, we call this telepathy. That is quite proper, but we seriously mislead ourselves if we suppose that we have thereby made these perplexing matters clear. We have taken a label or what is little more than a label for an explanation.

It seems evident then that words provide serious traps for the unwary. But what some sceptical philosophers have been apt to say recently is, not that we must be careful not to fall into error and confusion in that way, but that whenever we venture beyond the limits set by empiricism we are bound to be deceiving ourselves through the muddles engendered by misuse of language. In other words, it is thought to be clear as a matter of general principle that nothing can be meaningful if it claims to go beyond the reports of our senses, and thus the only question is why we should judge otherwise in any particular case; the answer is then given in terms of some linguistic confusion like the ones instanced. Instead of a warning we have an invariable principle and an alleged technique for explaining and exposing the bogus character of all non-empirical assertions. Examination of such assertions on their own account is pointless, the sole question from the start being what sort of confusion lies behind them.

This covers a great part of what has come to be known as linguistic philosophy—at least in the early stages of this mode of thinking. Claims have more recently been made for a more open and less sceptical view of linguistic philosophy, but how far the alleged new 'moves', as they are sometimes called, are really different is not easy to settle. We shall return to the question shortly. In the meantime we must concern ourselves with the more expressly sceptical or destructive side of linguistic philosophy which seemed to be at least the main form of it at the start.

In the extreme versions of this philosophy the very meaning of some statement would be identical with the observations by which, as we would normally put it, it would be tested. A statement about the past is thus in effect a statement about what we would find if we took certain observations in the future. Thus 'Caesar crossed the Rubicon' would mean that if we open *De Bello Gallico* we shall find certain words there and so on. Few however, of even the most daring *avant garde* philosophers were prepared to hold for long to this exceptionally paradoxical position,[1] and the general view came to be that no proposition was meaningful unless it could be verified by some factual test or observation. This was the famous 'Verification Principle'. There were two forms of this, a 'strong' and a 'weak'. For strong verification it must in actual fact be possible to provide the necessary test; we cannot at the moment, for example, apply this test to statements about the far side of the moon—we may of course be able to very soon by observing the moon from a sputnik or visiting it. But for weak verification it is enough if the observation is in principle possible, if we can understand what it would be like to make it. This is the form of the theory commonly adopted, and it was

1. The position is discussed by G. C. Field in 'Some Problems of the Philosophy of History', *Proceedings of the British Academy*, Vol. 24.

also given the name logical positivism; few would describe themselves in these terms today, and one of the best-known exponents of the theory, namely Professor A. J. Ayer, has changed his views in some important ways. But more of the substance and spirit of logical positivism persists than many would care to admit.

This is not the place to consider more closely the varieties and subtle shifts of emphasis of sceptical linguistic philosophy and logical positivism. It will be plain that, whatever survives the holocaust of the rigid and consistent application of these principles, the prospects for religion are poor indeed. In religion we seem to deal pre-eminently with an 'unseen' reality of some kind, God or Brahman or some state of Nirvana by which we escape the ills and frustrations of our present life. It is, moreover, in some inner life of our own that this unseen reality manifests itself as a rule, however important the visible world may also be for religion in its fullness. We have doctrines of the soul as well as doctrines of God. But in both these regards we appear to be outrageously non-empirical; if there is need for linguistic debunking of non-empirical claims, here is where we seem to have the field *par excellence* for it; and the linguistic techniques have thus to be invoked to show how men have persisted in thoughts of God or the soul or some other unseen reality through the confusions engendered by language and its forms.

I am reminded here of the advice given to my father when he went, as a young man, to take charge of his first pastorate. A senior minister in that locality urged him to preach a sermon now and again which no one could understand, the intention being apparently to maintain my father's reputation as a scholar and set him up as a thinker of great profundity. The advice, as it happens, was not followed. But what sceptical philosophers today have often maintained about religion is not unlike what my father's friend intended to happen. It is thought that religious people give themselves and others the impression of dealing with profound and significant matters when in fact they have only plunged themselves into utter darkness from which the kindly and enlightened philosopher is able to deliver them at last.

Another illustration which I have already used in print is this. Suppose I were to tell a story about a square circle. There clearly can be no such entity, but I might go on to say who invented this curious object, what his early struggles were like and so forth, I might say how the square circle was lost at one time and what crusades and pilgrimages were undertaken to recover it, what battles were lost and won, what fortunes made and forfeited. This story might be told with more live-liness by some than by others, some would give it more colour and romance, some would bring more eloquence and passion to it, some would tell it with much more intelligence and consistency than others and with a profounder understanding of human nature. But at the heart of it all there would be utter nonsense, for we cannot even conceive of anything being square and round in the same respect. So we have in religion inspired poets, gifted hymn writers, thinkers who far excel others in shrewdness and consistency, men of great psychological insight, and so forth. But at the heart of all this is irredeemable nonsense, and the time has now come to expose it and rescue what we can of the trimmings if we like.

Let us now look more closely at the course of this view of religion.

FURTHER READING

Language, Logic and God. Frederik Ferré (Harpers).

This is a very good introductory work surveying the various positions taken up recently in the philosophy of religion as affected by prevailing trends in philosophy today. It has much relevance to the chapters that follow as well as to the preceding one.

In a very well-known book, *Language, Truth and Logic* (Gollancz), A. J. Ayer made the position known as logical positivism very familiar to students of English philosophy. Much that he maintained in the first edition of this work has been qualified by the author in a later edition, and there are other ways in which the author has modified his position. *Language, Truth and Logic* should be read along with Ayer's inaugural lecture at Oxford at a more recent date—*The Philosophy of Language* (Oxford). Many facets of the change brought about in recent philosophy through the influence (initially) of the Vienna School are skilfully presented in another book already mentioned, *The Revolution in Philosophy* edited by Gilbert Ryle. Samples of writings in the same vein may be found in a work edited by Antony Flew, *Essays in Logic and Language* (Blackwell). Some of these will be difficult for the beginner. I should also much urge the student at this stage to get some impression of the personality of the thinker who lies behind so much in the fashionable philosophy of today, namely Wittgenstein. *Ludwig Wittgenstein: a Memoir*, by Norman Malcolm (Oxford), is a remarkably live and objective portrayal of a very unusual person by a disciple who knew him closely.

Studies in criticism of empiricism and linguistic philosophy are found in the following books.

Clarity is not Enough. Edited by H. D. Lewis (Allen and Unwin). The student will be specially helped at this stage by the contributions to this work of H. H. Price, C. D. Broad, Brand Blanshard and by the first of the contributions by C. A. Campbell 'Common Sense propositions and Philosophical Paradoxes'.

Contemporary Philosophy. Frederick Copleston (Burns and Oates) — especially Chapters I–IV.

The Modern Predicament. H. J. Paton (Allen and Unwin) especially Chapter II on 'The linguistic veto'. A vigorous and much discussed work in criticism of linguistic philosophy is *Words and Things*, by Ernest Gellner (Gollancz).

Other works in this field will be mentioned in the appropriate place later in this book.

CHAPTER EIGHT

RECENT EMPIRICISM AND RELIGION

The views I have just been noting were made widely known when they received a bold and impressive presentation in Professor A. J. Ayer's *Language, Truth and Logic*. In this book there is one chapter on the *Critique of Ethics and Theology*. In the course of it the author tries to show that ethical concepts are '*pseudo*-concepts'. He contends that 'the only information which we can legitimately derive from the study of our aesthetic and moral experiences is information about our own mental and physical make-up'.[1] The celebrated ethical theories of Kant and other writers have the essential defect 'that they treat propositions which refer to the causes and attributes of our ethical feelings as if they were definitions of ethical concepts'. 'Such aesthetic words as "beautiful" and "hideous" are employed, not to make statements of fact, but simply to express certain feelings and evoke a certain response.'[2] This view has been much criticized and it would not be in order to examine it more closely here. It concerns us now as the preliminary to an equally devastating rejection of religious knowledge. Professor Ayer has changed his mind on many matters, but not, so far as I know, on his philosophical objections to religion.

These begin with the insistence that only *a priori* propositions can be certain, but *a priori* propositions, so it is here maintained, are tautologies, that is they only set out what we know already and do not tell us anything new, they certainly do not establish for us any matter of fact. That could only be done by empirical evidence. Such evidence can never prove anything with absolute certainty, there is always the possibility of being mistaken about matters of fact; we must be content with probability, although in many matters this is of a very

1. op. cit., p. 171.
2. op. cit., p. 170.

high order indeed and gives us all the certainty we need. Religious people often claim certainty, but the truth is that we cannot have even a degree of probability in religious matters. For here we go beyond the sphere in which empirical evidence is relevant. Ayer himself puts it thus:

It is sometimes claimed, indeed, that the existence of a certain sort of regularity in nature constitutes sufficient evidence for the existence of a god. But if the sentence 'God exists' entails no more than that certain types of phenomena occur in certain sequences, then to assert the existence of a god will be simply equivalent to asserting that there is the requisite regularity in nature; and no religious man would admit that this was all he intended to assert in asserting the existence of a god. He would say that in talking about God, he was talking about a transcendent being who might be known through certain empirical manifestations, but certainly could not be defined in terms of these manifestations. But in that case the term 'god' is a metaphysical term. And if 'god' is a metaphysical term, then it cannot be even probable that a god exists. For to say that 'God exists' is to make a metaphysical utterance which cannot be either true or false. And by the same criterion, no sentence which purports to describe the nature of a transcendent god can possess any literal significance.[1]

The substance of this argument is that the moment we claim to pass from empirical matters to some reality beyond them we are bound to make a metaphysical utterance which, in terms of the author's general philosophical position, can have no meaning. The rejection of religion follows inevitably from the rejection of metaphysics in the sense of non-empirical utterances.

It follows also that the position of the sceptic, as represented here, is different in one very radical way from the position which sceptics have generally been thought to adopt. In the past the sceptic would not usually be thought, by himself or others, to have no understanding of what the believer maintains; he would simply be denying the truth of it. It is as if someone were to hold that there is a man in the moon. Others of us hold this to be highly improbable, there is no evidence for it and the evidence we have makes it extremely unlikely that there could as yet be anyone living on the moon.

1. op. cit., pp. 173 and 174.

But we all know what it would be like for there to be a man there, and what sort of evidence would prove it. There is no difficulty at all about understanding what is meant. It was in this spirit that there were great debates about religion in the last century. In the celebrated words of Laplace, many thought they could 'dispense with the hypothesis' of God. Phenomena could be explained in other ways, and there were matters like the spectacle of nature 'red in tooth and claw' which told heavily against a religious view. But both parties thought they understood what was at issue, they simply took different sides about it, some sceptics wondering whether after all they were wrong and wishing to be convinced.

The sceptic of today, as represented at least by Professor Ayer, takes a very different attitude. He does not concede the slightest possibility of his opponent being right. For what he holds is, not that the reasons for believing in God are very inadequate or that the evidence against is overwhelmingly strong, but that it makes no sense at all to speak of God; the word 'God' conveys nothing to him; and he does not agree that it can convey anything to the alleged believer either. There is, in strictness, nothing to argue about, nothing which has even a remote chance of being true. The believer is put out of court from the start.

This is indeed radical scepticism. It seems, moreover, to reflect well the attitude of many who are indifferent or opposed to religion today. It is not so much that they find themselves unconvinced but that most that religious people say and do is altogether without meaning to them. Just how novel this situation is may be hard to determine. But it certainly sets the religious apologist and the preacher and priest a very exacting and perplexing task. There is not much consolation in being assured that the position of the sceptic, so far as he firmly denies the truth of affirmations about God, is also without foundation. 'If the assertion that there is a god is non-sensical, then the atheist's assertion that there is no god is equally non-sensical.'[1] But the atheist will not be much perturbed by this, and the believer will find small comfort in it.

1. op. cit., p. 175.

I believe, however, that it is when we take a bold look at this kind of scepticism and grasp the full implications of it that we shall begin to understand how the case for the soundness of religion can be properly made. This is however to anticipate matters which can be set forth more effectively later.

Professor Ayer takes the same rather 'short' way with those who believe in an after-life. He declares that 'to say that there is something imperceptible inside a man, which is his soul or his real self, and that it goes on living after he is dead, is to make a metaphysical assertion which has no more factual content than the assertion that there is a transcendent God'.[1] One does not of course have to locate the soul strictly 'inside' a man, but it is usually claimed that it is non-empirical and cannot be literally seen, and so it comes fairly under Professor Ayer's axe if we grant his premisses.

Many other writers have followed Professor Ayer in stressing the impossibility or, as it is sometimes put, 'the logical impropriety' of basic religious notions. One of these is Professor J. N. Findlay. Unlike Ayer, Professor Findlay has deep sympathies with religion and he has an exceptionally close familiarity with the literature of it. But he does not think that religious beliefs, as we normally understand them, will bear the slightest examination today. He stated his position very challengingly in a short but much discussed article in the journal *Mind*, under the title 'Can God's existence be disproved?'[2] Professor Findlay here sets out to do almost the opposite of one of the most famous arguments for the existence of God, the ontological argument to which I shall refer later. Whereas Anselm and others had tried to show that the very idea of God implied His existence, Findlay contends that the way we have to think of God in religion logically precludes His existing. The ontological argument is made to stand on its head. The discussion goes as follows.

If God is to be the sort of being we can worship He 'must not be limited in any thinkable manner'. He must not be 'dwarfed in thought by still mightier superiorities'. He must

1. op. cit., p. 177.
2. The article is reproduced in *New Essays in Philosophical Theology* (Ed. Flew and MacIntyre).

have 'an *unsurpassable* supremacy along all avenues'. 'The proper object of religious reverence must in some manner be all-comprehensive; there mustn't be anything capable of existing, or of displaying any virtue, without owing all of these absolutely to this single source'. But an object of this kind cannot be one which 'merely *happens* to exist, nor one on which all other objects merely *happen* to depend'. 'God mustn't merely cover the territory of the actual, but also, with equal comprehensiveness, the territory of the possible. And not only must the existence of *other* things be unthinkable without Him, but His own non-existence must be wholly unthinkable in any circumstances'. We could respect and admire a lesser being, but it would be idolatrous to *worship* him. And in this it seems to me that Professor Findlay is altogether right. He shows a very fine understanding of the religious frame of mind. I shall return to the point again, but in the meantime it will be enough to concede Professor Findlay's initial point that a being who merely happened to be, whom we could at least think of as not existing, would be less than what we understand by God, a being conditioned by nothing outside Himself.

But if this is the way in which we must think of God, then, according to Findlay, we run at once into very grave difficulties. For, he maintains, the only sort of knowledge which has a necessary factor in it is that which concerns the connections of abstract truths with one another. We see that the sum of the angles of a triangle must be 180 degrees or that three fours are twelve. But this does not tell us that there is any actual triangle or inform us in any way about any qualities it has beyond those which it must have by the formal necessities of mathematics. We may learn certain things about actual objects from mathematics, but only if we know independently what sort of objects they are and that they exist. There is not, in other words, strict necessity about our knowledge that things are real. We find out that in fact there are certain things and not others, and that they have this or that empirical property. We find that there are swans and that usually they are white, but that there are no unicorns. It is conceivable that there should be unicorns; if we learnt that there were creatures such as we have in mind when we picture a unicorn, in some unexplored part of the world or in another planet, we might express surprise, since it is odd that we should have been thinking of such a creature without ever meeting it, but we should not say that it was impossible. There are not, to our knowledge, winged horses. But there could be. We find in fact that there are not, and that the laws of biology make it highly improbable. But what is improbable in our limited experience often turns out to be the case, as in the weightlessness of men 'in space'. What is, and what is not the case, and the rules for the way things behave, depend in fact on what we find, on what the evidence determines. We know in the same way that there are certain persons. Not even the completest and most vivid description could prove to us that some person was real and not a person in fiction. Someone would have to see him or have some other evidence of his existence and nature. It does not follow from the way we think of things and persons that they have to be. Necessity does not seem therefore to belong to existence at any point. And accordingly it seems improper to think of any necessarily existing being. There seems thus to be a fatal contradiction at the heart of religion. It seems to demand something which it is logically impossible that there should be. It is logically 'inappropriate'.

To put this in Professor Findlay's own words, 'those who believe in necessary truths which aren't merely tautological, think that such truths merely connect the *possible* instances of various characteristics with each other; they don't expect such truths to tell them whether there *will* be instances of any characteristics'. The religious frame of mind is for this reason 'in a quandary, it seems invincibly determined both to eat its cake and have it. It desires the Divine Existence both to have that inescapable character which can, on modern views, only be found where truth reflects an arbitrary convention, and also the character of "making a real difference" which is only possible where truth does not have this merely linguistic basis. We may accordingly deny that modern approaches allow us to remain agnostically poised in regard to God; they force us to come down on the atheistic side. For if God is to satisfy religious claims and needs, he must be a being in every way inescapable, One whose existence and whose possession of certain excellences we cannot possibly conceive away. And modern methods make it self-evidently absurd (if they don't make it ungrammatical) to speak of such a Being and attribute existence to him.' So, as in the case of Professor Ayer, we seem forced to conclude that the idea of God is literally non-sense, an idea which we cannot even begin to conceive, like that of a square-circle.

To feel the force of Findlay's contention we need not sub-scribe to the extreme view that 'necessity in propositions merely reflects our use of words' and is just an 'arbitrary con-vention'. We may hold that there are in mathematics and logic necessary statements which are not mere tautologies. For the true force of the argument really derives from the fact that such necessity is not found when we think of individual existing things. Nor need we consider here the alternatives which Findlay offers to the orthodox religious view. He sug-gests that we should substitute for an existent God an 'imagin-ary focus' or 'inexhaustible object of aspiration' for our own actions, and I shall come to that, along with kindred sugges-tions, in due course. In the meantime it must suffice to note one further instance of the way modern philosophers discredit the usual or accepted religious attitudes by claiming that the notions on which they seem to depend are 'logically improper'.

Similar views to those of Professor Findlay are advanced by Professor J. J. C. Smart in an article entitled 'The Existence of God'.[1] He also declares that 'the concept of a logically neces-sary being is a self-contradictory concept, like the concept of a round square'. He contrasts 'necessary propositions' with 'contingent propositions'. The former 'are guaranteed solely by the rules for the use of the symbols they contain. In the case of propositions of the second class a genuine possibility of agreeing or not agreeing with reality is left open; whether they are true or false depends not on the conventions of our language but on reality. ... So no informative proposition can be logically necessary.'[2] We may not accept the view which makes necessary truths a matter of conventions and rules for

1. *New Essays in Philosophical Theology* (as above).
2. op. cit. p. 38.

the use of symbols, we may think that there is more to it than that. But we would still find it hard to deny that 'An existential proposition must be very different from any logically necessary one, such as a mathematical one, for example' and that it is 'reality which decides' whether or not we affirm or deny an existential proposition. It appears thus hard to deny that 'the demand that the existence of God should be logically necessary is thus a self-contradictory one.'

Professor Smart has, like Findlay, an alternative which he thinks will meet our requirements in religion. But discussion of that had also better be postponed for the moment. Nor shall I consider here how, if at all, we can get out of the 'quandary', as Professor Findlay put it, that we seem to think of God as a being who cannot but exist and at the same time have no justification for asserting existence except as contingent fact dependent on the available evidence. I shall hold later that the quandary is a very significant one for religion. In the meantime it will be well for the reader to ponder it on his own and consider what, if anything, can be done about it.

Another very celebrated presentation of the view that religious affirmations can have no meaning but must, on the contrary, be vapid, may be found in a paper by Professor John Wisdom entitled 'Gods'.[1] In this paper Wisdom sets out to confront us with cases of sharp and important disagreement which we would not attempt to settle by recourse to facts. He considers for example the way we appraise a picture and suggests that we settle disputes in such matters 'by talk, perhaps' which helps us to see the picture differently. This is not, to my mind, very helpful philosophically unless we are told more than the author ventures to give us about the sort of talk which matters here. Another example is that of deciding whether the doer of an action, whose factual character we know, showed reasonable care. The ruling in a court of law, for example, could be very important—'a game is lost or won' with it. But, it is held, the argument is not 'a case of demonstrative reasoning'. I am not at all certain where these considerations lead us, or are meant to lead us, and I question the helpfulness of bringing together, as samples of the same

1. Reproduced in the author's *Philosophy and Psychoanalysis.*

kind of fundamental difficulty, problems which differ so sharply in many respects as those selected by Wisdom. But what concerns us at the moment is that we are brought, by way of these sample problems, to a view of religious statements as not admitting of any sort of factual verification.

The crux of the paper is a much discussed parable of 'the invisible gardener'. This is forcibly reproduced by Professor Antony Flew in a paper[1] which set off a further spate of discussion. The parable tells of a clearing in a jungle which looks like a garden which someone must be tending. But no such gardener is ever seen or heard. The disputants set up a fence and electrify it, they patrol with bloodhounds. But there are no shrieks or other signs of an invisible climber, the hounds never give cry. Yet one explorer insists that there must be a gardener. In Flew's words[2] 'Yet still the Believer is not convinced. "But there is a gardener, invisible, intangible, insensible to electric shocks, a gardener who has no scent and makes no sound, a gardener who comes secretly to look after the garden he loves." At last the Sceptic despairs, "But what remains of your original assertion? Just how does what you call an invisible, intangible, eternally elusive gardener differ from an imaginary gardener or even from no gardener at all?"'

The suggestion here is that religious assertions are qualified to the point where they have no significance, in Professor Flew's pointed phrase they 'die the death of a thousand qualifications', they are 'eroded' until they are not assertions at all; and it must be admitted that this is very like what happens. We say that God loves us, but there is appalling evil which we would expect a God of love to prevent. But, it is said, God's love is not like ours, it is inscrutable. Whatever happens we shall still believe that God loves us. But in that case does the word 'love' retain any meaning? Is there any point, Professor Flew asks, at which we would surrender our belief in the love of God or in His existence? If not, if our assertion is such that no evidence could upset it, can we be thought to be saying anything? If I affirm that a cat has been hidden in the room, I know that this must make a difference at some

1. *New Essays in Philosophical Theology*, Chapter VI.
2. op. cit., p. 96.

point to what I would find or hear. If it did not, the statement would be pointless. But what would have to be different for there to be or not to be God? The believer may refer to the good in the world, to prayers that have been answered, and so on. But when we note that there is evil and many prayers not answered, the qualifications begin, and Professor Flew's suggestion is that the qualifications go on being made to the point where nothing is different because there is, or is not, a God. But a statement that is compatible with all facts whatsoever, or with any and every evidence, seems to be a statement without any content or substance, in short not a statement at all but empty words.

Professor Flew follows up this attack with another. He observes, in a further article,[1] that Christians usually hold that God is 'all-powerful' and also 'all good'. But how then do we account for evil? In the past one answer has been that God allows evil in making us free to do good or evil—evil comes about through our misuse of our freedom, and we must not blame God. Now I think that this does cover a great deal of evil. My own objection to it would be that there is much evil, unavoidable suffering of men and animals for example, which we do not bring about ourselves. The free-will answer is only a partial one, and much remains to be considered in some other way. But Flew does not think that the free-will answer is even a partial one. It is 'broken-backed', because God could, it is held, have made us free and guaranteed that we always did what was best. This seems very paradoxical. How can we be free and yet bound to act in a certain way?

The answer is a very linguistic one. We are invited to consider what is the standard or 'paradigm' use of the word 'freedom'—the 'appeal to the paradigm case', as this procedure has now come to be known. In the paradigm use we might say that I am free in writing this passage now. No one drags my hand along the page, no one holds a pistol at my head. I am writing 'of my own free will' and can stop if I wish. And yet my friends who saw me go up to the study, or whom I refused

1. 'Divine Omnipotence and Human Freedom', in *New Essays in Philosophical Theology*.

to join in a game because I was going to work, could have said in advance where I would be and what I am doing. Indeed we anticipate some actions months and years ahead; in Flew's example, we know that an engaged couple are going to get married in the normal course of things, but we still affirm when the time comes that they are doing so of their own accord and freely. Compulsion would imply at least that their parents (or someone else) were putting pressure on them. In short we rely on one another, there is some continuity in conduct, people act in character and so on; and yet we speak of being free.

Now this is much too vast a problem in itself to be examined on its own account here. We should have to ask whether there were occasions when we did not act in character, and whether this constitutes freedom in some special sense. I shall at least touch on the problem again. But what should be noted at the moment is the easy way in which Professor Flew disposes of this problem and all its complications by simply noting that we do, in ordinary parlance, speak of being free in situations where we seem also to be doing what persons of our sort are bound to do. But this is to give up at the start, to shelter behind 'ordinary usage' when we should be seeking to probe deeper and trying to sort out the matters which are not properly reflected in what we say for ordinary purposes from day to day.

Here then are some examples of attempts to show that basic religious notions are inherently impossible and only seem meaningful when we confuse different levels of discourse or depart from the thinking which is reflected in the talk that directly reflects our day to day experience. Many other examples could be provided. Indeed we could well fill the entire space of this book with the present subject, so much has it occupied the minds of some philosophers of late. But then we should be neglecting equally important topics, and I must content myself now with urging the student to consider carefully as much as he can of the material suggested for further reading at the end of this chapter.

I have concerned myself mainly in the preceding pages with difficulties about the existence of God and the main divine attributes like love and power. But there are obvious difficulties also when we consider the more specific affirmations made in the various religions, for example that God is One and also Three Persons, that Buddha lived on and died of ripe years long after the enlightenment that released him from temporal ills, that we may be called to account for our deeds although everything happens by the will of Allah. These 'mysteries', as they are sometimes described, also invite the attention of the sceptic armed with his new techniques and determined to expose confusion at every point. It is, however, to the basic issues that consideration has been given mainly: and this is not strange, for if it can be shown that the ideas of God or of the soul or of divine love are inherently impossible ones, there seems not much point, in the Christian religion for example, in troubling our minds much about the rest. But we shall be considering the more precise affirmations of religious faith later when I have said more about the basic notions.

The question which now arises is whether there is some general line of defence to be taken against the claim made by the sceptical linguistic philosopher, namely that the basic religious assertions admit of no verification in terms of what we find in the world and that they are bound to be confused or vapid. Can we go further than questioning particular procedures like those of Professor Flew? What reply can be made to Professor Findlay with whom I have already expressed some agreement? What are we to make in general of the parable of the gardener as Professor Flew reproduces it? I think that there is a reply to be made to the empiricist and to those who follow him in seeking to make out that religious notions are inherently misleading, and I think further that it is in finding this reply and meeting the basic challenge about the meaningfulness of religious assertions that we shall begin to understand religious matters properly and see how more constructive work in religious thought may be undertaken.

Before we undertake this task, however, account must be given of the attitude adopted by many thinkers who believe that the criticisms of which I have given some examples could not be directly met but that what matters in religion is not affected by this, that we can concede to our critics the substance at least of what they say and yet hold on to religion. This seems to be a somewhat desperate remedy, but it has been vigorously commended by very gifted and influential philosophers of our day. Let us now look at some of their views.

FURTHER READING

Much in the book by Frederik Ferré already mentioned will be relevant to the theme of this chapter. An admirable critical survey of the positions just discussed will be found in *Words and Images* by E. L. Mascall (Longmans) — a short but very readable work; and samples of these positions will be found in *New Essays in Philosophical Theology*, edited by Antony Flew and Alasdair MacIntyre (S.C.M. Press) and in *Faith and Logic*, edited by Basil Mitchell (Allen and Unwin). Some impressive reactions to the empiricism of today will also be found in the last two volumes, and I should like to draw attention especially to the notable essay by Ian Crombie in *Faith and Logic* — 'The possibility of theological statements'. In *Christianity and Paradox* (Watts), Ronald Hepburn provides some very challenging objections to religion along the lines outlined in the preceding chapter; and a sustained defence of religion by a writer who shares many of Hepburn's assumptions is found in *Religion and the Scientific Outlook*, by T. R. Miles (Allen and Unwin). Other books which have much relevance here are *Religious Belief*, by C. B. Martin (Cornell University Press) and *Faith and Knowledge* and *Philosophy of Religion*, by John Hick. The student might also consult here my own 'Survey of Recent Work in the Philosophy of Religion', in *The Philosophical Quarterly* for April and July 1954.

CHAPTER NINE

EMPIRICISM AND ATTENUATIONS
OF FAITH

Among those who have felt the appeal of empiricism today have been many religious persons. Their position has obviously not been an easy one. For how could they remain religious if they were also to be consistent empiricists? Should they give up their religion? Many were reluctant to pay that price, but it was also plain to them that they could not hold on to religion in the way this is normally understood. The dilemma became acute, as the conflict of science and religion in a different form was distressing to many in the last century. We saw that some took refuge, in an earlier day, in a kind of 'double-think', a 'truth of the heart' as well as a 'truth of the mind'. Nothing quite as crude as this has happened today, but out of a sore and desperate strait there have emerged several attempts to understand religion in ways that did no violence to empiricist principles. One could again, it appears, have the best of both worlds, one could stay in the prevailing philosophical fashion and be firmly, in some cases indeed ardently, religious as well. How was this to be accomplished?

One of the boldest attempts to achieve the desired reconciliation of religion with an empiricist view of truth appeared in an article to the journal *Mind*[1] by the Rev. David Cox. The article had the title 'The Significance of Christianity', and this was a little startling in a philosophical journal of a severely professional and somewhat 'tough-minded' character. But it was not hard to see where the appeal of the article lay. It began with a firm exhortation to Christians to adopt the principles of logical positivism. This does not, for the author, require us to confine ourselves strictly to what our senses report ('experience' can be taken in a wider sense than that), but we must all the same dispense with any reality beyond

1. *Mind*, April 1950.

or outside our present experience, any 'transcendent' object of worship as it is sometimes put. The author indeed affirms that 'Originally Christian doctrine was not intended to provide a description of what might be called "transcendent reality"'. Its function was 'to safeguard Christian experience'. The suggestion that doctrine should be considered in close relation to experience seems to be a sound and important one. But Mr. Cox believes that experience is best safeguarded by doctrine by the formulation of rules for the use of terms in what he calls 'theological jargon' and by 'empirical hypotheses' 'which can be verified by human experience'. The serious trouble about this is that human experience is understood for the purpose in question as involving nothing that is more than human; and this it is that sets Mr. Cox on his further course to outline a means of restating the main Christian doctrines in terms that accord with his principles. He does so as follows.

We are first told that the word 'God' is only rightly used in phrases like 'meeting God' or 'encountering God', and the rules for the use of the word will thus be rules for describing the experiences mentioned. Accordingly 'God is loving' could be restated as the formal rule that 'no experience of meeting a person who is not someone who loves you can be rightly called "an experience of meeting God"'. As an alternative we could have the empirical hypothesis that 'some experiences called "meeting God" will probably be experiences of meeting a person who loves you'. I do not know how far these statements could be warranted, even in the little (from the religious point of view) that they say. Would not religious people say that they are meeting God even when not meeting someone who loves them? But the main difficulty is that the role of God Himself becomes a very ambiguous one in Mr. Cox's restatements—does God come properly into the transaction at all? The suggestion seems to be that we can dispense with Him. The word 'God' is just one that happens to be useful in describing merely human experiences.

Mr. Cox goes on to declare that the doctrine 'God created the world from nothing', 'is, at first sight, a particularly non-significant statement', but that it can be made significant if understood to mean that 'everything which we call "material" can be used in such a way that it contributes to the well-being of men'. I am puzzled again as to how we would establish this claim about material things. But we have obviously travelled very far here from what anyone would normally understand as the meaning of the words 'God created the world'. I shall be attempting to show later that, far from being 'non-significant', the idea of creation, though very peculiar and in some way elusive, is about the most significant there is. But for the moment it must be enough to wonder whether anything of a properly religious character remains in Mr. Cox's suggested translation. He has achieved his aim of preserving Christianity 'from the limbo to which metaphysics is being exiled (rightly, as I believe) by the logical positivists'. But is it any longer Christianity? One can understand better the attitude of Professor Ayer. As he deems the word 'God' to be devoid of meaning he does not pretend that he can have any sympathy with religion. This is a consistent and honest position. We know what Ayer thinks, and we know where we stand with him—believers and atheists alike. Can anyone say the same of the Rev. David Cox?

There are many who have followed a course similar to that of Mr. Cox. Some of these make very explicit use of alleged linguistic techniques. For example, I have heard it argued that when we consider a statement like 'I believe in God' in the Christian creed we should pay more heed than has been customary to the words 'believe in'. The suggestion is that we must distinguish between 'believing in' and 'believing that', i.e. believing that something is the case. There is an important half-truth in this. Christian belief, for instance, in its fullness involves trust and a commitment of some kind. It is like believing 'in' your doctor or your friend; you are prepared to take their advice and rely on them. But surely we do not 'believe in' anything without 'believing that' as well. If I believe in my doctor I go to see him when there is need, and if I wait some time in his surgery it is in the expectation that in due course he will appear. I could not believe in him and not believe that he existed and was available. Similarly, if we believe in God we must believe that He is real, and if we believe in Christ we must consider some Christian teachings to be true about Him. Otherwise, why should we believe in Him rather than anyone else?

Others have tried to be rid of the 'propositional' element in religion, that is the factor of belief and its problems, by making the emotional element the central one. This is in line with much that has been written in recent ethics as well. One of the subjects most debated in ethics has been whether there can be 'ethics without propositions'.[1] It has been suggested that ethical assertions do not make affirmations about some property like goodness but only have the form of assertions when in fact their aim is to express or to arouse emotions. We caught some hint of this earlier in our reference to Professor Ayer. A similar view has been adopted by some writers on religion. It has been maintained, for example, that the point of a religious practice, like going to Church, is that it satisfies 'religious emotions'. There is some precedent for this in religious thought in the past. Some have supposed, for example, that the eminent religious thinker Schleiermacher[2] was commending a religion of feeling as distinct from a religion of belief. I do not think this is fair to Schleiermacher,[3] for although he gave prominence in some of his work to what he called the 'feeling of dependence' this was not to be understood in a way that was not directed to something beyond itself. Schleiermacher was indeed suspicious of dogma, especially when the dead letter of it tended to replace live religion and genuine piety. But he did not wish to make religion solely or even mainly a matter of feeling. That is however how he has often been understood, and some of his followers have taken the view thus ascribed to him to be the truth of the matter. In this they were preparing the way for those who wish today to turn the edge of the epistemological difficulties of religion by presenting it as a matter of satisfying certain religious emotions.

1. This is the title of a well-known paper by Winston F. H. Barnes in *The Proceedings of the Aristotelian Society*, Supp. Vol. XXII. Barnes does not, however, defend an emotivist view; cf. also Jonathan Harrison. 'Can Ethics do without Propositions', *Mind* 1950.

2. and 3. See references at the end of the chapter.

The objection to this procedure is that an emotion can hardly be understood by itself. There is rarely, if ever, a mere emotion. If I have, for example, the emotion of fear, this is because I believe I am menaced by something. The belief may be without foundation and perhaps extremely irrational. Many factors may come into it, as in some of the unhealthy states described by psychologists when people almost enjoy their fear or desire it in some way. But even in these perverted states a fear must have something, however posited, on which to feed. Even if I cannot express my fear it must in some vague fashion be fear *of* something, even if only of something within myself or the disapproval of my friends. Likewise, if I love I must love someone or something, even if I have only a very vague feeling of elation which I cannot properly describe, and, if some state of merely physical well-being has much to do with this, my joy takes its character from something which in some way I take to be the case, within myself or in the world about me. Normally we can specify fairly explicitly what causes us joy or fear. I am glad because I have passed my examination, frightened because there is danger, hurt because I have been snubbed, in love with a particular young lady because of what she is like or at least what I 'find in her' as the saying goes—no other would do. Our emotions thus feed on something beyond themselves.

Must not this be true in religion? However prominent a place emotions may have in it, there must surely be something which determines what sort of emotion it is. How otherwise could we recognize or characterize a religious emotion? What would distinguish it from any other? But if we have to go beyond the emotion, to what can we go other than some complex of experiences in which the factor of belief has a part, normally a prominent one? If we go to church to satisfy emotions these are surely the emotions centred on the reality we worship, on God for example and what we believe God has done for us; and if someone were to attend a religious service for the satisfaction which the music or some colourful spectacle afforded him, but without a belief in some other reality which was symbolized or encountered in such ways, then we would say that at best he was having a poetic or aesthetic experience, not that he was worshipping or having a religious experience. Nor would I agree that even poetic or musical experience is merely an emotional matter. It has more body than that, but however important that may be, and however close, as I think it is, to religion, religion requires something more which it takes to be of central importance. We cannot avoid the problems which arise from this by simply saying that we are religious to satisfy religious emotions.

It is not however to religious emotions that philosophers have mainly turned in recent attempts to reconcile empiricism with religion. There is a further expedient which has received more support and publicity. It is that commended by Professor R. B. Braithwaite in his Eddington Memorial Lecture under the title *An Empiricist's View of the Nature of Religious Belief*. This lecture has already been widely discussed and criticized very recently. But a reference to it in this book seems warranted as a way of indicating the courses which some philosophers are prepared to adopt today as a way of adjusting religion to the philosophical empiricism to which they subscribe.

The first part of Braithwaite's lecture is concerned more with ethics than with religion. In common with many others today he wishes to commend 'a form of ethics without propositions'. But his is 'a conative rather than an emotive theory: it makes the primary use of a moral assertion that of expressing the intention of the asserter to act in a particular sort of way',[1] for example to maximize happiness. A utilitarian is thus not asserting any proposition nor evincing any feeling of approval, 'he is subscribing to a policy of action'.[2] The merit of this is taken to be in particular that it alone provides a satisfactory answer to the question: 'What is the reason for my doing what I think I ought to do? The answer it gives is that, since my thinking that I ought to do the action is my intention to do it if possible, the reason why I do the action is simply that I intend to do it, if possible.'[3] On other views there is a 'mysterious gap' 'between the moral judgement and the intention to act in accordance with it'. On Professor Braithwaite's view there is none.

Whether it is an advantage to close this gap, mysterious or

1. op. cit., p. 12.   2. op. cit., p. 13.   3. op. cit., p. 14.

otherwise, I must leave largely to the reader. For I cannot go closely into ethical questions at this stage. But it seems to me plain that to close the gap in question as completely as Braithwaite does is just to make an end of ethics. Does not morality depend on our being able to act contrary to our convictions? And if intention to act and conviction go together as closely as Professor Braithwaite expects are we not bound to approve all intentions, or at least all policies of action equally, those of Hitler as much as those of Ghandi? Many writers, including Mr. R. M. Hare, who is a prominent advocate of a conativist ethic, have tried to meet this objection; and the reader may wish to examine their work.[1] I can only say here that they do not seem to me to come within any length of succeeding.

Having dispensed with propositions in ethics Professor Braithwaite turns to religion. This is for him very closely related to ethics—one might almost say that the two are identical. For the main thing in religion is also the intention to act in a certain way, but here we are thinking not so much of specific intentions taken by themselves but of a system of intentions, a policy, a way of life as a whole. It is thus 'the intention to behave which constitutes what is known as religious conviction'[2] and 'the primary use of religious assertions is to announce allegiance to a set of moral principles'.[3] Thus 'conversion is not only a change in the propositions believed—indeed there may be no specifically intellectual change at all; it is a change in the state of will'.[4] This is frankly described as 'assimilating religious assertions to moral assertions'.

In presenting this view Professor Braithwaite makes much of the very close relation there has usually been thought to be between religion and ethics. In this I, for one, go entirely with him. Few things seem to me more regrettable than neglect of this close relation of religion and ethics, and I have ventured on more than one occasion to voice some very vigorous protests against the tendency of some theologians to obscure or distort the ethical factor in religion. Morality, in some form, lies at the heart of most religions. But it is one

1. See Further Reading appended to chapter Two.
2. op. cit., p. 16.   3. and 4. op. cit., p. 19.

thing to say this, and to be concerned about it, it is quite another to claim to give an account of all that matters in religion in ethical terms. That is what Braithwaite seems to do.

He does indeed note some important differences between moral and religious assertions. The latter give more place to concrete examples, like the story of the good Samaritan, and they concern themselves more with inner behaviour, with the heart as well as the will. I am not sure how far these contentions are sound, but they do not take us in any significant way beyond ethics and our behaviour in the present world.

We are thus driven to ask what account Professor Braithwaite would give of aspects of religion that appear at least to go beyond morality. When the Christian, for example, professes his belief in God or the doctrine of the Trinity, when we speak of redemption and reconciliation and of eternal life and so on, just what are we doing? When we speak of divine providence or of the grace of God, when St. Paul says that 'it is not I but Christ that worketh in me', how are these matters to be understood? Can they be jettisoned altogether? Can we think of Christianity solely in terms of loving one another in the right way?

Professor Braithwaite certainly thinks that the essential differences between religions turn on the moral policies they recommend. He believes the Christian religion, with its particular policy of love or *agape*, excels in this respect and he has become for this reason a prominent member of the Anglican Church. But as for the other ingredients of religion to which the churches normally attach importance, these can be treated as no more than 'stories' which stimulate us to behave in the right way. We need not take the stories to be true in any sense, it is enough if we 'entertain' them, or let our minds dwell on them, sufficiently for them to set us on the right way of living. Religions differ according to the stories they tell in this way. Part of the stories will be believed as a matter of fact, like some of the historical statements to be made about Jesus, for example that he died on a cross in the time of Pontius Pilate in Judaea. But it is not strictly necessary to believe even these things. The important thing is that 'the story' should be given its chance to do its work.

The use of the term 'story' is quite deliberate. It is preferred, for example, to the word 'myth' of which so much has been heard of late in theology. For a myth is consistent with a truth of some sort being involved. We speak thus of the creation stories being myths and we mean that they must not be taken in a literal sense—we do not mean that we give up the idea of the world's being in some sense created by God. But the term story is quite neutral here, and with much frankness and clarity Professor Braithwaite prefers it for that reason.

The stories in question are, moreover, all of them stories which must be understood empirically or verificationally, that is 'in terms of human beings—mythological beings, it may be, who never existed, but who nevertheless would have been empirically observable had they existed'.[1] The author sums up the matter thus himself.

But my contention is that belief in the truth of the Christian stories is not the proper criterion for deciding whether or not an assertion is a Christian one. A man is not, I think, a professing Christian unless he both proposes to live according to Christian moral principles and associates his intention with thinking of Christian stories; but he need not believe that the empirical propositions presented by the stories correspond to empirical fact.

But if the religious stories need not be believed, what function do they fulfil in the complex state of mind and behaviour known as having a religious belief? How is entertaining the story related to resolving to pursue a certain way of life? My answer is that the relation is a psychological and causal one. It is an empirical psychological fact that many people find it easier to resolve upon and carry through a course of action which is contrary to their natural inclinations if this policy is associated in their minds with certain stories. And in many people the psychological link is not appreciably weakened by the fact that the story associated with the behaviour policy is not believed.[2]

We are reminded of the influence of novels like those of Dostoevsky or of other frankly fictitious works like Bunyan's *Pilgrim's Progress*. Braithwaite concludes:

It is *all* the thoughts of a man that determine his behaviour; and these include his phantasies, imaginations, ideas of what he would

1. op. cit., p. 25.   2. op. cit., p. 27.

wish to be and do, as well as propositions which he believes to be true.[1]

This leaves us in no doubt where we are invited to stand. The Bible is not radically different from *Pilgrim's Progress* or the novels of Dickens. There is nothing that must be strictly believed but only ideas to be entertained for the moral inspiration they provide, and all such ideas must admit of being understood exhaustively in terms of this world and the lives of men. This has the considerable advantage that it much simplifies the problem of religious belief—indeed it almost disposes of it altogether. There is no epistemological problem that would not arise in the ordinary way in science or some other branch of secular knowledge. The peculiar difficulties of religious belief have all gone, the mysteries have been dissipated. But at what cost?

I do not know how anyone can suppose that those who wrote the Bible at various times, and those who read it afterwards, thought of God, for example, as He figures in 'the stories', entirely in terms of some picture in their minds of bodily creatures like ourselves—and if the matter were pressed, as it will be later, are we not ourselves more than physical observable realities? We may read of God speaking 'out of the whirlwind' or of the word of God 'coming' to this or that prophet, but has anyone at any time, even in remote days, taken this seriously to be more than metaphor? If they did the Bible itself would provide ample corrective. Was it not made very plain to Moses that God was invisible, do we not read again and again of 'a God that hides himself', has not Professor Braithwaite ever pondered the eighteenth or the hundred and forty fifth psalm or the book of Job, or the description of the call of Isaiah? Does he think that God was supposed to hide himself literally in the clouds? Metaphor and poetry may sometimes have taken too firm a hold of men's minds, and it may not be possible for us to dispense altogether with mental pictures—that is a very moot point. But it is hard to think that even the most simple-minded believer thought of God entirely in terms of the pictures by which we represent Him.

1. op. cit., p. 28.

And what of more mature minds? Does Braithwaite seriously believe that the great doctors of the church thought of God as a being who descended from the sky to address men? Is that how the educated believer of today thinks of Him? Let Professor Braithwaite say that such belief is without foundation, or if he likes without meaning. But he is certainly naïve in the extreme if he supposes that believers do not at least claim to encounter some Being who has not a terrestrial form at all. The great Christian painters may have thought 'of the three persons of the Trinity in visual terms'[1] and the poets presented them as talking to one another. But that is what poetry and painting are like. No one supposes that everything so portrayed must be strictly visible and audible. Is the purported redemption of man, his being 'bought at a price', an entirely witnessable transaction, is the 'work of the Spirit' reducible solely to what can be observed in the lives of men now? This is certainly not what Christians suppose—or have ever supposed. And if Professor Braithwaite thinks he has simplified our problems for us that can only be because he has cut away the substance of Christian belief. Christianity does not begin to be recognizable in his picture of it.

And what of other religions? Does Professor Braithwaite suppose that when the Hindu speaks of the 'One *Atman* Who is Everything', of the *Karma* which determines our lot in a particular life and of the state of *nirvana* by which we are released from the wheel of rebirth and united with the One which is our own true reality—does he suppose that all this can be understood in terms of what we find by observation in the world around us? Is it not expressly taught that the world of empirical experience is illusory and evil? We may dismiss these doctrines, if we like, as nonsense, although I would not do so. But to suppose that they can be presented in terms of stories about human life as we witness or imagine it in our present experience seems to me about as wide of the mark as any theory could be. There may be substance in the claim that Hinduism is excessively other-wordly. That it can be thought of wholly as a way of life in this world must surely

1. op. cit., p. 29.

startle anyone who has the slightest familiarity with it.

The same could be said of other religions, not excluding Confucianism to which Professor Braithwaite makes a casual allusion. But it appears to be the Christian religion and Buddhism that he has mainly in mind, and it seems to me that he could hardly have referred to two religions which lend themselves less readily to his emaciated account of what religion is like in essentials.

I must leave the student to judge further on his own, hoping that he will look closely at Braithwaite's lecture and some of the discussions of it listed below. But we have not done by a very long way with attempts to solve the problems which confront us in religion by emaciating it and reducing the substance of it to what we can observe in 'the here and now'. The views I have just been noting have at least the merit of being explicit and easy to grasp, and this makes their deficiencies all the more apparent; there is no prevarication. But I have now to note some more subtle and elusive variations on the same essential theme and some positions which seem to concede more to the traditional view although in fact little of the substance of traditional notions survives in them.

FURTHER READING

An Empiricist View of the Nature of Religious Belief, by R. B. Braithwaite (Cambridge). This is carefully discussed by E. L. Mascall in *Words and Images,* and by A. C. Ewing in a contribution to *Philosophy* for July 1957 — the whole of this number of *Philosophy* is devoted to the subject of empiricism and religion and has much relevance to the themes of the present part of this book. In amplification of the reference to Schleiermacher the student should read Schleiermacher's *On Religion: Speeches to its Cultured Despisers,* now available as a paper back (Torch Books). A new appraisal of this work is attempted by me in a contribution to *Theology* for March 1962.

An influential Swedish philosopher, Hägerström, who flourished at the turn of this century, put forward ideas very similar to the positivism typified by Ayer in his early work. It is interesting that Hägerström should have arrived at ideas which were to be developed independently and made so influential later by the Vienna Circle and its English followers. It strengthens the view that there is much in the life and culture of our times to direct men's thoughts into these sceptical and anti-metaphysical channels. Hägerström was sharp in his denunciation of metaphysics. But, unlike Ayer, he thought this was an advantage to religion and he put forward views much in line with those discussed above. His thought was welcomed by religious leaders and not taken to put religion in any jeopardy. This shows how strong, in certain circumstances, the appeal of the 'short way', as I have called it, can be. A selection of the works of Hägerström has been made recently by Robert Sandin and translated into English. It has just been published, with a memoir of Hägerström by C. D. Broad, under the title *Philosophy and Religion* (Allen and Unwin). It will be interesting to compare this work with its English counterparts.

CHAPTER TEN

THE APPEAL TO LANGUAGE

Some reference has already been made to the influence of Wittgenstein. Among the ideas derived from him is that of metaphysics as some kind of plan or model of our experience as a whole. This is understood to mean that there can be no reference beyond the reality of the world as we find it in present experience; there can be little, that is, of metaphysics in the old sense, but there can be some helpful over-all way of viewing the sort of experience which we all in fact have. This does not add anything strictly to our information, it provides some conspectus, a map or grid which helps us to get the significance of what we do know. Such a suggestion is not altogether new, it may owe more than some realize to one side of Kant's thought. Nor is it easy to determine what limitations Wittgenstein himself would place on this approach or just how sceptical he intended to be in commending it. But the main intention, as taken up by some of Wittgenstein's most eager followers, is clear enough. It is a conspectus of present experience that metaphysics really provides, and so far as there was significance in the high debates of system builders in the past, this was because they were taking an indirect way to carry out a task whose nature we understand much better now. When Plato spoke about 'forms' or ideas as the true reality, when Spinoza spoke of 'infinite attributes' and the idealists of the universe as being one universal mind or will, and when pluralists denied this, there was no sense at all in what they were doing at its face value, but it had importance (and retains it for us) in so far as it provided various models for the way we are to view the course of the lives we actually live in this world; and some go so far as to suggest that the thinkers in question had often a shrewd understanding of where the true significance of their work, as now represented, lies.

To illustrate this suggestion a reference is often made to pictures or natural objects which we can view in widely different ways. We have all seen pictures of staircases which could also be seen as cornices, of boxes which can be made to appear in reversible perspectives, according as we look at them; most of us have seen various things in the fire or joined in a game of counting the number of faces we can find 'concealed' in a picture which at first look has nothing of the kind in it—a picture of a tree perhaps. I remember being present once at a lecture by a very gifted follower of Wittgenstein who had great skill in drawing such pictures on the board. At one stage he drew for us the picture of a very glamorous young lady and then, turning round to his audience, he said: 'You see this old hag'; and lo, from that moment, that was all we could see. Now the speaker had not cast any sort of spell on us, nor had he quickly touched up the picture in any way, rubbing a little out or adding a little here; the lines on the board were just the same, but now we saw it all differently, and with some effort we could go back and recover our picture of a glamorous young lady. It all depended entirely on how we looked at the picture.

Now this is not, in my view, quite as simple a matter as it seems. For when we look at the picture differently we are in a way doing something to it, the way we focus our eyes on it brings different parts of it into prominence and we are thereby in a subtle way doing something not unlike the process of actually touching up the picture. But the suggestion made by those who use this illustration is that in no way are the facts different when we see the picture differently, it is entirely a matter of the slant or conspectus we have on it.

This is thought to be true of metaphyscis as well, and it has been applied with vigour to religion and its problems. There is not, it is contended, any reference beyond our present experience in religion, perhaps nothing that cannot be described in strictly scientific terms. But there are various conspectuses we may have of the world, we may think of it in a Buddhist way or in a Christian way or in a Marxist way. There is nothing factually at issue here, the facts are the same for all, and likewise when some take up the Hinayana view of Buddhism and others the Mahayana, when some hold by orthodox Islam, and some become Sufi Mystics, when some become Catholic Christians and some Protestants, when some subscribe to Barthian theology and others to Modernism, there is no question of fact involved, nothing to which the distinction of true or false properly applies, but only the different slants we have on the same reality. When someone is converted he does not now really believe something to be the case which he thought was not so before, it is simply that he sees everything he saw before differently, all is 'made new'.

A careful and very readable presentation of this position may be found in Professor T. R. Miles' book, *Religion and the Scientific Outlook*. I cannot offer here a close account of Professor Miles' views, the student should examine them for himself; but the substance of Professor Miles' position can be seen very clearly in the following passage.

Now it is commonly supposed that those who believe in God have in their possession some factual knowledge which is not available to unbelievers. It has been one of the main purposes of this book to argue that such a view is mistaken. The word 'God' cannot be thought of as the name of an extra para-physical entity, since the notion of a para-physical entity makes no sense. However important the insights of the religious believer and the mystic, we cannot claim that they are the possessors of extra factual information which the unbeliever lacks. Two people may have access to exactly the same factual information, may feel the same joys and sorrows, may be confronted with the same good fortunes or disasters, and yet may tell different and conflicting parables. It is not that one person is better informed on his facts than the other; it is rather that they see the same facts, as it were, through different spectacles.[1]

Elsewhere in the same book we read:

There need be no factual disagreement between those who accept the parable of the incarnation and those who do not; but those who accept it are claiming, among other things, that the agreed historical facts require to be understood in a special way.[2]

I am not quite certain what this amounts to. Theologians do often speak of 'the fact' of the incarnation, and they also describe it as something which 'happened', a 'once-for-all

1. op. cit., p. 176.   2. op. cit., p. 199.

event'. But they would not, as a rule, imply that this was an event to be established in quite the same way as it might be shown that Jesus was in fact nailed to a cross or Napoleon sent to St. Helena. How, in that case, we can establish such things as the incarnation is a question I must leave for discussion later. But clearly there are facts besides the more obvious kind of brute fact, that one person loves someone else for example. And however strange a fact the incarnation is found to be, those who affirm it do take something to be the case, and a fact at least in that sense, about the person of Jesus which cannot be exhaustively described in terms of his life as a man.

It might be thought that Professor Miles allows this in saying that the facts are to be understood in a special way. But this is a very vague admission, and in the context it is plain that the author is not intending to admit that there is something further to be affirmed for which the agreed facts, in Professor Miles' sense, provide some of the evidence. This would be more than using the facts as a parable.

So also with the belief in God which the doctrine of the incarnation implies. One can understand the reluctance to speak of God as 'a fact', He is certainly not the sort of fact we establish from day to day or in science; and if Professor Miles were merely tilting against those who have a crudely anthropomorphic view of God—as a Being up in the skies for example—then the most we could complain about would be that he was wasting his time, most of all in talking to Christians today. There are not many today, nor I should be disposed to think in the past, who understand by the incarnation that 'the same ghost which occupied God the father came also to occupy Jesus'—it is certainly a more subtle doctrine than that. But if Professor Miles merely wished to enjoy himself attacking preposterous theological windmills, we might leave him to it. The trouble is that when he, and many like him today, have disposed of crude misconceptions which they take to be common, they conclude that there is nothing left but 'parables' and ways of viewing secular facts. We may have to use the language of parable and metaphor in religion, but the reference all the same is to something we take to be real. God is not a fact in the sense of being part of the world He sustains, but does it make sense to say that we believe in Him unless we take Him to be some kind of reality?

Professor Miles, it will be noted, believes that there can be no 'para-physical entity'. This raises difficulties at once about immortality. On this Professor Miles' position is not clear. He writes: 'If the problem is a factual one at all, it certainly cannot be settled by watching the behaviour of things called "souls". We should not know what to look for; it seems quite impossible to say how "The soul is immortal" could be given "cash value".' This is bound up with the assumption that bodily continuity is at least one essential criterion of personal identity. But it is on the other hand allowed that the notion of 'experiences after death' is a factually significant one, although it would, presumably for Miles, involve bodily continuity as well. The trouble with it, in his view, is that we cannot verify the assertion until we die, and we have a firmer indication of his true position in his statement that the words 'occur' and 'experiences' may be 'appropriate in earth' but not 'in heaven'. Perhaps they are not, and no one wishes to deny that 'after-life' must be a great mystery. But is there any point in affirming it at all unless it can be given some cash value? Professor Miles, I am sure, does not want to entertain seriously the notion of the literal resuscitation of our corpses, but must he not then have at least some notion of the soul which makes it capable of surviving the disintegration of the body? If not, the parable of the resurrection, which Professor Miles is quite happy to tell, appears to be very far removed from any meaning we would normally give it—one wonders indeed what meaning is left in it at all.

There are very similar difficulties when we turn to the work of Professor I. T. Ramsey. He has written a great deal about religious language, and if we are to understand his approach to the subject we must note a change that has come about in the course of linguistic philosophy. At first it was mainly, as we have seen, a technique for exposing claims which were taken from the start to be groundless because they went beyond the limits of possible verification. At a later stage, due largely to a change in the teaching of Wittgenstein himself, a somewhat more open and less sceptical aim was given to linguistic analysis. It was still thought that the clue, or at least one of the main clues, to the understanding of the questions raised by philosophers was the study of language. But now the 'open texture' of language was stressed. Linguistic expressions may function in a variety of ways, and while it is important on the one hand to expose the confusions that arise from mixing these, it is also necessary to plead the case of linguistic practices which do not conform to the commonest patterns and which are in danger of being deprived of their place altogether in the stress on ordinary or accepted usage. The language of art or religion is not like the language of day-to-day exchanges or statements of ordinary fact, and a proper place must be kept for them.

This was certainly an important advance and philosophy has undoubtedly felt the liberalizing influence of it. But the main preoccupation would still be with language and the supposition that it was by looking very closely at various linguistic usages that we would find the answer to our questions. Critics of this procedure, including myself, have wondered what progress could really be made unless we broke away more completely from the domination of severely linguistic studies and regarded the study of words and forms of speech as merely ancillary to considerations which could proceed also on their own and had their own discipline. In the event, it has appeared also that those who practise the more open kind of linguistic philosophy have failed to break away as much as this new policy would allow them from the limitations of the severely empiricist assumptions with which linguistic philosophy was so closely associated at the start. This seems to me well illustrated in the work of Professor Ramsey.

He stresses the 'oddity' and what he sometimes calls 'the logical impropriety' of religious utterances. These should not be assessed like ordinary statements of fact, even when they seem so in form. The significance of them must be found in certain kinds of situation called 'disclosure situations'. There are many of these besides the expressly religious ones, although I suspect that, for Professor Ramsey, religion is never very far when you have a disclosure situation. Professor Ramsey provides in his books a wealth of lively and homely illustrations of those special situations, and no one can fail to be entertained as well as informed as he reads about them. There is, for example, 'the man in the bowler hat who comes to sit next to us in the train'. From time to time we learn more about him, that he invariably orders Double Diamond, that he does the crossword in fifteen minutes, that he has a wife and three children and so on. 'But one day he says, offering his hand: "Look here—I'm Nigel Short." At that moment there is a "disclosure", an individual becomes a "person", the ice does not continue to melt, it *breaks*.'[1] Then there is the case of Mr. Justice Brown for whom the word 'Penny' has a special significance because he and his wife found a penny by the first stile which they crossed on the first day of their honeymoon. The word is now 'currency between them for all that which is most *characteristically personal*'; it would be 'in violent contrast to the language used normally in the setting of the High Court', and when it is used 'the situation is more than "what's seen", it has taken on "depth", there is something akin to religious "insight", "discernment", "vision" '.[2] We are told again of the situation in which the Judge suddenly recognizes the prisoner before him as an old acquaintance—the poignant situation again takes on depth, there is more in it than 'what's seen'.

A difficulty that arises at once about these examples is that of deciding what the 'more than what's seen' involves. Professor Ramsey is drawing here upon the work of the writers known as 'existentialists' one of whose theories is that there can be 'encounter' with persons which is distinct from 'knowing about' them. The outstanding exponent of this view is Martin Buber whose short book *I and Thou* has already become a religious classic. It is full of fine insights and a prophetic quality which characterizes much in the other work of this notable thinker. At times one feels that *I and Thou* should be read as poetry rather than religious philosophy. An attempt to commend the same view in a more detached philosophical way is found in Karl Heim's much admired work *God Transcendent*, and a very lively theological restatement of the

1. *Religious Language*, p. 26.   2. op. cit., p. 20.

position may be found in a recent book by Professor N. H. G. Robinson, *Christ and Conscience*. All these writers make it plain how important is the situation of 'encounter' and 'meeting'. But the question still remains—how far does all this help us to solve our problems?

For while we can all, for rough and ready purposes, distinguish between 'knowing about' a person and really 'meeting' him, are there not problems attending this idea of 'meeting' as well, and how sharp is the distinction between 'knowing about' and 'encounter with'? May not my encounter with some persons come to be through knowing more and more about them, even though I never 'meet' them in the common meaning of this word—meeting 'face to face' and so on? And is there not some element of knowing about in the 'more' which encounter involves? Is there not something new we learn, something rather subtle or elusive perhaps but real all the same, in the disclosure situation?[1] And if so, we have still some kind of affirmation to justify, we have not got rid of the problem of belief or knowledge but come across it in a novel and exceptionally difficult form.

This is a difficulty one feels very sharply when one considers Professor Ramsey's account of the more specifically religious situations of disclosure. He shows how these involve a 'total commitment' by contrast with the partial commitments of other situations and, with this as his main clue, he brings out the alleged 'logical impropriety' of terms like 'unity', 'simplicity', and 'perfection' as applied to God; and he deals in a similar way, again with lively illustration, with the language of the Bible and of Christian doctrine. Where so much turns on significant illustrations it is not easy to do justice to the author's position, and the student should read Professor Ramsey's books and judge for himself. But my own impression at the end is that it is not enough to exhibit the peculiarity of religious utterances without saying more about the sort of meaning they do have and how they are validated. It is well to be reminded that a belief in the Resurrection is 'no logical kinsman of "Did Queen Anne's death occur?" ', but this

1. For amplification of this point see my 'God and Mystery' in *Prospect for Metaphysics*, Ed. I. T. Ramsey.

seems to be the beginning rather than the end of problems, and while it may well be true that confusions have often resulted in the past from thinking of religious assertions as if they were strictly like ordinary statements of fact, can we say that we can give Christian assertions such 'a logical structure as by-passes many traditional confusions and controversies which are in fact from this standpoint mere brawling'—do we by-pass the old controversies altogether?

This difficulty seems to me to become very sharp when we turn to a book[1] devoted entirely by Professor Ramsey to two main questions, freedom and immortality. We are told here of situations of decision to which someone gives a 'personal backing' which 'cannot be netted in the language of objects'. There is 'a response to objects and more', the situation has ' "depth", becoming observables and more.' Such decision is also said to be 'spatio-temporal and more'. But the question really is, 'what do we make of this "more"?' Our decisions surely take place in time, and if, in our forethought and so on, we transcend the present, this is a metaphor which does not prevent our act from being an occurrence. Nor is the strictly religious side of this clear when we read that we are to use the word 'God' as the 'ultimate category' when it is seen to 'integrate the various words and phrases which are attached to the diverse routes by which distinctive situations are evoked'. But if the word 'God' does function in this way, we have still to ask how that comes about and whether the word refers to some reality beyond the situations whose evocations it integrates. What, in short, have we beyond certain sorts of human situation? The question becomes very insistent when we read that 'we are in fact using such a phrase as "God's will" to give us an alternative description for what confronts us when we are aware of obligation, an alternative description which seeks to do justice to the fact that there are distinctive disclosure situations other than those in which "Duty" is pegged'.[2] Religion is more than morality, but how much more on Professor Ramsey's view?

Professor Ramsey draws a sharp distinction, in the same

1. *Freedom and Immortality.* p. 53.
2. *Freedom and Immortality.* p. 53.

vein, between immortality and some 'property' of a thing called the soul which goes on and on. There is point in this; immortality is a great mystery and we may fall badly into error if we think about it closely in the terms appropriate to the here and now of this life. But are we not in danger of going to the other extreme and making the idea of immortality empty of all precision and significance when we say that 'it is in so recognizing duty as something which transcends the spatio-temporal, that we recognize our own transcendence of the spatio-temporal, our own immortality'. The way we may be said to transcend time in responding to duty, even if we allow that there is sense in this, does not give us what we mean by 'life eternal'; that cannot be understood in terms of some aspect of what happens to us now.

The merit of Professor Ramsey's procedure is that it brings out strikingly the need for caution in dealing with religious issues. For here we are concerned with matters which go beyond our full understanding, and it can be very misleading to suppose that we talk about matters which involve God and 'the world to come' in the same terms as we use in thinking of the world around us. This will be much stressed again in a moment. But it is one thing to stress the elusive character of religious realities and the mystery which lies at the heart of religion, it is another to take out of religion any reference to a reality other than peculiar situations in the present life; and that is what Professor Ramsey comes dangerously close to doing at times. There is a tendency also to conflate religious and ethical matters, although never in the outright way we found in the case of Professor Braithwaite. How far Professor Ramsey manages to escape these dangers and retain in the notion of disclosure situations, and the total commitment and the encounter these involve, a reference to some genuine reality beyond what is 'observable' is a truly difficult question, and those who read his books ought to have this question very much in mind. Has he got us, in any substantial way, beyond the notion of a special way of viewing the course of merely human experience?

A closely related difficulty is that of knowing how we distinguish between different, and sometimes conflicting, religious claims in terms of Professor Ramsey's approach. I have already shown that what he says about freedom tends to be the same as what he says about immortality, and might we not then be in danger of reducing all the different affirmations made in religion to one insistence on the peculiarity of what appears in a disclosure situation? How, in the present view, are we to approach the rival claims of Catholics and Protestants or of traditional doctrines in conflict with 'Modernist' theology? How do we justify being Christians rather than Hindus or Muslims—or the other way round? There is something of substance at issue between these faiths, but it could be said of all of them that they are making peculiar claims and using odd language. This last consideration may be a good starting-point in religious thought, but unless we get beyond it are we not in danger of disregarding the distinctiveness of particular religious claims and treating all religious utterances as if they came ultimately to the same thing? For some that might be the truth of the matter, but it is certainly at odds with much that we think and it is a very implausible position for a Christian theologian to take up. I am sure that Professor Ramsey does not wish to do so, but how far does he manage to avoid it in his philosophical approach to religion?

In discussing Professor Ramsey's position elsewhere[1] I have described him as walking on a very slim tight-rope between, on the one hand, the abyss of the empiricism which makes religion altogether a matter of this world and, on the other, the deep pit of the caution which ventures to give no body at all to distinctively religious claims, to venture to say nothing at all. These dangers were once described by a very fine thinker, Edwyn Bevan, as 'the pit of anthropomorphism', and 'the pit of agnosticism'. The religious apologist is always in danger of toppling into one or the other of these, and we shall see more clearly soon how this comes about. Perhaps Professor Ramsey just manages to keep his feet, but some of those who, like him, make the peculiarity of religious language central to their apologetics are certainly apt to hurtle headlong into the pit of agnosticism.

1. *Freedom and History,* Chapter XVI.

Take, for example, a well-known American theologian, Professor W. Poteat. He typifies an extreme form of the linguistic approach to the task of religious apologetics. This may be seen to good advantage in an article he published under the title: 'I will die: an analysis.'[1] The main aim of this article is to show the logical absurdity of the notion of survival after death. The argument proceeds by way of what purports to be a close examination of the logical behaviour of the verb 'to die'. It is that, while I can properly say — 'I will die', 'he died' and so on, I cannot, as in the case of the verb 'to run', use the past tense first person and say 'I died'. It is absurd to say 'I died' or 'I am dead', for, so the argument implies, here I am alive to make this assertion. The statement 'I died' is a contradiction in terms. I do not think in fact that this curious argument holds at all. If I were to survive, and we cannot rule that out at the start in an argument intended to disprove its possibility, I could well, in principle at least, refer to my death in talk with some other departed spirit or, in principle at least whether or not there is reason to believe it can actually happen, in a communication to the living. I am sure that questions about survival and about the meaning of 'after-life' and the reasons for believing in it cannot be settled as slickly as Professor Poteat, and many others, suppose today by study of the forms and behaviour of words in the way suggested.

But what is remarkable is that these arguments are advanced not by writers like Professor Ayer or Professor Flew to show how impossible it is to maintain a religious view. It is the argument of a theologian trying to turn the tables on his critics by directing their sort of argument to the defence of religion. How does he do this? If the idea of survival in any form is a logical monstrosity, what do we say of the Christian hope of resurrection and all that we read at a committal service? All we are told on this crucial issue is that we can affirm all that is customary here in an existentialist sense of which it is not possible, it seems, to give a proper indication. But the effect of this kind of apologetics, it seems to me, is to play straight into the hands of the sceptic. Here, if anywhere,

1. *Philosophical Quarterly,* January 1959.

the argument has died 'the death by a thousand qualifications' and nowhere have we greater need of Professor E. L. Mascall's wise warning against trying too easily to prove our own conclusions from the premisses of our opponents. The effect of denying that the soul is some kind of entity and that it can in some form survive the dissolution of the body is to deprive any talk about resurrection of genuine significance. We escape being caught out by refusing to bat, but I do not think many people can be interested in a defence of religion which speaks of an 'existentialist commitment' out of which all the content has been made to evaporate.

We have not done, however, with the present 'short way' with unbelief. Indeed the same desperate expedient has been adopted quite as recklessly by some writers who lie more on the theological than on the properly philosophical wing of Christian apologetics. These provide a striking counterpart to some of the fashions that prevail today in the philosophy of religion. It will be well to look briefly at some typical instances.

FURTHER READING

Religious Language. I. T. Ramsey (S.C.M. Press).

Freedom and Immortality. I. T. Ramsey (S.C.M. Press).

On Being Sure in Religion. I. T. Ramsey (Athlone Press).

The second of these books is discussed in some detail by me in Chapter XVI of my *Freedom and History*.

An Analytical Philosophy of Religion. W. F. Zuurdeeg (Allen and Unwin).

This is an elaborate work and more severely linguistic in its principles than the books of I. T. Ramsey.

'I will die: an analysis', by W. H. Poteat in *The Philosophical Quarterly*, January 1959.

The view that there can be a relation with others which does not involve 'knowledge about' them had its classical expression in Martin Buber's *I and Thou* (translated by R. Gregor Smith, S.C.M. Press). A more severely philosophical defence of the same position is found in *God Transcendent*, by Karl Heim (translated by E. P.

Dickie, London). There are many English presentations of this position. One of the most vigorous of these owes much to general 'existentialist' notions and is also cautiously aware of difficulties — it is *Christ and Conscience*, by N. H. G. Robinson (Nisbet). I disagree with much in this book but I also commend it as an impressive presentation of a widely held view.

CHAPTER ELEVEN

ATTENUATIONS OF FAITH AND ETHICS

Not many theologians of our day have won more the confidence and esteem of their fellows than the late Professor
John Baillie. He was for many years a leading ecclesiastical
figure and famed for his defence of the Christian religion in a
number of books which have been widely read and much
admired. He was a considerable scholar as well as a thinker,
and he could command a lively and agreeable style in speech
as well as in writing. Here then we might expect clear Christian guidance and a good sample of the way a balanced and
judicious exposition of Christian claims is to be provided for
intelligent and earnest seekers in our time. The expectation
is not always disappointed, there is much helpful instruction
and moving thought in Baillie's work, and it all carries the
stamp of a strong and attractive personality. But it all tends
to revolve around one central theme which seems to me a
very questionable one and symptomatic of a widespread
tendency to make religion acceptable and relevant to our time
by drastic surrender of some of its essential ingredients.

The main theme that runs through Professor Baillie's work
is that everyone is a believer at heart. He himself puts this in
words that come repeatedly like a refrain in his main books,
namely that we may deny 'at the top of our minds' what we
none the less believe 'at the bottom of our hearts'. This is
closely allied to the distinction 'between knowing and knowing that we know'. The main contention then is that the
unbeliever really does know God although he does not always
know that he knows this. Baillie is able in this way to admit
that in some sense there are genuine atheists and agnostics.
He does not have to impugn the honesty of the unbeliever.
He would not maintain that A. J. Ayer or Bertrand Russell
were practising some collossal deceit upon the rest of us. But
he would have to insist that these and thousands like them

are totally mistaken about what they do in fact believe. What they sincerely profess is not in this case the truth about themselves. Everyone is a believer, and indeed a Christian believer, at bottom.

This is certainly a bold line to take, and the student would do well to begin his thinking about it by considering how far, and in what ways, it is possible to draw a distinction between what we know (or believe) and what we think we know. How far can we be deceived about what we believe? In what ways are we most liable to self-deception, and what are its limits? Unfortunately there is little help to be obtained at this point from Professor Baillie himself. For although the present distinction is the basis of much that he maintains in his major works, he does not subject it to close analysis.

I think, however, that there are certain ways in which it is plain that we may be deceived about ourselves and not the best judges of what we are doing or believing. One simple case is this. We may not understand properly what is meant by certain terms we use in repudiating or professing certain beliefs. If someone were given an exhibition of an orator, perhaps a Hitler-like one, swaying a hysterical mob and told that government by this means was the essential thing about democracy, then he might well declare himself opposed to democracy. But it does not follow that he would be opposed to democracy in the form of representative government which allowed for the consultation of expert opinion and a wide range of experience and so on. Words like 'freedom' and 'democracy', 'liberalism', 'capitalism' and 'communism,' are notoriously vague and this could easily lead to a situation in which we may appear at least to be affirming or denying something quite at odds with what we really think. When correction or clarification has done its work we may then find ourselves saying, 'Yes, I believed all along what I seemed to deny—and meant to deny—until I understood better what was meant'.

This situation could easily arise in religion, for here there are also notoriously confusing terms and ideas. Do we believe in providence? 'Yes, if you understand this by it, not if it means that.' The failure to arrive at clarity of thought on such issues has sometimes led to bitter and needless religious controversy, and this, incidentally, is one of the main points at which philosophy can be helpful to the proper practice of religion. Such confusion may, moreover, cloud for us the basic issue of whether or not we have some religion at all. If someone, for example, thought that the word 'God' meant some wrathful despot looking down at us from the skies and seeking opportunities to sentence us to unspeakable and unrelieved torment, especially for being disrespectful to Him, then he might scornfully repudiate a belief in such a being and ascribe it to superstition or some distorted sadistic impulse in our nature. But if he were encouraged to think of God as an infinitely wise and loving being on whom all else depended, remote and invisible and baffling but also mysteriously present, then he might say, 'Yes, I believe there must be something like that, it tallies with the experience I sometimes have'. Or if God is thought of even more elusively as 'a spirit' that 'rolls through all things' and so on in the sense of Wordsworth's famous lines, or as a power that works mysteriously for righteousness in the world, in the way the Taoists thought, then someone might say, 'Oh, Yes, I always inclined to think that way and now that you have put it to me I certainly believe in God if that is how you understand the matter.'

He *might* say this, but he *need* not. He might just reply — 'Well you are offering me something more plausible and less offensive now, but I am still quite unable to accept it.' In much the same way we may find ourselves sharply at odds about matters like democracy or socialism, even when the confusions have been removed and it is reasonably clear how the terms are used. It would be interesting to know how many cases there are, a few or many (or perhaps none), of people who have believed all along in God in the sense which enlightened or subtle thought might give the term while at the same time, because they understood something very different by 'God' and 'religion', firmly denying that they had any religious belief. This would also be a good topic for further reflection by a student or for discussion in a class.

My own impression is that we would not find many cases of the state of mind in question, although I do think it very likely indeed that when people who are averse to religion, or who might describe themselves as spiritually dead, are given improved ideas of what religious belief truly involves, they may well have got over the main obstacle to becoming religious or be well on the way to acquiring a religious belief. But that would be quite a different matter, and one which could point us again to a very vital function of philosophy in religion; it would not entitle anyone to say, or us to say it for him, that he had in fact been a believer without knowing it all the time.

There are however other ways in which we may be mistaken about ourselves beside the ones engendered mainly by confusions of thought and language. We may, for example, be mistaken about our dispositional attitudes. By this I mean our tendencies to react in certain ways in various situations. I may consider myself a bolder or a more timid person than I really am or, more precisely, I may think myself little afraid of some ordeal I have to endure but find myself reduced to abject terror when the time comes, as Fagin's courage, or as much as he had, oozed out at sight of the gallows. I might then say 'I did not realize I was such a coward or weakling'. Others might add: 'We had guessed it all along, you put up a bold front and took yourself in, but you gave yourself away to the shrewd observer long before you came to the final test, indeed your very show of boldness was itself a symptom of your fear.'

There can be no doubt that we do sometimes delude ourselves in these ways, on occasion of course doing ourselves less and not more than justice. To what extent we do this is another matter, and a very difficult one to settle. How far is it true that other people may know us better than ourselves? Can we also be mistaken about what we are actually feeling or thinking at a particular time, in distinction from being mistaken in our recollection of what we were like earlier or in anticipations of the future? Can a man hide his fear or his hatred or his love or joy from himself at the time when he is actually feeling these things? It is hard to believe that he can, although he can of course misdescribe his state—which is another matter. Yet we do say of a person that he is afraid when he himself appears unaware that he is. Should we conclude that he is just pretending? Or is he even now deceiving himself? Should we say, perhaps, that there are many sides of our nature and of our experience at some time, and that one side of us may be frightened, the other not? I, at any rate, find it hard to believe that we can be seriously mistaken about whatever is uppermost in our experience at a particular time.

At this point we are bordering on the vexed and difficult question of the 'unconscious'. This has bearings on religion in many ways which I cannot follow out here. Nor can we consider closely the many ways in which the idea of the unconscious has been understood or the confusions with which it has often been fraught. Some have tended to think of the alleged unconscious as if it were a kind of subterranean duplicate of conscious experience. But the best psychologists tend (with occasionally rather grievous lapses) to think of the unconscious[1] in terms of dispositional tendencies of which we are not fully, if at all, aware but which modify our actual experience and behaviour and which may be mainly due to occurrences of which we have no recollection. It is these that analysts try to consider as at least part of their work. To what extent we are influenced by unconscious forces of this kind is not easy to determine. I suspect that the influence of the unconscious on our conscious life is much exaggerated. If its influence were as extensive as some suppose, if our actions were due little to overt purposes and determined more by 'unconscious motivation', there would be created the most serious problems for ethics and our understanding of moral responsibility. But here, as elsewhere, we must resist the occupational temptation of philosophers, namely to follow out closely the many questions into which the original question splinters.[2] It must suffice at the moment to concede that there

1. For an excellent discussion see C. D. Broad, *The Mind and its Place in Nature*.
2. The way this happens can be seen very clearly in some of Plato's works. He was fond of pleading with philosophers to take ample time to follow the 'long route', and in some dialogues, notably the *Republic*, he provides excellent examples of the way philosophical problems lead on to others and can yet be held together in a comprehensive view by a writer of genius.

seem to be unconscious factors, however precisely understood, at work in our lives and that in this sense also we may
be unaware in some fashion of what we are truly like in
thought or deed.

But again it must be added that the fact that we may be
mistaken about ourselves, in this or that regard, does not
prove that we are. It would be paradoxical, to say the least, to
suggest that our ordinary notions of what we believe and
aspire to are totally wrong, and I do not for a moment believe
this to be the case. What the more cautious, and I should add
judicious, psychologist usually claims is that we can be pre-
sumed to be deluded about ourselves, as a group or as individuals, when there is *reasonable evidence* of this. He does not
accuse us of self-deception at random. If I am thought to be
afraid when I announce, with seeming sincerity, that I am not,
it is because I whistle too loudly (to suppress my fear) or
tremble and blanch or snap irritably at my friends. There
must be these or some other ways in which I give myself
away—and the same holds for more persistent and deep-
rooted delusions about ourselves.

How does this bear on religious belief? Can we have such a
belief without being aware of it? I suppose that this could happen where the belief is dim and intermittent. But I am also
inclined to think that it must be rare. One might be on the
point of having some religious awareness, and one might be
subject to the confusions already noted. But the difference
between having and not having some religious awareness,
whether made explicit and articulate or not, is so vast and
affects us in such radical ways that it is hard to see how one
could fail to note it in one's own case. The most likely
deception comes about, I suspect, when some practice of
worship is continued in a social and conventional way when
the life has gone out of it, but how much do we deceive
ourselves as well as others in that case?

Professor Baillie, however, is not contending that in some
cases we may be mistaken about what we believe and in need
of careful nurturing if the belief is to become mature and
firm; he goes much further and maintains that in all cases of
professed unbelief there is an element of self-deception. The

atheist, even the most intelligent and clear-sighted, really believes 'at the bottom of his heart'; and this seems to me an astounding claim.

My first comment on it is that it induces the apologist to offer quite unnecessary hostages to fortune. If he is to talk of self-deception, so may his opponent. The appeal to what we really believe, in distinction from what we seem to believe, can cut in more than one way, and it is well known that Freudians have often taken the line that religion is something we manufacture ourselves to allay deep-seated fears and insecurity and that we persuade ourselves that God is real although in fact he is no more than a projection of ourselves. When this argument is deployed I counter by appealing to what I myself understand of my own convictions and what seems forced upon me as religious belief. I claim to be aware of some reality which is not at all a projection of myself—or of anything human—and proceed to indicate further what form this takes. But if this is to be allowed to me, if I am not to be ruled out of court at once on the score of self-deception, I must allow the same to my opponent. I can quite properly affirm that his belief is mistaken, but as to whether he holds, or does not hold, a certain belief, that is surely a matter which any fairly clear-sighted person must be allowed to settle in the final analysis for himself.

If we overlook this we shall be in serious danger of directing the main religious controversies into a shadowy land where the real strength of the case for either side is never properly weighed. The real issues will be more fairly judged in the open—and by direct confrontation of what they involve. And if the advocate of religion is to suggest in all seriousness to his opponent that he does not really believe what he sincerely professes then this accusation must at least be backed by weighty evidence. This, it seems to me, is what is lacking in the case of many well-known unbelievers. What evidence is there that David Hume faltered in his unbelief? He certainly looked on his destiny (or the lack of one) with great calm and good humour when Boswell taxed him about it on his death-bed. Is there a shred of evidence that well-known atheists of today are anything other than they profess to be?

Is Bertrand Russell a secret believer? If he is, then where is the evidence? I should think it would be quite impossible to find.

The same goes, not only for outstanding thinkers, but for the masses who seem today quite indifferent to religion. They may be ripe for conversion, if for example there are attitudes disclosed in social activities or modes of entertainment which only religion can meet or if fiction exhibits some deep-seated longings which only religion can satisfy. But this has to be carefully shown, and even when it has been shown it does not in the least follow that the people in question entertain a religious belief now or are in some other sense religious already. The simplest account of the facts, as they appear to the lay and the expert eye alike, is that the bulk of the population in Britain, for example, today have no religion at all (except in some misleadingly loose use of the word) and are largely indifferent to its claims. This seems true also of most European countries and there is obviously extensive irreligion in America. Russia appears to be in the main a God-less community, and while it may not be true today, as it has been quite recently, that religion is severely persecuted in Russia, it is clearly at a grave disadvantage and it is not likely that the bulk of the people there have any true sense of its nature and claims. Most of the younger generation have, one would suppose, been well indoctrinated against it. In other places also religion has lost much of its hold, except when revived as a political force, and the main religion would not in any case be the Christian one—which makes it very hard indeed to affirm that all are *Christian* believers at heart. Is the young Hindu peasant who has barely, if ever, heard of Jesus a Christian believer? How then does Professor Baillie deal with these obviously awkward facts?

To a large extent he deals with them by ignoring them. But he does also advance arguments which bear on our theme. Some of these arguments fail to do him justice at all as a thinker and scholar. He observes, for instance, that 'it is quite impossible to live in this country today as if Christ had never come'. We still close our shops on Sunday and date our letters from the birth of Christ. But what does this prove? In these senses no one could live as if Julius Caesar had never been or even Adolf Hitler. But there are two weightier arguments which Baillie uses.

The first of these refers to 'the case-books of the psychologists', and I will not add here to what I have already said on this score; the appeal to the unconscious, if that is how we wish to proceed, needs substantial and explicit support and it seems to me also very doubtful from the start as a main line of defence. The second expedient is to divert attention to mainly ethical matters. Everyone has 'an uneasy conscience' we are repeatedly told and we are also told that 'ultimate reality meets us not in the form of an object that invites our speculation, but in the form of a demand that is made upon our obedience.'[1] Now there may be such a demand and it may be possible to show that everyone has an 'uneasy conscience',[2] although this is far from obvious. But even if all this were plain how much does it give us? We may wrap it in religious terminology, conferring on the 'Absolute Obligation'[3] the dignity of capital letters. But have we in effect anything of substance which goes beyond the 'religion as morality' of Professor Braithwaite? Admittedly Baillie speaks in more orthodox terms and converts the voice of conscience sometimes into a haunting numinous presence.[4] But when we look at the substance of what he says, especially when it becomes hard to prove the universality of religious belief, it is the allegedly inescapable character of a moral sense that is really stressed. Even here the ground may not always be firm, there are moral as well as religious sceptics and there are many who do not believe in an absolute duty. But even if we could get over these ethical difficulties how far would we have gone to establish the claims of religion? Professor Baillie's procedure is indeed high-lighted in his reference to 'L. P. Jack's shoemaker who spent his breath proving that God did not exist, but spent his life in proving

1. *Our Knowledge of God*, p. 157.
2. It is remarkable how, in spite of the emphasis on absolute duty, very much in the style of Kant, we have also in the thought of John Baillie a strong inclination towards the 'Socratic Ethic' whereby 'virtue is knowledge'—that is we are bound to seek the good if we know it.
3. op. cit., p. 161.
4. op. cit., p. 4.

that He did'. The point seems to be that no matter what the shoemaker sincerely professed his fine conduct amounted to religious belief. That is, I think, how this cryptic remark is to be taken in its context, and if I am right we have at any rate come dangerously near that attenuation of faith which equates it with merely moral beliefs and attitudes.

It is of course true that morality lies very near the centre of religion, and there is a sense, as we shall see, in which the voice of conscience may also be regarded as the voice of God; but in that case there must be more involved than the voice of conscience as such, and this is what tends to become rather faint when Baillie seeks to establish the universality of belief on the basis of an alleged inescapable consciousness of duty.

FURTHER READING

I have referred mainly in this chapter to John Baillie's position as he expounds it in his *Our Knowledge of God* (Oxford). But the same views are advanced by him also in a recently published posthumous work *The Sense of the Presence of God*. The latter work is reviewed at some length by me in *The Journal of Theological Studies* for April, 1964, and by Fred Berthold in *The Christian Scholar* for 1962. Another discussion of John Baillie's work is by D. D. Evans in *Mind* 1961.

The way we should think of the unconscious is considered closely in a way that has rarely been surpassed by C. D. Broad in *The Mind and its Place in Nature*, Chapters VIII and IX. Other helpful works on this subject are: *God and the Unconscious* by Victor White (Collins) and Freud's own *Introductory Lectures on Psychoanalysis* (Allen and Unwin).

The reader could also benefit here by reading Freud's *The Future of an Illusion* (Hogarth) and considering how far it provides, in reverse as it were, the sort of argument on which Baillie relies. An outstanding presentation of Freudian views is found in J. C. Flugel's *Man, Morals and Society* (Duckworth).

CHAPTER TWELVE

ATTENUATIONS OF FAITH AND RECENT THEOLOGY

In presenting the view we have just been noting Professor Baillie makes considerable reference to the work of J. Cook Wilson, an eminent and influential philosopher who flourished at the turn of this century.[1] Indeed Baillie's leading ideas are derived very directly from Cook Wilson. The latter maintained that there were certain things we knew without adducing reasons for them. A common term for this kind of knowledge is 'intuition', although the term has certain other uses and can be misleading.[2] It is alleged that we know the distinct steps in an argument in this way, we must just 'see' the point when it is put to us; and some, including prominent ethical philosophers, hold that we know ultimate ethical truths in this way.[3] Cook Wilson held that we knew some matters of fact in this direct way also, and that this includes some knowledge of one another, at least of the existence of other persons. This is held by many to be doubtful. Do we not depend for what we know of other persons on what we observe of their bodies, including of course the sounds they utter? I cannot go into this closely here, but it must be added that Cook Wilson

1. Cook Wilson held the Wykeham Chair of Logic at Oxford and had much influence on the thought of other eminent Oxford philosophers, especially H. A. Prichard and W. D. Ross. There is an interesting account of his life and work at Oxford in Volume I of *Statement and Inference*, a posthumously published collection of his writings, edited by A. S. L. Farquharson.

2. We speak, for example of 'a woman's intuition', or the intuition by which an old salt tells what the weather will be like; these are shrewd guesses, sometimes based on close observation and wide experience. Then there are wilder surmises, purporting sometimes to have an occult origin, like 'Hitler's intuitions'. We must not confuse these popular uses of the term with its more technical use in philosophy.

3. Such thinkers differ however in their view of the way intuition functions—there is a marked difference in this respect between the views of G. E. Moore and W. D. Ross.

believed we had some indisputable certainty about God as well as about men. How then do we ever come to have doubts about God? Why do people deny that He exists?

Cook Wilson implies that this doubt is a 'philosophic' one. What then do we mean by 'philosophic doubt'? Briefly this. Philosophers, as is well known, have had many strange doubts. They have doubted the existence of an external world or their own existence. This is not because they were foolish people or had had some extraordinary experience which disclosed to them, as some mystics[1] have claimed, that this world is not real. They were usually claiming to offer an account of what we all find our experience in the world to be like. Thus when Berkeley denied the existence of the material world he was not calling the ordinary facts of experience in question at all, he was not claiming that he could walk through a brick wall or that he would not be dashed to bits if he jumped from a high cliff. He simply held, on the basis of illusion and perspectival distortions (the round tower looking square in the distance and the railway lines seeming to taper—in a post-Berkeleian instance) that while we had experiences which happened in inescapable ways there was strictly nothing real besides these experiences and their coherence and necessity and so forth. I shall not now ask[2] how far he was justified, but it is plain that while he was, in one way, a very radical doubter the doubt itself depended on certain familiar things being basically accepted. Likewise, when Hume denied the existence of 'the self' he was not denying that there were persons like himself, but only affirming that persons were little more than their passing experience. Doubt of this sort is not of course a trivial matter, but it does imply that Hume would take himself to be as real as the next man for all ordinary purposes. He did not doubt his own existence outright.

This is, moreover, according to Cook Wilson, the way atheists and sceptics doubt in religion. Their doubt springs from difficulties which appear at a certain sophisticated level of

1. See Chapter Eighteen.
2. The reader will be familiar with some of the answers if he has examined some of the books listed at the end of Chapter 1.

reflecting upon experience and does not seriously affect or eliminate a basic certainty. Cook Wilson is not out to show that all of us are Christian believers. His concern, in his writings at least, is with general theistic belief, not with expressly Christian belief. Nor is he quite as explicit as his follower, John Baillie, in claiming that all of us have some direct awareness of God. But that seems to be his main intention and, where common experience is concerned, he seems convinced that it contains some direct awareness of God. But where is this awareness found? It is here that the attenuation begins again. The basic thing in religious experience is a 'unique' feeling, 'a solemn reverent attitude'. This feeling, we are told, 'is only possible because we are convinced of the presence of something entirely transcending everything human', and the feeling moreover 'points to the reality of the experience'. If this means that our feeling guarantees the reality of some entity to which it is directed, this is curious reasoning—have we not, for example, on occasion 'irrational' fears of things that do not menace us or may not exist at all? But what I wish to note especially is that in seeking to show how inescapable is the situation in which God is thus known Cook Wilson tends to empty the experience itself of everything that is more than human. Are there not he asks, pursuing his argument, 'actual experiences of our own' such as 'times of great emotion, when, as the saying is, we seem lifted beyond ourselves. Times, it may be, of great trouble, or of great joy'? Here we seem down to entirely human matters. The agnostic need not question them. Who has not had times of great emotion or of great joy? If someone has not he can easily learn about them from poetry and drama. But how does God come into this? To answer that we must do a great deal more than indicate features of experience which Professor Ayer or Bertrand Russell could acknowledge as readily and consistently as any.

Here again then we seem to be putting the agnostic out of court by changing the plea, in the course of defending it, to one the agnostic has no concern to dispute. It is a pointless victory that is gained in this way.

The same comments apply to much theological teaching

that has had wide publicity of late, the work of Paul Tillich, for example. It is not easy to pin Tillich down to a precise position and it is thus not always clear in his case when criticism has got to its mark. Tillich, like Karl Barth and other Continental Theologians (as they are called), does well to insist that God is not to be found as 'an object among objects', He 'transcends the world of objects as well as every subject'. The last remark is a little cryptic, but it seems certainly true, as will be seen again shortly, that God is somehow beyond the world and our experience of it, He is transcendent or absolute, to use terms to which I must return later. But it is one thing to allow and stress this. It is another to suggest that 'the God beyond God', in Tillich's rather quaint phrase, is not an entity or reality other than ourselves. God is a great mystery but He is not so elusive as to be nothing at all in Himself. But we come perilously near to saying that when we speak of God as the object of 'an ultimate concern'. The unbeliever can have an ultimate concern, and in some cases a very noble one. Tillich does indeed speak also of God as 'the Ground of our being', and if this is understood in the traditional sense no objection can be taken to it. But how does Tillich understand it when he also writes as if this 'Ground' was not some reality distinct from ourselves and the world but something ultimate in the depth of our own being. Tillich is likewise evasive where the more specific Christian affirmations are concerned. Traditional language is often used but in a way that seems far removed from its traditional meaning. It is not certain for example how far he thinks the life which Jesus lived on this earth has importance for Christian faith. He seems at times at least to attach more importance to the concept of the 'new being' as it appears in the experience of the early Church and of Christians afterwards. He certainly does not believe in a vague amalgam or syncretism of all creeds and religions but he none the less writes as follows at the close of one of his latest works:[1]

Christianity will be a bearer of the religious answer as long as it breaks through its own particularity.

The way to achieve this is not to relinquish one's religious

1. *Christianity and the Encounter of the World Religions.*

tradition for the sake of a universal concept which would be nothing but a concept. The way is to penetrate into the depth of one's own religion, in devotion, thought and action. In the depth of every living religion there is a point at which the religion itself loses its importance, and that to which it points breaks through its particularity, elevating it to spiritual freedom and with it to a vision of the Spiritual presence in other expressions of the ultimate meaning of man's existence.

This, according to Tillich, is what Christianity must see in the present encounter of world religions. Most Christians would find the element of particularity much more radical than this and incapable of being eradicated at any depth of their experience.

In terms of the attitude I have indicated Tillich expects us to 'lift ourselves above the problems' of theology and religious thought, and here again we see the lure of the 'short way'. It would be good in one way not to have to cope with difficulties. But the difficulties are there and faith is profounder and firmer in the long run from having to cope with them. A point where Tillich's attitude bears very closely on our present theme is where he maintains, like John Baillie, that there are no serious atheists. 'Their seriousness in trying to be atheists,' we are told, 'witnesses against their claim to be atheists.' But what force can this statement have? We can think of many serious and gifted atheists of today and of the past. Was not Gilbert Murray as serious-minded a person as any—or C. D. Broad or Barbara Wootton today? There are no doubt superficial and frivolous atheists, but there are also profound and sincere ones. The only way in which we could make Tillich's statement plausible would be by identifying belief in God with seriousness. We could make people Christian in that way easily 'by definition', but would anything be gained? This is the confusing attenuation of faith to which I have referred as the standing temptation of liberal-minded thinkers anxious to gain recognition of Christian truth and adherents to it.

This is even more evident at popular levels as in the much discussed book *Honest to God* by Dr. J. A. T. Robinson. Intelligent people will readily agree with Dr. Robinson in rejecting crude notions of a God in the sky or 'out there' in the sense in which an astronaut might find Him. It is indeed doubtful whether many people have ever thought seriously of God in this way, although the figurative language we use might suggest that. No enlightened religious person thinks of God as a being in space. But having tilted, needlessly it seems to me, at the man of straw on which humanists are also apt to waste much ammunition, Dr. Robinson seems to swing to the other extreme of writing as if God were not a reality other than ourselves at all. 'Theological statements', he declares, 'are not a description of "the highest Being" but an analysis of the depth of personal relationships — or rather, an analysis of the depths of *all* experience "interpreted by love".'[1] 'The necessity for the name "God" lies in the fact that our being has depths which naturalism, whether evolutionary, mechanistic, dialectical or humanistic, cannot or will not recognize.'[2] 'Belief in God is a matter of "what you take seriously without any reservation", of what for you is ultimate reality.'[3] The support of Tillich is invoked in the quotation 'The Divine, as he sees it, does not inhabit a transcendent world *above nature*; it is found in the 'ecstatic' character of *this* world, as its transcendent Depth and Ground'.[4] These quotations claim to take us beyond the naturalism which recognizes no reality other than this world, but they do not unambiguously acknowledge a reality which is other than ourselves and not just some profound aspect of our own being.

We shall see a little more fully in a moment what gives some plausibility to pronouncements like those of Tillich and his disciples. Many similar pronouncements on other features of religion could be culled from the same sources, and it would be a good exercise for the student at this stage to go through a book like *Honest to God* and consider how far it may be fairly accused of sacrificing indispensable elements in religion, or making them very uncertain, out of a misguided zeal for making religion acceptable without too radical a change of the climate of thought today or too drastic a surrender of prevailing sceptical attitudes.

Samples of one further position must be noted before

1. op. cit., p. 49. 2. op. cit., p. 54.
3. op. cit., p. 55. 4. op. cit., p. 56.

closing this chapter. This is a much more consistent position and it has attraction for many. It is that of frankly rejecting religion, in the normal meaning, but retaining some of its features as useful ingredients of a this-worldly outlook. This applies especially to the emotions aroused by religion and to the imaginative colourful language which religion uses. The psychologist J. C. Flugel, for example, used to contend that 'religious emotions must be largely or entirely secularized and be put in the service of humanity. The religion of humanity is surely the religion of the nearer future.'[1] I myself doubt whether religious emotions can be made to function in this way. Will not their significance and power be lost when they forfeit their distinctive religious character? I have similar misgivings about the position of Professor Ronald Hepburn[2] who is anxious to retain the symbolism of religion in the form of over-arching symbols which help us to give form and direction to purely human enterprises, continuing for example to think of life as a pilgrimage and so on. It is certainly possible to put some colourful religious metaphors to a secular use, but much of the vigour of the metaphors will be lost in the process. We have also to be careful, if we adopt this procedure, not to carry over strictly religious overtones of the religious expressions we borrow and exploit their power in ways no longer warranted. Professor Hepburn himself has issued a powerful warning to his fellow-humanists in just these terms,[3] but even he himself tends to fall foul of his own warning in his allusion to the concept of the holy as one which the secularist could retain. In the main, however, his position is a fair and consistent one. But it is not a properly religious one and for that reason I shall not discuss it further here. The student will find it profitable to study a position

1. *Man, Morals and Society*, p. 275.
2. See his 'A Critique of Humanist Theology' in *Objections to Humanism* (Ed. H. J. Blackham).
3. *Christianity and Paradox*, Chapter XI. This is discussed by me in *Our Experience of God*, Chapter V. Professor Hepburn's position has much in common with that of Erich Fromm in his *Psychoanalysis and Religion*. With this should be compared also the views of Professor J. N. Findlay in *Values and Intentions*. He writes "Religious objects are no dispensable luxury, but are essential to the descriptions and actual existence of our

like that of Professor Hepburn and compare it with the allegedly religious positions reviewed in this chapter and the previous one. Which is the more consistent, Braithwaite or Hepburn? Such comparisons will help us to determine how far the other attempts to accommodate religion to the outlook of men today have exceeded reasonable limits.

But if we are not to meet the empiricist and secularist by attempting to conceive of religion in terms which they are able to accept, how shall we proceed? To this question I shall now turn.

FURTHER READING

Two books by E. L. Mascall deal in a close and penetrating way with several of the positions and thinkers considered in the preceding chapter. They are: *The Secularisation of Christianity* (Darton Longman and Todd) and *Up and Down in Adria* (Faith Press).

---

life of impersonal valuation, which can neither be thought of nor be except as pointing towards them. If such objects are non-existent, they are not for that reason to be ignored or misprized: *their* non-existence is in some sense an infinitely important sort of non-existence, more important than the *being* of the orientations which involve them in their description." p. 403. Chapter IX of Professor Findlay's book will repay close consideration and as it is a position which the author is making more positive in certain ways, the reader may wish to go on to the same author's more recent *The Discipline of the Cave* and *The Transcendence of the Cave.*

CHAPTER THIRTEEN

THE LIMITS AND LESSONS OF EMPIRICISM

We have been concerned with attempts to come to terms with empiricism and the positions associated with it in contemporary thought. There are many, however, who believe that this is not the proper course to take. They think that empiricism can be refuted and that this opens the way for a less tortuous defence of religion and the affirmation of its claims afresh in senses not so radically different from their normal and traditional meaning as the compromises which we have just been noting. The refutation of empiricism takes two main forms. One is to bring out internal strains and inconsistencies in the presentation of the empiricist position. These appear especially when claims of a general or universal nature are made, for example the insistence that *all* knowledge must be derived from sense experience or based on observation. How do we know that these conditions *must* apply to *all* knowledge? Is there an empiricist way of establishing this principle itself? Can the 'principle of verification' be verified? Attempts are made to counter this by describing the principle of verification or some other less rigid form of empiricism as statements of a rule or method of procedure or as a convention which does not itself claim truth. But this is a difficult position to justify without opening the door to many things which the empiricist does not usually want to admit. Nor does it seem to me very plausible in itself as a defence of a philosophical view. The second way of meeting the challenge of empiricism is a more direct one. It consists in noting features of our thought or experience of which it is extremely difficult to give an exhaustive account in empiricist terms. Of these the following are outstanding examples.

Firstly there are the principles of logic itself, including the law of contradiction. We take it to be absurd of us to contradict ourselves, and a common feature of all controversy is the attempt to show that one's opponent is not consistent. No one wants to plead guilty to out and out inconsistency. We may find a use for suggestive paradox, we may affirm things which seem inconsistent, or are verbally so, without being inconsistent in fact. But how do we know that we must not contradict ourselves, that it is absurd to suppose that I am in this room now and, in the same sense, elsewhere? There seems to be no answer to this question. We just see the absurdity involved. We do not derive it from some kind of experience. We must of course have some experience to know when we are contradicting ourselves, and we shall also have the unpleasant experience of finding ourselves in much practical difficulty if we set consistency at naught. But these are not reasons which convince us that it is absurd to contradict ourselves. I know without further ado that I cannot be in this room and playing on the lawn, except in some unusual and metaphorical use of one or the other of these terms, as when I may be said to be 'in thought' playing tennis outside. The principle of contradiction is, in technical language, *a priori*, that is the validation of it does not depend directly on experience. But this principle is basic to all our thinking, and there seems thus to be something non-empirical at the centre of all thought and experience.

We may take a similar line about further truths of logic and about mathematics. We do not know that twice two are four because that is how it has always turned out in our experience. We know that the answer *must* be four and that this is true of every situation or world of which we can think. It just cannot be otherwise. We could, of course, in a quibble, say that two rabbits, in breeding, produce many more, but this biological fact has nothing to do with multiplication in the strict mathematical sense. Likewise we prove that the sum of the angles of a triangle is 180 degrees without thinking at all of sampling various triangles to see whether this is true. We know something in these cases in some way which is quite different from the knowledge we have that flames are hot. We can conceive of flames being cold; this might be difficult but the idea is not at any rate self-contradictory. We know that two and two just could not be five. Sampling is unnecessary and irrelevant here, and as soon as we have understood the matter we know that the angles of a triangle *must* be 180 degrees.

In reply to this, it is sometimes maintained that these principles of logic and mathematics do not claim truth in the proper sense, they are definitions, tautologies, rules of procedure, and so on. As such they are also variable. There can be 'alternative logics' and 'alternative geometries'. This seems to me very hard to sustain. That twice two are four seems so evident the moment we understand what is meant that it might seem plausible to regard it as a tautology, that is as containing no new information. But this is much less plausible when we turn to more complicated calculations in arithmetic or geometry. We know what 245 and 367 mean without having any notion what they will yield when multiplied. That would take time to discover, and the solutions to some problems require exceptional gifts, and in some cases genius, to discover them. Surely we learn something new in the process. As for the notion of alternative geometries and logics, I believe these will be found, on proper inspection, to involve alternative systems which do not in fact come to the same thing at all, that is they do not really contradict one another or provide strict alternatives.[1] This would take long to debate, it is one of the central matters in controversy today in philosophy, and the reader should try to pursue it further on his own account. I must content myself here with indicating logic and mathematics as spheres of truth and understanding which it is exceptionally hard to bring within empiricist terms.

Is not this also true of our judgements of worth and kindred matters in morals and aesthetics. We certainly do require knowledge of facts in these cases, but must we not have more? Am I, for example, to work for the abolition of capital punishment? To answer I must consider whether there are likely to be more murders if this punishment is stopped and whether the lives of policemen are put in jeopardy and so forth. But I must also believe that human life is worth preserving and have some

1. There is a very fine discussion of the basic question involved here in C. A. Campbell's 'Contradiction—Law or Convention', *Analysis* March 1958.

more detailed notion also of what counts most in human life. At some point I must pass some judgement on the facts. I may know, for example, that some act will cause pain, but how do I know that it is wrong to cause pain when this does not lead to some compensating good? Answers have been given in terms of our own reactions, the rules and conventions of society, our basic commitments and so on. But those who do not find these 'naturalistic' answers satisfactory will find in ethical judgements at some point a factor which goes beyond empiricist terms of any kind. The same is true in aesthetics. In judging a work of art we certainly must know properly what it is like; it is an advantage to have our attention drawn to features of a poem or painting which we are apt to overlook, and the art critic can do much to help us here. But it is not enough to know what the poem is like, for its beauty belongs to the poem in virtue of what it is but is also more than what the poem itself is. If this something more is not just our feelings or some other attitude of ours, it looks as if the beauty of the poem involves something more than the facts of what things are like.

All these are difficult and highly controversial matters. A proper study of them would require at least one book to itself. At the moment it must suffice to give these further indications of points where the critics of empiricism feel that this kind of philosophy is put to considerable strain. A similar point is found when we think of the self or the soul. It may be that we only know other persons by observation of their behaviour, but does not their behaviour disclose to us something 'inner' akin to what we find ourselves, in direct experience of ourselves, to be? This is also a most controversial matter at present, and anyone who wishes to mount a full-scale attack on empiricism is bound to have a great deal to say about it. Perhaps it is here more than anywhere that the most certain limit of empiricism is reached. We shall touch on this matter again, as it bears very closely on some religious issues.

It should be added that in seeking to meet the claims of the empiricist, and above all in considering fairly what makes them plausible, we learn a good deal about the way to present other positions. We shall not, for example, if we have learnt our lesson, speak too crudely of the self as if it were just like some object in the external world and we shall avoid such pitfalls and travesties as those involved in much loose talk about 'a realm of values' and so on. We acquire more of the caution and subtlety which is needed for a truly philosophical handling of various matters, this being one of the main ways in which philosophical controversy advances the subject.

I do not, however, wish to undertake here a close examination of empiricism. It must be enough to indicate some of the main ways in which its opponents have found it wanting. But one point should be noted. It is that in seeking to rebut empiricist claims in the respects just noted one does so by controverting them fairly directly, that is we expressly affirm that the empiricist is altogether wrong about certain matters, there are things we all recognize, however hard to understand in some ways, which seem to go beyond the limits the empiricist sets himself. In religion the position is more subtle, and although we pass here, in my view, more certainly than anywhere beyond the limits of empiricism, there is also more to be learnt in religion from taking the full impact of the criticisms advanced by empiricism today.

This is because there is some point in religion where we seem to pass, not merely beyond the sort of facts the empiricist can admit, but beyond all that we encounter in our experience of the world and in our understanding of it—and of ourselves. At the heart of religion there is, as a rule at least, some reference to a reality 'beyond', and in most cases this 'beyond' is understood in a very strict sense. There is a God who is not in time but eternal and uncreated, absolute and without limit. He may be thought of in personal or theistic terms as is common in the West, but we may also be told more vaguely still of the Supreme Self, the One, the Ultimate, which has none of the limitations to which we are subject. But what sense can we make of this? If the God we are to worship is altogether 'beyond' the sort of experience of things we have, if He is perfect in such a way that none of our conceptions apply to Him, how can He come within our thoughts at all?

Must He not remain an unfathomable mystery? But if He is such a mystery can we even say that He exists?

This is not a new problem. Thinkers have been acutely aware of it down the ages. But it has been very much sharpened of late. This has come about when empiricists have pressed upon us the question of how religious affirmations are verified. Their presupposition has been that the verification must be in terms of some natural or other observable reality of the kind which the scientist studies. We have seen reason to question this presupposition. None the less a problem remains. For, granted that there is more to the life and experience we have than the empiricist admits, we have only to broaden the question and ask what the test of truth can be for affirmations which pass altogether beyond the sort of reality we meet in experience and which our minds are capable of handling. We cannot meet the infinite or unlimited Being as if it were some specific or limited entity within the world: the Creator is not part of the world He has created. But in what other way can God be met and known? By putting the question insistently in their own restricted terms the empiricists have forced us to become more acutely conscious than ever of a problem which lies at the centre of religious thought and which is inescapable whether we are verificationists in the strict contemporary sense or not.

The accentuation of the problem in question, and with that an exceptionally shrewd appreciation of the way it should be met, marks, in my opinion, a major advance in religious understanding today; and this illustrates well how advance is made in philosophy by sharp controversy and heed to the insights found in positions with which we may not have much sympathy. The defender of religion owes much to his empiricist critics today at the point where his own thought can be most constructive.

This comes about especially when persistent critical questioning forces many to abandon the half-way houses in which they might otherwise seek a less disconcerting place in which to rest. For there are many who would not, on the one hand, wish to come to terms with empiricism in the way we have been noting in previous chapters, but who are averse, on the other hand, to making the object of worship in religion so different from anything else we encounter that it seems to elude us altogether and have no relevance to the life we lead now. They thus tend to represent God, or whatever takes His place in their religion, as a spiritual reality far exceeding what we find in fact in the world around us and in human life but not altogether different in nature from other finite things. This is sometimes described as the theory of 'a finite God'. One of the main attractions of this theory is that it makes it easier, in one respect, to deal with the age-long problem of evil, that is the problem of accounting for various forms of evil in a world alleged to be under the control of a Perfect Being. For while we would still say that God is 'all-good' we can now add that there are some things which thwart Him—at least over a period. He is not strictly all-powerful. This however does not accord well with what religious people feel. They tend to feel they can rest in the absolute goodness of God as being also superior to all ills, although it does not come within their comprehension how this can be. It is moreover very hard to show what reason there can be for believing in a finite God. The way things happen in the world does not require us to postulate him. There may be creatures in the universe superior to ourselves. But have we any firm evidence of their existence?

The case for there being at least one overwhelmingly superior but not absolute being is usually made to rest on the presence of design or order in the universe and the preponderance of good. This is known as the 'teleological argument' for the existence of God, and I shall comment further upon it in Chapter Seventeen. At the moment it must suffice to note that it has little appeal to thinkers of any school today. Perhaps there are features of it that have more relevance than we realize. But in general it has been largely discredited because critical thinkers have argued that if we are to proceed along the lines suggested we must observe the same standards of evidence in principle as we require in seeking to establish the existence of the sort of entities we normally find in the world. The movement of thought involved is the same. But when the alleged evidence is considered it is found to be vague and uncertain and, on some presentations of it, to amount to no more than indications of interesting features of the world from which nothing in particular can be inferred.

It is also urged that the attitude adopted by religious people is usually sharply at odds with the uncertain and tentative character of the teleological argument and kindred reflections. At the centre of his religion, although not always elsewhere, the worshipper normally claims an unshakeable certainty. He does not just hope, he believes without shadow of doubt. 'I know', not 'I opine', or 'it seems likely', is the basic language of religion. And what is known is, moreover, not just some reality superior to ourselves, a being much greater in power and wisdom, but some altogether Supreme Reality, an infinite, eternal or absolute Being, one who is not in any way subject to our limitations but perfect and self-contained in a way that is not possible for finite entities like ourselves and all that we find in the world around us.

This is the central point of the insistence that 'no man hath seen God', that 'His ways are not our ways', that God is inscrutable and beyond our comprehension, and it is in the context of thought of this kind that we encounter perplexing doctrines such as the notion that God is one God but also three persons. It is not expected that we should be capable of rationalizing these notions and explaining closely and exhaustively what they mean. They belong to 'the mysteries of faith'.

Our critics have, on the one hand, forced us to be more unambiguous and explicit about this central and exceedingly perplexing aspect of religion. They have done so in part by noting that this is how religious people have generally thought and spoken, they have brought us back from what, in our more rationalist moods, we would like religion to be and made us more conscious of its true accents, not in variable incidentals but at the heart of it. But it has also been urged relentlessly that the attempts to reason our way from the facts of the world as we find it, including its more distinctive and significant features, to some superior reality akin in nature to itself have the faults already noted. Nothing seems to be explained in these terms which could not be better explained otherwise. The evidence is either meagre or so qualified as to yield no distinctive result.

I shall amplify this later. But in the meantime contemporary criticism has not only forced the religious apologist to regard the object of worship in religion, and the basis of the saint's sense of absolute security, as being in some way altogether beyond the world as we comprehend it, an eternal uncreated reality, it has also insisted with equal vigour that a reality which falls so completely outside the sphere in which our own minds are at home can mean nothing to us. If we affirm that God is not known as other things are known, if there is no inference to Him from the way the world goes, if He stands in no specific relation to other entities and does not admit of being known and characterized in that way, does it make sense to suppose that we know Him at all? In short, if we say that God is a total mystery we may have well evaded one horn of the attack upon us but only to be firmly impaled on another; we have no longer to provide reasons for believing in God and make these run the gauntlet of criticism, but has not the affirmation which remains been emptied of all content and significance? We cannot think a total mystery, and in insisting that we indicate how our affirmations are understood and what considerations, whether strictly empiricist or not, are relevant to their appraisal, our critics seem to have closed with particular firmness the only avenue of escape that seems possible. I submit, all the same, that by forcing us ruthlessly into this particular dilemma they have done us a great service and opened out for us the way to real understanding. How does this come about?

The answer to this question takes us to the very centre of the philosophy of religion, especially in the course it takes today, and we must therefore attend very carefully to it, as I shall now attempt to do.

FURTHER READING

Many of the papers in *Clarity is not Enough*, already mentioned, set out to exhibit the inadequacies of empiricism. So do two other books mentioned already, namely Errol Harris' *Nature, Mind, and*

Modern Science and Brand Blanshard's *Reason and Analysis*. A further book which may be much commended in this connection is *Essay in Christian Philosophy*, by Illtyd Trethowan (Longmans). The limitations of empiricism in ethics is well brought out by A. C. Ewing in *Reason and Intuition* and by the ethical writers noted above (in Chapter Two) as sharing his point of view.

The difficulties which empiricism encounters in dealing with the problems of the soul and self-identity will be noted in Chapter Twenty-four below, and suitable further reading will be appended to that chapter.

A symposium dealing with the question 'Can philosophical theories transcend experience?' was published in the *Proceedings of the Aristotelian Society*, Supplementary Volume XX. *Christianity and Paradox*, by Ronald Hepburn brings out exceptionally well the quandary to which the defender of religion is reduced by shrewd empiricist criticism; and the way to meet these is well exemplified in a major religious work of today, *Selfhood and Godhood*, by C. A. Campbell. The reader should consider especially Chapter xvii on 'Supra-rational Theism'.

Further reading on the problem of evil will be provided below but, in the meantime, reference may be made here to discussions of the notion of 'a finite God' mentioned in the text. This notion is defended in well-known writings by William James, such as his essay on 'Pragmatism and Religion' in his *Pragmatism* and *The Will to Believe*, where we have the description of God as 'one helper' among others and only *Primus inter pares*. The same view is found in parts of James' *The Will to Believe*, and in works like *The Realm of Values* (Cambridge) by one of James' most distinguished followers in religious philosophy, R. B. Perry. Explicit criticism of the notion of a finite God is found in the last chapter of C. A. Campbell's *Scepticism and Construction*.

The most thorough attempt to present a religious view without exceeding the limits of a broad empiricism is that of F. R. Tennant in the two volumes of his notable *Philosophical Theology*. These, and other works by Tennant, deserve to be more widely read and discussed today than they seem to be. A discussion of the problem of evil by Tennant is found in Chapter XXIV of Ninian Smart's *Historical Selections in the Philosophy of Religion*. Examination of these and other works by Tennant will bring out the strength and also the limitations, as they seem to me, of even a very broad empiricist view of religion.

CHAPTER FOURTEEN

GOD AND MYSTERY

Let me first insist here even further on the absolute character of the mystery involved in religion. There are other mysteries. When for example the conjurer takes a rabbit out of what seems to be an empty hat or puts a watch in a box which proves to be empty the moment it is opened, we may be quite bewildered; but we know that there is some explanation. We may never learn what it is, but the conjurer knows and can repeat his trick as required—there is no mystery in it for him. We find similar mysteries in detective stories. Someone has been stabbed in a room where all the entrances were sealed and remain so. How did the murderer enter? We may be quite baffled, but the author will not play fair unless he makes it all clear to us at the end; we know again that there *is* some explanation. There are similar mysteries in science, and to some of these no one has yet found the clue. But the scientist continues his investigations in the confidence that there is a solution to be discovered. Mystery at all these levels is relative. It depends on how much we understand already. The solution when it comes may surprise us and require much adjustment of earlier ideas. But it is all the same an explanation. This is no less true if reference is made to very unusual phenomena, as might happen in our murder case if the victim had been hypnotized beforehand (perhaps from a distance) and ordered to stab himself. This would be a strange explanation but we would accept it as being in accord with certain sorts of things, odd though they may be, which we have reason to believe do sometimes happen.

In all these regards, explanation is a way of putting things together to give a consistent account of the way they happen, and we proceed on the assumption that even the oddest and most bewildering occurrences do somehow make sense in this fashion, whether we can discover the solution or not. But however comprehensive such explanations may be, there seem to be still further questions to ask. Every discovery prompts us to look for another and even if we felt, as seems very unlikely, that profitable investigation had come to its end, we would still ask why the whole system of things is such as we find it to be—or 'why is there anything at all?' This is not a demand for further explanation of the sort we normally provide. It is a very strange question, but it lurks in all the solutions of all our problems. A is due to B, B to C and so on, but this process could go on without end at its own level, the sort of explanation provided is not exhaustive, it tells us of certain ways in which things are related to each other, but why there should be such relations we do not discover except in the sense of seeing more and more completely what those relations are. And yet we hanker for more. There seems to be a kind of 'why question' which normal explanation does not begin to answer.

This 'why question' is as much the bafflement of the child as of the philosopher. If a child asks questions about his own birth (or more simply 'who made me?'—or his brother or sister) he will probably be told today as much of the biological facts as he can understand, but many will still ask questions about this to which the harassed parent may give some version of the traditional answer: 'God made us this way in making the world what it is.' To which the reply will usually be, 'who made God?' This disconcerting question may be met in various ways, but whether the child is satisfied or not he is in his simple fashion feeling his way to the perplexing situation whereby we feel we must persist in seeking explanations while at the same time being increasingly aware that nothing that can normally be said will content us. It needs a sophisticated person to give formal expression to this perplexity and to distinguish between explanation in the normal sense and the curious sense of explanation or of 'ground' or 'cause' which is relevant to the questions 'Why is there a world?' or 'Why is there anything at all?'

This question arises from the existence of anything, no matter what, a speck of dust as much as the life of a saint. It does not depend on any particular feature of the world—

harmony or beauty or goodness. This is why it is not in the same realm of discourse, as it were, as the teleological argument, taken strictly. Everything, in the sense of our present question, points to God or, as some put it, is 'luminous' with God. God is everywhere and in all things, not, in the first instance, as some recognizable formative influence, but as a reality wholly unseen and unknown which is involved in all things and is beyond all things. God invests the world in this way at all points but is not the world or any part of it. As some philosophers put it, 'We see the finite breaking into the infinite' as well, although we have no notion what the infinite in itself can be.

When God is thought of in these terms he is invisible in a much more radical way than an invisible star or planet the astronomer may discover for us. For the astronomer can learn about some planet, before there is a telescope adequate to find it, by inference from what he can observe. He postulates the planet to explain the movements of other heavenly bodies. We may likewise postulate remote and obscure realities to explain things in other realms also. But we know something about these realities, that is they must have the character which is required for them to be plausible explanations of other things. They are not, as we say, quite indeterminate. But whatever 'explains' the whole system of things within which other explanations are possible must fall outside that system and nothing can be explicitly known about it except that it must *be* to account, in this special sense, for the way things are as a whole — or for there being anything at all.

There are many, however, who say that they do not feel the need for 'explanation' in the present, very unusual, sense I have been noting. Why, they will say, not just accept the way things are, as we find them, and leave it at that? Is there any substance in your peculiar 'why question'? We know what it means to have this or that explained, or to ask why this or that is such as it is. But is there any sense in asking for more, is there any question that we can ask other than questions which are in some way specific?

There is no easy answer to this point. We cannot prove that our very radical or ultimate question is significant, we cannot lead to it directly from other questions. But there are devices by which we can awaken in others the sense we have of there having to be something to account for the world in some way which involves being itself ultimate and perfect as nothing within the world can be. We can ask, for example, 'Do you think that things ultimately just happen to be?' It seems to me at least very odd to suppose that this could be. It is not that we find it disconcerting or distressing in some way to think that everything is ultimately due to some colossal chance. That might be, but there is more than distress here. We seem to see that in the last resort the world just could not exist by some extraordinary chance or just happen. And if that is so there must be 'explanation' in a way that goes beyond the sort of explanation we could ever grasp, some reality altogether beyond in which present reality is none the less rooted.

This consideration may be made a little more explicit, or given a little more body, by reflections on time and space of the sort noted earlier. In one way it seems there can be neither beginning nor end to either of these, and yet there is something altogether mystifying about the notion of time, for example, which never began anywhere. Are there, then, not pressures of these kinds which bring our minds to the point where they acknowledge, not merely that there is much in the world that is bewildering, but also more positively that all that we encounter points to a Reality which is complete and self-contained and which is the ultimate ground or condition of all the conditioned, limited reality we find ourselves and the world around us to be?

This sense of the Unconditioned has sometimes been described as 'a feeling of dependence'. But if this phrase is used we have to be very careful. For it is not just a feeling that we have, but a conviction or insight, a sense that something must be, a cognition in more technical terms. It is not easy to find an adequate name for this particular cognition or awareness. A common designation of it is intuition. 'Intuition' in philosophy stands for the knowledge we sometimes have without adducing further reasons for it, seeing each step in an argument, for instance, or the soundness of the principle of contradiction. Seeing that there must be the ultimate is direct in this way; it is, as I have put it elsewhere, 'one leap of thought'. But the intuition of God is peculiar in other ways which set it apart from insights into this or that specific matter. Moreover, some people have held that we can have direct confrontation of God or know Him as He is in his own nature or essence, and they sometimes use the word 'intuition' of this. But if I am near the truth at all, 'intuition of God' in this sense[1] is just what is most certainly impossible. Provided we avoid that mistake, however, I see no serious objection to the use of the term 'intuition' in this context. No terms can be adequate, but what matters most is that we should fully understand that it is knowledge or insight that is involved and that we should realize just what sort of insight this is, just how we appreciate that there must be the Ultimate Reality in question.

We can now also understand various observations which philosophers and theologians have traditionally made in this connection, for example that essence and existence are one in God and that the essence of God cannot be known. It is not part of the nature of anything normally that it must exist. We find that there are certain things—we could not deduce this from the concept of them. We also sense that in the last resort nothing could just be by chance, but the element of necessity here is not found directly in finite things themselves but in a Reality beyond themselves and in their dependence, in some way we cannot further comprehend, upon it. It is thus part of the nature of this Ultimate Reality that it must be; and this, along with the perfection which this kind of existence carries with it, is all that we can know directly about God. He is a Being who exists by necessity, but what it must be like further to be this sort of Being we cannot from the nature of the case ever know. We do not know the essence of God.

This would not be the case if we knew that God existed by inference from the way the world goes or what we find in it; for then we would have to postulate a certain kind of Being to account for this or that. But we seem impelled to think of God

1. Another name for this position is 'ontologism'. It is generally regarded as a heretical position.

in a much more radical way to account, not for this or that, but for everything or for there being anything at all. He is involved in the being of everything besides Himself, but not involved as terms are related in an inference but in a quite peculiar relation of dependence of all things upon Him. He is closer to all things than distinct finite things ever are to one another, and also remote beyond all conception. This we see, not as inference, but in one insight or leap of thought.

For the same reason we know that God exists with a certainty we do not have in learning about other things. We know that there are certain things in the world from the evidence or our experience of them. We find that we ourselves and other persons and things exist. The evidence is often so overwhelming that we never doubt it for a moment, but what we attain all the same is an overwhelmingly high degree of probability. Even when we know our own existence directly in being ourselves, we know this as something certain which could be otherwise. But we are certain of God because we know that He must be.

This is an important part of what is meant by saying that God is unique. He is not like ourselves and other things we find in fact in the world. Fact and necessity meet in Him as they do not in anything else, and this has a further peculiar consequence, namely that if we understand properly what is meant by 'God' we at one and the same time see that He must be. This does not mean that unbelievers are just stupid. For the understanding involved is not a matter of drawing the correct deductions and so on, it is a matter of acquiring a very special sort of insight—or of having it elicited. But it does follow that the task of the apologist or others in commending religion to the atheist, or seeking to convert him, is initially, or where the existence of God is concerned, not that of getting him to agree that there is some being corresponding to the idea of God which he understands well enough, but to get him to sense what this idea means. He cannot do that without, in that act itself, seeing that God must also be.

In this regard God is unlike everything else. We may understand the concept of many things, or learn what types of things they are. These may be concepts of things which we know to exist, or they may be concepts of things which may exist but of whose existence we have no conclusive evidence— and perhaps much evidence against it. We may thus form the concept of a dragon. We do not find it hard to understand this concept or to give a rough indication of what it means. But it has then to be settled, as a further matter, whether there are such creatures, whether there are instances of this concept. In the case of God, to understand the concept is to see, in the very same thought, that there must be one instance of it and that there cannot be more than one.

The last point may need further stress. It might seem a perfectly proper and sensible question to ask 'Is there just one God or are there many?' Men certainly seem to have worshipped many gods at the same time. But I shall contend in a moment that this is a simplification of a very complicated situation and that, where genuine worship is involved, there can only be one object of worship. If the object of worship is the sort of ultimate Reality about which I have just been writing, it can clearly not be one among many of its kind. It must be beyond the relatedness of other things and retain in itself the principle by which other entities stand in relation to one another. If it had a duplicate the relation of the two realities to one another would have to be understood again in a way that pointed beyond both to some more ultimate and radically different sort of being which is itself limited by nothing. God is not *primus inter pares* but absolute.

I have said that to see that there must be God is not a matter of ordinary understanding. It requires a certain attitude of mind. If our thoughts are wholly engaged with the course of things about us, if the daily round and the whirl and excitement of all that happens today completely fill our minds, then it is not surprising that many become unaware of any other reality and never perceive in the reality of the present world any intimation of anything other than itself. The extending boundaries of ordinary understanding and knowledge content them and they do not become sensitive to the sort of absolute boundary which presents itself directly in all knowledge and experience. It is thus not surprising that so many people find religion today, not so much implausible, but meaningless, and that others should be trying desperately to make it meaningful by making it something quite different from what it really is (in ways indicated earlier). We see also how peculiarly important for religion is the current preoccupation with meaning and how those who have drawn attention to the problem of meaning, even if they came to it with very restrictive empiricist presuppositions, have helped to direct attention to the right quarter in religion. But here the remedy is not a wholly intellectual one. Intellect and sophistication are certainly involved, more so indeed than at any time; and philosophy has an increasingly important part to play in bringing out the sort of considerations of which I am giving an indication in this book. But there are other conditions of insight and there are pressures which may be brought on our minds to induce the awareness of an ultimate reality involved in a peculiar way in all else there is.

Some of these pressures are among the more disturbing and disruptive experiences we have in the world—disappointment, sorrow, fear, bereavement and loneliness and so forth; and it has been argued that while these are as fundamental a feature of experience today as ever, we are also much cushioned against them and have means of turning away their edge. How much they make their impact felt at other levels of life today than the superficial round may be well discerned in contemporary literature. We thus find ourselves in a very ambivalent state; on the one hand in our more conscious thoughts and overt habits we are drifting, as societies, very far from religion and becoming insensitive to it or unaware of what it means; at another level we are acutely conscious of pressures which bring us close to religion and find our creative writers using quasi-theological terms and sometimes borrowing expressly the language of religion.

This is not the place to pursue this important theme further. It must be enough here to note that religion requires, for its proper furtherance, certain conditions of living, including those which prevent us from lapsing into glamorized impressions of the world which cover up its starker and more unsettling aspects. There must also be conditions which conduce to the sort of contemplation which can lead our thoughts beyond the here and now.[1] What these are cannot be considered here, but it should be evident that they are best fulfilled when there are proper opportunities for worship and inducement to it. This is the element of truth in much that is written about commitment in religion today, a truth so much misrepresented in the notion that we can just commit ourselves to a belief. It is also the source of one of our worst practical dilemmas.

The dilemma is this. To be sensitive to religious realities we need to move within an environment which is conducive to awareness of them. When we pass to more specific religious matters than the basic one of the existence of God, this is even more evident and the need greater. But how can we come 'within' and sense the atmosphere of holy things if we have not already some conviction? How can the honest agnostic take part in acts of worship? I am not sure what is the answer to this question, but I am sure the answer will involve the arrangement of some types of religious services which can be attended in a more non-committal way than is possible at present. This is however a matter of evangelical and missionary strategy which does not concern us closely here. For our present purpose it must be enough to have indicated various aspects of the insight by which we become aware of the ultimate and unconditioned Reality which is 'beyond' the world it conditions, in a very special sense of beyond, and in its essential nature beyond any grasp of our understanding. We know that it must be, but how it is and must be we do not know beyond its completeness and per- fection which themselves elude our comprehension.

1. E. L. Mascall writes wisely as follows in *He Who Is*, p. 80: 'Under modern conditions of life, people very rarely give themselves the leisure and the quiet necessary for the straightforward consideration of finite being. They never really sit down and look at anything. This diagnosis is borne out by the common experience of people making their first retreat, that after the first day or so natural objects seem to acquire a peculiar character of transparency and vitality, so that they appear as only very thinly veiling the creative activity of God. But what is possible after a period of repose and silence in the atmosphere of a retreat-house is very difficult to achieve if one spends one's working life in a stockbroker's office or a steel foundry and one's leisure time at the pictures or dancing to the accompaniment of a saxophone-band.'

The sense of there being this Beyond is at the heart of all religion. There may seem to be religions which lack it and I shall comment on that later.[1] But it is certainly plain that some discernment of a supreme and ultimate Reality is very marked in many religions. The God of Judaism, Christianity and Islam is obviously 'beyond' in the present sense, or, in a more technical term, transcendent. But so is the One or Supreme Self of Hinduism; and I think we shall also find the same sense of the transcendent, in a subtle and highly significant form, in most varieties of Buddhism. It is indeed remarkable how early in the life of societies the sense of the Beyond is found. There are explicit intimations of it in very early records, such as the first Vedic writings[2]; and it is reflected in many other aspects of early culture.

This does not mean that there is overt formulation of the notion of an Ultimate or Absolute Reality among the peoples of very early times. We could not expect that without much sophistication and some rudiments at least of philosophy. But we have also seen that the sense of a Reality altogether beyond the world as we know it is not the result of elaborate ratiocination, it comes directly in the impact of certain experiences upon us, and simple-minded folk are in some ways more open than others to the thrust of the Beyond into their lives in this way. There is certainly ample evidence that this has happened, and that in turn has brought about a considerable change in the study of the history and the origins of religion.

This is reflected especially in a justly celebrated work which all students of religion should consider carefully, namely Rudolf Otto's *The Idea of the Holy*. Our sense of a Reality mysterious and fascinating — the famous words are *mysterium tremendum et fascinans* — is carefully analysed by Otto, and he also shows how much this notion has presided over the origins and development of religion. This may be contrasted sharply with the view of religion which held the field in the nineteenth century. It was then thought that religion had

1. Chapter Twenty-seven.
2. A good account of these and other early Indian scriptures may be found in the Introduction to *The Principal Upanisads*, by Radhakrishnan.

begun with the personification of natural objects and the worship of our ancestors or their ghosts and had only acquired the notion of one supreme deity at a late and very sophisticated stage. A classical expression of this view had been formulated in advance by David Hume in the eighteenth century in another celebrated work, *The Natural History of Religion*; and while I cannot pause here to consider these books closely I would like to urge the student to read these two books, both classics of their kind, together and compare them to see which impresses him as the more plausible approach to the subject. Some of the evidence relevant to the problem will be found in some of the books listed at the end of this chapter.

Nowhere is the sense of God's transcendence more explicit and sharp than in the religion of the Hebrews. The patriarchal stories, the stories of Jacob at Bethel and Peniel for example, the psalms and the prophecies – very notably the account of the vision of Isaiah[1] – reflect it extensively. But there is perhaps no passage in the Old Testament which is more significant or celebrated in this connection than the story of Moses at the burning bush.[2] For here we read of Moses seeking desperately to have God disclosed to him as He is in himself, to know His name and how to describe Him. This would provide Moses, so he expected, with the assurance and authority he needed for his task. But this is also what he most certainly cannot be given. He is not, as the story puts it, to see the face of God or know His name. He can be told only that God is 'He Who is' or the 'I am'. And it is remarkable indeed that, at least at the time the book of Exodus came to be written (and no doubt before that), the Hebrews had thus acquired a very explicit awareness of the impenetrable mystery of God and realized that whatever may be known about God we cannot reduce the mystery of what He is in Himself. He is the One who *is*, who must be, and that, as involving His perfection and holiness,[3] is all we can directly know about Him. For the same reason the Hebrews had a profound aversion to even uttering the name of God. That would make Him too much

1. Isaiah VI.
2. Exodus III.
3. On this see the book by F. Sontag listed at the end.

like ourselves, it would not be consistent with the majesty and holiness of God.

The remarkable early understanding reflected in the Exodus story may be contrasted with the attitude of some of our contemporaries to religion. The late Professor J. L. Austin, the moving spirit in much recent linguistic philosophy, is reputed to have referred to the famous story in a lecture. His comment was that if God said to Moses 'I am', then the proper reply should have been 'You are what?' There is obviously shrewdness here. No one utters a meaningful remark normally by just saying 'He is' or 'I am'. The context may supply more; we may, for example, be answering a question and saying in effect 'I am hungry' or something of that sort. But there is no meaning at all in just 'I am' without indication, if not in words in some other way, of who the person is and what is being affirmed about him. Affirmation of this sort must in fact take the form of ascribing some predicate, however vague, to a subject which can in some way be identified. This is what our thought is like, and to try to go outside this is to utter words without meaning.

But what Professor Austin seems to have overlooked is the peculiarity of religious utterances. In so far as these are about God they are about a unique Reality which falls altogether outside ordinary discourse. What holds without exception of finite things does not hold of God; He is the supreme exception, just because He is God, and this is what Professor Austin's procedures obscure. The insight of the Hebrew writer seems to me much profounder.

Equally profound is the Hebrew understanding of the world as a created world. It may not be easy to determine how exactly the Hebrews understood the 'Creation Stories' in Genesis. But it is certain that in their ripened religious awareness creation was not to be assimilated to ordinary making or fashioning; it was a great, indeed irreducible, mystery. But the Hebrews also understood particularly well that the absolute or transcendent character of God did not mean that everything else was in some way taken up into His own nature. They appreciated with surprising shrewdness that the unqualified nature of the mystery of the being of God was consistent with, indeed required, our being distinct and separate existences, and we shall shortly see that this has particular importance, especially for the discussion of mysticism.

We are now in a good position to see what makes it plausible if also misleading, for Tillich and others to speak of 'a God beyond God' and to maintain that God is not one object among others, since the relation of subject and object is transcended in the case of God. All this is proper provided that it is understood that God is truly real although His reality passes incomprehensibly beyond the sphere where proper discourse, affirming specific predicates of limited subjects, is possible. The trouble is that many today, Tillich and his disciples in particular, oscillate confusingly between this way of understanding God's transcendence and supposing, or vaguely suggesting, that, as God is not a subject of predicates in the normal sense, He is nothing at all in Himself and must be thought of therefore as some fundamental aspect of our own existence and not as such any reality on its own account.

This procedure appears to relieve us of grievous problems, especially those which concern the specific claims we make about God—at least in some religions. But it is also, as we have seen, the short way which solves our problems at the expense of the reality we are most concerned to preserve.

A statement of much importance in this connection is that 'all determination is negation'. This sounds highly technical and puzzling. But it is a form of words which the student is almost certain to encounter in further reading on the problem of God's existence and nature. It is not in fact as difficult as it may appear. It means this. In affirming anything of some subject we are excluding other predicates not compatible with the one affirmed. If I say that a book is here I imply that it is not over there, if I add that it is blue it follows that, while it may be light or heavy, it cannot be red—in the same part. All discourse involves limitations and negations of this kind, as Plato was particularly anxious to stress in his discussion of truth and knowledge. To 'determine' an object, in the sense of making it precise and clear, is thus, in the present sense, negation. But God, it is rightly claimed, is not determinate in this sense. He is not, however, indeterminate in the sense of being nothing at all but in the sense of being beyond all limitation, of being complete in Himself as finite limited reality cannot be and being, for this reason, beyond the proper grasp of our intellects.

But here we come back to our original problem and paradox which our critics have sharpened for us today. For if God is as elusive as has just been made out, how is it possible to think of Him at all, even to affirm that He exists? We have either to bring him within the sphere of ordinary discourse or find that He has vanished altogether and become nothing. If we take the former course we have something less than God, and the claims normally made about God become impossible to sustain when referred to a lesser reality—if He is a postulate in the normal sense the evidence is inadequate, if He is a First Cause that cause seems to need a cause in turn, and so on. But if we avoid problems of this kind, does not our critic hold us in his cleft stick all the same? For we have now made God so unlike everything else, so 'wholly other', that He does not seem to be anything at all.

It is tempting to bluster or wriggle our way out of this cleft stick without reckoning fairly with the force of the grip which holds us in it. But we must not attempt to do that, we must come fully to terms with our dilemma and realize that wisdom in religious thought begins with clearly acknowledging the force of the considerations which present us with this dilemma; we must not seek rashly to moderate them. God is not an object we can characterize like finite things, He is, in the term oft repeated by a very notable philosopher of today,[1] 'supra-rational', but on the other hand we must not admit that He is nothing. We do not know what His essence in itself is, we cannot particularize the divine nature, we know Him only in the inevitability of His being as the transcendent ground or condition of the limited conditioned existences which we can understand and discuss in the ordinary way. It is not that our thought here is empty or without content, it is

1. C. A. Campbell. See specially the discussion of supra-rational theism in his *Selfhood and Godhood*.

the richest thought of all, but from the nature of the case we cannot make it more explicit than the affirmation of there having to be Supreme or Ultimate Being.[1] That is all we know directly of God.

But if God is as incomprehensible to us as religious thought and religious experience and prophecy alike make Him out to be, if He is essentially hidden and invisible, how do we come to make such intimate claims about Him as we do in much of our religious life and worship? Why, for instance, do we speak of God as 'Him', that is use a distinctly personal term, rather than 'it'? The reader must feel impatient for an answer to these questions. I must however plead with him to remain patient, for if he is to be fully in the picture he must now attempt to see how the famous arguments for the existence of God, the traditional arguments as some of them are called, appear in the light of the position we have now reached. That is the topic to which I now turn.

FURTHER READING

The views advanced in this chapter are presented at more length in my 'God and Mystery' in *Prospect for Metaphysics* already mentioned and in the first part of my *Our Experience of God*. The further reading provided at the end of Chapters Thirteen and Fifteen will be relevant here also.

1. I have put the point elsewhere in these words: 'There is a content to our thought (about God), otherwise it would not be thought at all, but it nevertheless falls outside ordinary discourse; we are not affirming predicates of an entity already characterized and recognized in some fashion, nor are we claiming existence for some entity with a nature in some way determined. Subject and predicate are not relevant here, yet our thought is not empty, it has, in a fashion, the richest content of all. But it is not the apprehension of distinct characteristics, but of the inevitability of there being the completion which finite thought lacks or the perfection of the world as we find it. In what this completion consists we do not know at all, we are not having any glimpse behind the scenes—and we could not. Any light on things we can receive, as finite beings, is the sort of light they have partially already; what we can grasp is the kind of thing we now grasp. There can be no means therefore of determining what it is to be God. We have not even a partial reduction of that mystery. The nature of God is in this sense altogether hidden. We know him in the necessity of his being as the other and positive side to the impossibility of ultimate fortuitousness.' *Prospect for Metaphysics*, p. 225.

Of the importance of the idea of God's transcendence in recent theology and in Eastern thought a very good account is given in W. S. Urquart's *Humanism and Christianity* (Edinburgh) and in his *Vedanta and Modern Thought* (London). *The Theology of Crisis,* by Ulrich Simon (S.P.C.K.), is a sympathetic exposition of Barthian transcendentalist theology. A good instance of such theology is Emil Brunner's *Revelation and Reason* (S.C.M.). Reference could also be made here to *The Principal Upanisads,* by Radhakrishnan (Allen and Unwin). This contains selections of notable Hindu Scriptures and a most informative introduction by the editor. *The Paradox of Nirvana,* by Robert Slater (University of Chicago Press), will also have much relevance to the theme of the preceding chapter and link it with some of the questions to be considered later; *Divine Perfection,* by Frederik Sontag (S.C.M.), is a recent book which deals in a scholarly and suggestive way with some of the topics of this chapter.

CHAPTER FIFTEEN

THE FIVE WAYS AND THE ONTOLOGICAL ARGUMENT

There are many variations on the main arguments for the existence of God. All these have been subjected to much criticism from time to time, and there are not many persons today who believe that the arguments provide a strict and conclusive proof of the existence of God. This does not mean, however, that the arguments are of no account. Every student of the philosophy of religion should make himself familiar with them. Nor is this merely a matter of historical interest in the development of the subject. A careful examination of the traditional arguments can be very instructive to the student today. For it is not an accident that the arguments have impressed so many people in the past, including some of the greatest thinkers of all time. If the arguments are not strictly successful they do, none the less, in some versions especially, direct our thoughts in the right way and point to something of the utmost importance for our understanding of God.

If the arguments, or some of them, were strictly successful, this would naturally put the apologist or any other defender of the faith in a very strong position. We could not convince everybody but we could set forth the truths of religion with the sort of assurance, and the expectation of their general acceptance, which we find in science or mathematics or logic. This has indeed been the ideal and hope of some notable thinkers who have put forward formulations of the main arguments. The attractiveness of their expectation is plain. But alas religious truth is not of this order. It is in some respects simple, but this is not at any level the simplicity of a trim argument. We should understand by now why this is so. At the centre of religion is the idea of a transcendent or Absolute Being who, from the nature of the case, is beyond the sphere in which we relate things rationally to one another. He is beyond the unity of system as we know it, and thus it is out of the question to know Him by argument of any kind. We can only know Him directly, in the way indicated, as involved in all possibility of argument and the existence of anything at all.

All the same the arguments, in spite of their being unavoidably in conflict with their own purpose of proving that which, rightly understood, goes beyond all argument, have reflected men's discernment of there having to be a 'Beyond' in the sense in question; and the point at which the arguments fail most sharply helps to exhibit for us the peculiar way in which God is elusive and transcendent. The arguments are thus important, both in respect of what they reflect of man's insights and convictions and as an exhibition at the same time, by their own inadequacy, of the proper scope and significance of these insights.

I shall now offer a brief review of some typical and well-known forms of the traditional arguments. This will be designed to open up the subject for the reader and to illustrate the points I have just been making. It will obviously need to be supplemented by other reading.

The Five Ways of St. Thomas Aquinas. These are five famous proofs of the existence of God advanced by St. Thomas in the First Book of his *Summa Theologica*. The first three of these have much in common, and they can be regarded as variations of what we generally know as the Cosmological Argument, that is the argument from there being a world or cosmos which seems to need something that will account for it.

(*a*) The argument from movement. We find that certain things are in motion, and others at rest. Something must have started the movement. But this must itself have been set in motion by something else. We cannot, however, go on in this way *ad infinitum*. The series of 'moved movers' implies thus 'an Unmoved Mover', a Mover that is not itself moved by anything else, and this, the argument concludes, must be God.

This is not the version of the basic argument that is likely to impress us most today. We are conscious of problems about the nature of motion which would not have occurred to

Aquinas. With our knowledge of modern physics it is not so clear to us that the conditions which we could describe as static could not have initiated movements of some kind. In addition, we find it hard to draw a distinction of an absolute kind between being at rest and in motion. Are not the things which are relatively stable in motion in relation to other things, and is there not movement of some kind involved in the ultimate composition of all physical reality? We may thus conclude, for these and kindred reasons, that St. Thomas has not here chosen the best starting point for his argument.

This might not, however, be thought to affect the substance of the argument. Change is after all a fact of experience, and it seems reasonable thus to ask what accounts for this. But here we meet a more basic objection, namely that if we begin with the principle that everything which initiates change must have been initiated in some way itself, this must apply to the alleged First Mover also. So it does not mean that we can stop anywhere in our explanations or the postulation of movers of movers. We are back with something like the apt retort of the child — Who made God?

In a way this last objection is fatal. It is fatal, that is, if we begin with a series of finite events, together with a principle which governs them, and hope to find, on that basis or in these terms, an original event which is not subject to the same regulation as the others. This is what the argument, in the strict form of an argument, seems to require. In approaching the issue in that way, however, we may be missing the point. For what makes us feel that, however open to objection as it stands, there is still something in the argument, is the possibility of the reference being, not to some exceptional member of the series of 'moved movers' itself, but to some Reality of a totally different order altogether outside the series and not itself subject to the conditions which govern it. Dr. Mascall maintains that this is not something we may find suggested to us today by the argument, but that it was the intention of St. Thomas and those who have followed his lead. In Professor Mascall's own words:

The point is not really that we cannot have an infinite regress in the order of nature, but that such an infinite regress in the series of moved movers would necessitate an unmoved First Mover not *in* the order of nature but *above* it.[1]

This seems to me to put the matter admirably.

(*b*) The second way is the argument from 'efficient causality'. This is sometimes known as 'the aetiological argument'. The idea of efficient causality is this. We can think of a cause as something which is just invariably connected with another event, the effect, adding if we wish that this invariability is a necessary one, that is that the effect is bound to happen when the cause occurs. There has been much controversy among philosophers about the element of necessity in causal connections, and I shall refer to this again. But invariable connection, whether strictly necessary or not, is one thing. It is another to think of a cause, as not merely preceding the event in some regular way or found always in correlation with it, but as itself actively producing the effect, being properly accountable for it. For normal purposes, including science, all we require are the connections and correlations which our observations establish. But we are apt also to think of a cause as involving more than this. Some have argued that this expectation comes about from the cases where we ourselves are the causal agents and produce things. But the question of how we come to think of a cause as more than regular or necessary antecedent, and whether there is justification for this, is a hard one. I leave it aside for the moment, as it will be enough at this point to indicate how the idea of efficient cause is to be understood.

St. Thomas believed that everything that happens must have an efficient cause, but in that case every cause must in turn have another efficient cause to bring it about. It is impossible, however, to go back in this causal sequence to infinity. There must be a terminus in the form of a First Cause which is not itself caused by anything else. This First Cause is that to which 'everyone gives the name of God'.

This argument invites the same sort of comment as the previous one. For even if we find no difficulty in the notion of an 'efficient cause', the objection arises that if we begin

1. *He Who Is*, p. 44.

with the principle that *everything* must have a cause we cannot, without contradicting our initial assumption, exempt the First Cause; and to this the reply must be made that, while there is no answer if the argument is meant to proceed as a strict argument in terms of what we find in the world around us, the objection fails if the reference is not to some extra-ordinary member of the causal series but to the necessity of there being something not itself a cause in the normal sense at all which accounts for there being the causal series itself, a Cause of causes as it were. This, it is held (I think rightly), is what St. Thomas himself meant.

I shall add a word in another context about the notion of efficient cause and the place of this in the movement of our thought from finite things to a transcendent reality beyond them. I also leave aside for the moment any further difficulties in the notion of a causal series. For I do not think that those affect the substance of what St. Thomas is maintaining.

(*c*) The argument from contingency — '*e contingentia mundi*'. This is also often known as the cosmological argument, but it has been pointed out that the first three ways are all themselves variations on the theme of what is generally understood by the cosmological argument. This argument starts from the fact that some things certainly do exist — we ourselves and the world around us exist. But there is nothing in the nature of the entities we find in the world to make them exist, or to require that they must exist. In fact they come into being and they pass away. But this cannot be the whole truth about them, it cannot be true of the totality of things that they just happen to be. If that were the case there would have been a time — and St. Thomas would have said that there would have had to be one — when there was nothing at all. But then nothing could have come into being or begun — from nothing nothing could come. The existence of beings which, from considera-tion of their own natures alone, are just found in fact to exist, in other words contingent beings, implies that there is some 'necessary being' to account for them. If we suppose that the necessity of such a being is bestowed upon it by another, we still cannot extend this *ad infinitum*; there must thus be some necessary being whose existence is necessitated, not by something other than itself, but by its own nature or essence. Such a being, St. Thomas concludes again, 'all men speak of as God'.

This argument has the merit of bringing us more directly to the heart of the matter. It makes no use of any special notion of causation. The temporal reference in the argument and the postulation—if St. Thomas really meant it—that contingent existents considered solely in themselves would have implied a time when there was nothing at all—are dispensable. What remains irrespective of any particular way of formulating the argument is the immediate apprehension, not thus an argument with distinct steps, that nothing could just happen to be and that everything must thus involve the transcendent in the way indicated earlier. St. Thomas may have made the presentation of this insight more elaborate than he need, but there seems to me to be little doubt that 'the third way' comes very close indeed to what I attempted to describe in the last chapter.

(d) The argument from degrees of being. This argument is coloured more than the others by ways of thinking and speaking that were more common in medieval times than they are today. We are not accustomed to think of anything having a degree of being or reality. Either an entity exists, or it does not—that seems to be all. We are likewise reluctant to speak of degrees of truth. A statement is true, or it is false; it cannot, in the same particular, be something in between. We do, however, speak metaphorically of certain things as being more true or more real than others, just as we say that some people are more alive than others or speak as the Bible does of having life more abundantly. What we mean is that some things are richer in content and more significant than others, and so on. In the last century the idealist thinkers I mentioned earlier[1] maintained that the more complete some reality was, the more it contained in a systematic way in itself, then the more it partook of the one whole of reality and the more real it was. So the notion of degrees of reality (and degrees of truth as well) was very common in philosophical debates in the last

1. Chapter V.

century.[1] We are much more averse to it today. Medieval thinkers did not have explicitly in mind the sort of considerations which led Hegelian thinkers to speak of degrees of reality, but incipiently they had many of them. In particular they tended to equate being with goodness, and in the case of goodness the notion of degrees is not only appropriate but unavoidable. We do not just ask whether things are good but also how good, moderately good or supremely good and so on; and if being and goodness are equated it becomes more natural to speak of degrees of being. The notion of being and goodness as being identical or at least coincident is of course a very difficult one, and it meets a particular difficulty in the fact of evil—the solution usually sought at this point consisting in regarding evil as a mere lack or a 'privation of good', a suggestion I myself find particularly implausible in any normal reference. I shall refer to it again in a moment. But it must suffice here to give this brief indication of how some thinkers come to speak of degrees of being and truth as well as degrees of goodness.

What is the next step? It is to point out that an ascending scale of being and truth and goodness must have some limit in a Being who has these qualities in a supreme degree in relation to which the rest becomes possible, in other words the cause of there being such qualities in all other beings, the cause of all other perfection, as St. Thomas would put it; and this again 'we call God'.

This argument has the merit of bringing the goodness or perfection of God into prominence. It will none the less seem to us much more artificial than the other arguments. The identification of being and goodness, together with the notion of degrees of reality, presents obvious difficulties. Nor is it evident why a scale of goodness and corresponding reality, however we understand this, should, as such, presuppose some absolute limit. For consideration of the absolute in this sense arises, not in respect of this or that feature of reality, but in respect to any reality at all, that is it has nothing specifically to

1. A celebrated work on this theme appeared in the first decade of this century. It is H. Joachim's *Nature of Truth*. The reader should also consult A. C. Ewing's *Idealism*.

do with goodness. On the other hand we cannot dissociate from the nature of ultimate or transcendent being the idea of perfection. Whatever can serve as the ultimate ground of all else, however much it passes beyond our understanding, must be thought of as complete and adequate in itself in every way; and thus the idea of ultimacy at this point passes into the idea of perfection. This brings us very close to what we shall also find in a moment in another very famous mode of argument for the existence of God, the ontological argument. For the present it must be enough to add that if the 'fourth way' is taken, not as an argument proceeding from certain conditions thought to apply specifically to the notion of goodness and involving questionable notions of degrees of reality, but as expressing the insight that beyond all we can meet and conceive of in the world lies some transcendent reality which must also, from the nature of the case, be supremely perfect, then it also puts us on the right road; and there is, I believe, a case for maintaining that this is how the matter shaped itself mainly in the mind of St. Thomas himself. But in that case we are back again at something less complex than the particular arguments in the specific form each takes, something which lies behind them all and which they imperfectly express.

(*e*) The argument from design or the teleological argument. This, as St. Thomas intends it, is not quite what we understand by the teleological argument. The name denotes for us the argument which proceeds from alleged indications of design or purpose in the world, the structure of living organisms or the course which evolution or history as a whole may be thought to take. For St. Thomas the argument is more *a priori*. It does not depend so much on inspection of the facts of the world as on the general principle that everything, however insignificant, must have a purpose. This was part of the metaphysical framework of the thought of St. Thomas and his contemporaries and it owed much to what they had derived from Aristotle's account of different modes of causation, and especially at this point the notion of a 'final cause', a cause not, as it were, propelling from behind but drawing on from in front in the shape of some end or purpose to be achieved.[1] The notion of a final cause, especially as applied to the world of nature in general, has not much appeal today, although it is not without some support. But if we grant this notion, a question presents itself at once. In the case of intelligent beings it may be said that, for their own actions at least, they set their purposes for themselves. But this can hardly be true of other creatures, least of all of inanimate ones. How then are their ends or purposes determined? St. Thomas contends that there must be some intelligent being who arranges the adaptation of things to their ends for the order of nature as a whole, and this he again concludes must be God.

There are serious defects in this argument. I shall leave aside now the difficulties in the notion of a final cause. But even if those are waived it does not seem that we have grounds for postulating anything beyond a being of superior knowledge and intelligence who need not be supreme or ultimate in the way we think of a being we worship as God. It is not even clear that there could only be one such being. There might be a number working together. At best we seem to have only an architect or governor of the world, someone able to manipulate things in certain ways but not an absolute Lord or Creator on whom objects depend for their being and all they have in them. The fifth way, in short, could at best only guarantee the existence of some further finite being, a being much greater than ourselves no doubt, but not an infinite being. And this, as we shall see, is the weakness of the teleological argument in its somewhat different modern forms as well.

To make the present argument impressive we would have in fact to presuppose at the outset the notion of some absolute or ultimate source of all existence to which the cosmological argument points. We might then see such purposiveness as we find in nature as one manifestation of its operation. But this would add nothing of substance to the original notion, nor would it strengthen it in any way. That notion must stand or fall by itself.

Accordingly, even if the ideas we associate with the

1. The reader can learn more about this from Chapter III of W. D. Ross's *Aristotle*.

cosmological argument were in St. Thomas' mind in presenting the argument from design and were meant to give the latter the support it needs, we cannot regard the argument from design as having any success, on its own account, in what it sets out to do. Whether its main ideas can have significance in another context is another matter.

The Ontological Argument. This is very different from the sort of argument we have been noting hitherto. It makes no use of causal or quasi-causal considerations, and it is thus more completely *a priori* than the other argument; it is apt to strike the student at first as extremely abstract. Opinions about its merits differ very sharply, some people are profoundly impressed by it and others think it obviously absurd. The aim of the ontological argument is to put the existence of God beyond doubt by showing that it can be established by consideration of the idea of God itself, that is, we might put it, by analysis of the notion of God. This puts the matter on a level with logical or mathematical proof, at least in respect to certainty and independence of fallible observations of any matters of fact. It can be shown, for example, from the very nature of what we mean by a triangle that the sum of its angles must be 180 degrees—we need nothing further; and it can well be seen what advantages would follow for religious apologetics if the existence of God could be established in this way. How does the argument proceed?

In a famous formulation of the argument which made it widely known in the Middle Ages St. Anselm[1] described the idea of God as the idea of that 'than which nothing greater can be conceived'. But, he maintained, a God who is real is obviously greater than a God who exists only in our own thought. If we do not think of God as real we can think of something greater. To be real is thus involved in what we mean by 'God' and we thus cannot think of Him, as we do, except as existing.

To the argument thus presented there was an equally famous reply by a monk named Gaunilo, the main point of the

1. The reader can learn more about St. Anselm from A. E. Taylor's article on 'Theism' mentioned at the end of the chapter and the histories of philosophy listed earlier.

reply being that we could prove the existence of many other things in this way. We might think, for example, of an island than which none could be wealthier and better. If the island were just one in our imagination then it would be inferior in these respects to an island which was also real. Therefore there must be such an island.

There has been, and there continues to be, much debate about the question whether Gaunilo's seemingly knock-down reply misses something essential, as Anselm himself certainly thought was the case. Does Gaunilo's objection have force when we think not just of something supreme of its kind but of that than which there could be nothing greater anywhere? It was to bring this point out that Descartes, in what became centuries later the best-known statement of the argument, spoke of perfection rather than greatness. The idea of God is the idea of a perfect Being, or as Descartes would put it a being who has all perfections. But existence is a perfection, and in thinking of God as having all perfections we are bound thus to think of Him as existing. Not everyone agrees that this is an improvement, but it does enable the distinction to be drawn more effectively between that which is perfect of its kind and that which is absolutely perfect; and to some extent this seems to take care of Gaunilo's island. But Kant presented afresh what I think lies behind Gaunilo's objection when he questioned whether existence could be regarded as a perfection. The terms used here will seem a little alien to us; for Descartes, although he thought of himself as a very complete innovator, used many terms as they had been used from the Middle Ages on and was thus apt to equate 'perfection' with 'quality' or 'attribute', this being itself some legacy of the tendency to identify being and goodness. What Kant was therefore saying in effect was that existence was not a quality of the kind which could appropriately be included in the content of our idea of some object, it was something further to be affirmed, if at all, independently. Thus I might say that the idea of an orange is the idea of something round, having yellow colour, juicy sections inside and so on. But existence is not a candidate for inclusion in any list of this kind. It could not be part of what we mean by an orange or anything else. When we have learnt what is meant by 'orange', the question still remains whether there are any. This is what is meant by saying, in Kantian terms, that statements about existence are synthetic and not analytic.

It is plain that there is force in Kant's objection—and in the anticipation of it by Gaunilo. We would indeed be contradicting ourselves if we thought of something as a circle and denied that it was round. But we do not seem to contradict ourselves at all in denying that something exists. To be real is not part of what we mean by anything. If therefore the ontological argument proceeds on the initial assumption that existence can be treated as a property on all fours with colour, size, cleverness, and so on, the bottom drops out of the argument by our showing that there is no soundness in the initial assumption. But this is perhaps where the mistake is made, by defenders of the argument and critics alike. If we begin with certain principles thought to apply to finite things, such as we find in the world, and then try to proceed by argument from this to the existence of infinite Reality, we are bound to fail, and we shall almost certainly do this in the form of importing into our premisses considerations which have no relevance except in relation to our conclusion, that is we shall think of finite things in terms only appropriate to God. It was natural to attempt this course, and there are special reasons to be noted shortly why it was tempting for Descartes. But he should never have embarked upon it. He should have heeded more the radical difference between finite things and infinite or unconditioned Being, and he could then have pointed out that in the case of God we have a Reality of which we cannot think without thinking of it as having to be. But then this would not be an argument in the ordinary sense, it would be the insight already noted into there having to be the sort of Reality we understand by God.

St. Anselm indeed came very close to this at times. He pointed out that the trouble with the atheist is not that it is hard to convince him that God must be, but that he fails to grasp what is meant by 'God'—and in this St. Anselm, and Duns Scotus in making a similar point after him, were strikingly modern. The mistake of St. Anselm and Descartes was to try to dress out in the form of an argument what is in fact one insight of a very special kind about a Reality which is unique in the sense already indicated, namely by passing beyond the sphere where the normal distinctions and 'steps', such as we have in an argument, apply.

This is what makes assessment of the ontological argument, and of the many debates about it, exceptionally difficult. For on the one hand the argument seems trifling or absurd (and has often been denounced as such), while on the other it seems to say something profound and true. The explanation is that while as argument it is bound to fail, it does revolve round and obliquely convey the conviction that beyond all we can experience or think there must be one Supreme Reality which is perfect in a way that requires that it must exist.

This makes it a little hard to understand the cool reception of the argument by St. Thomas Aquinas. He sided with Gaunilo and contended that while the existence of God could be seen by God himself to be bound up with His essence this would not be self-evident to us who cannot know the essence of God. But do not the five ways, in so far as they take us to the goal at all, involve at least this, namely that while we cannot, in principle cannot, know the essence of God we are capable of seeing that the existence of anything requires that there be one Being who cannot but exist, a Being whose existence is necessitated by His nature?

It thus appears that, in the light of what makes them truly significant and accounts for their plausibility, the two types of argument which seem at first to be so different, the cosmological and the ontological arguments, in fact converge on the same ultimate insight; and this is a matter which has been brought to the fore most suggestively by several religious thinkers today,[1] including some well-known followers of St. Thomas. It is in my view a very helpful point of departure for the further study of the subject and for scholarly reviews of those arguments and the debates that have revolved around them in the past.

I should like now to take these observations a little further

1. See *The Christian in Philosophy* by Illtyd Trethowan, and the article by C. J. S. Williams, mentioned in the Further Reading.

by looking fairly closely at the form which the cosmological argument takes in the writings of the seventeenth century philosopher Descartes.

FURTHER READING

I know of no better short critical discussion of the 'Five Ways' than that provided by E. L. Mascall in Chapters IV, V, and VI of his excellent book *He Who Is* (Longmans). The same author's *Existence and Analogy* will also be found extremely helpful here. Chapter xxxiv, Vol. Two of F. C. Copleston's *History of Philosophy* has also a lucid exposition of the famous arguments.

A. E. Taylor's article on 'Theism' in Hastings' *Encyclopedia of Religion and Ethics* also provides a valuable survey of the themes of the present chapter.

There has been much renewal of interest in the ontological argument recently. It centres on articles by Norman Malcolm, starting with his 'Anselm's Ontological Arguments' in *The Philosophical Review* 1960, and on a difficult but suggestive work by Charles Hartshorne, entitled *The Logic of Perfection*. There are also interesting discussions of this subject in C. J. S. Williams's 'God and Logical Analysis', *Downside Review*, July 1956 and the same writer's God and Logical Necessity', in *The Philosophical Quarterly*, October 1961. Most histories of philosophy will have references to the 'traditional arguments' as they are treated in famous writings by St. Anselm, Descartes or Kant.

CHAPTER SIXTEEN

DESCARTES AND THE COSMOLOGICAL ARGUMENT

The study of modern philosophy commonly begins with Descartes. His is at least the first name of outstanding import- ance we meet in a study of the thought of this period.[1] He has been described as the father of modern philosophy, and he himself certainly thought that he was making a very clear break with the past, although he certainly claimed more for himself than is warranted here. He believed that thinkers in the past had gone astray and been sharply and needlessly at variance with one another because they had followed the wrong methods. In philosophy, he thought, it must be pos- sible to make a genuine advance and also put our results be- yond all doubt. This could be achieved, he further maintained, by adopting in philosophy a method strictly modelled on the procedures we follow in mathematics. We must begin from simple axioms and definitions and proceed through combina- tions of these to more elaborate truths. Provided we kept close watch on each step in the argument and kept ourselves to ideas that were perfectly clear and distinct we could not fail to arrive at irrefutable conclusions about philosophical matters.

The details of the famous method which Descartes put forward in this way cannot be set out and investigated here. It will be seen however that it puts absolute reliance on abstract reasoning, and it is in this sense that Descartes is understood to be the first of the great modern rationalists. The other main names are those of Spinoza and Leibniz. Descartes began his thinking by setting out to doubt as much as he could, a procedure sometimes known as methodological doubt. This means that Descartes was not really in a state of

1. The word 'modern' in this context stands roughly (since there can be no precise demarcations in matters of this sort) for the last 1500 years.

doubt but set himself to take up a sceptical attitude in order to discover the things about which it would prove impossible to be in doubt. He would scrape away the loose sand and stones in order to get at firm rock.

The first point where he found his doubt firmly arrested was his own existence, for whatever else he doubted he could not doubt that he himself existed while he was doubting or whatever else he might be thinking. *Cogito ergo sum* are the famous words in which he summed this up. There has been much debate as to what this argument strictly achieves. Descartes himself believed that he had established the existence of an entity distinct from the body and, as he went on to maintain, in interaction with it, a thinking thing as he put it. This notion has been widely challenged, especially of late, and the question of its soundness is one of the cruces of recent philosophy. I believe that Descartes was much nearer the truth than his recent detractors and that we must think of the mind or self as an abiding entity distinct from the body. I also think this very important for religion. But I do not think it is established in the quasi-mathematical mode of reasoning admired by Descartes. I believe we come to know of our own existence in 'living through' the various experiences through which we pass. This awareness takes a philosophical form in our reflection on what we find ourselves to be.

Having satisfied himself that he himself must exist Descartes took stock of the situation. How could anything else be known? If he was essentially a 'thinking thing' the reports of our senses could not be trusted very far and in fact Descartes found them to be very misleading where the true nature of external things was concerned. At best the external world was imperfectly mirrored in sense experience itself. Our senses could give us rough guidance for day-to-day purposes but not give us certain knowledge about the true nature of things. But in that case we seem to be shut in in a world of our own, the egocentric predicament. How do we break out of this?

We break out of it effectively, according to Descartes, when we become assured of the existence of God. For once we are certain that God exists we know that we can put every confidence in the faculties with which we have been endowed and in what we are strongly disposed to believe. For God can be no deceiver. In this Descartes is not altogether consistent; for he had urged already that we ought not, as rational creatures, to have confidence in anything other than what we understand with absolute clearness and distinctness, and, as he understands it, our strong propensity to believe in an external world more abiding than the fleeting impressions of our senses is not in this class. We can see, with clearness and distinctness, what a material thing must be, or what is the essence of matter, but we do not see with the same clarity that material things exist. But Descartes himself was none the less satisfied that once we were certain that God exists we need have no serious doubts about matters on which God has implanted as strong a conviction in our minds as the existence of an independent material world.

As a devout Catholic Descartes accepted the truths about Himself which God had revealed and which the Church preserved in its teaching. But he also held that some of these truths could be established in a philosophical way by the exercise of reason similar to the way we argue in mathematics. He believed that the ontological argument, to which I have just been referring, was successful in this way. I shall say no more of that, but I should like now to look at the details of Descartes' presentation of the cosmological argument. For the claims Descartes makes for this and the way it proceeds seem to me extremely significant and revealing where arguments for the existence of God are concerned.

There are two ways in which Descartes thinks the cosmological argument can be advanced. The difference between them is not especially important for our purpose and I shall confine myself mostly to the first form of the argument as Descartes presents it.

Descartes begins with certain pronouncements about cause and effect. In making them he seems unaware of many of the difficulties which other philosophers have felt about this subject. He takes it all to be a matter of clear and distinct ideas. At one level this seems plausible. We use the words 'cause' and 'effect', or their equivalents, every day. But as I have hinted earlier the subject is really full of difficulties. It seems a simple matter to say that everything must have a cause. Are we not all the time looking for the cause of this or that and quite satisfied most of the time when the cause is discovered? Why is there milk all over the table-cloth? Because the cat jumped on the table and upset the jug. Here we seem to have one specific cause for one state of affairs. But is this quite the case? Had the maid placed the jug somewhere else it would not have been upset. Had not my friend opened the door to the cat a moment ago it would not have been in the room. There seems in fact to be no end to the causes we may list in this way.

Take another example. A haystack has been burnt down, and we want to know how this happened. In answer we are told that a tramp slept there overnight and did not take proper care in knocking out his pipe in the morning. Some live ashes from that set the hay ablaze. This seems clear enough. We have discovered *the* cause. But then if it had been raining the ashes might have been douched before they reached the dry hay. If the hay had not been loosened at some point it might not have caught fire. If the composition of hay had been different it would not be so combustible, if there were no oxygen in the atmosphere there would be no blaze. Again, if the tramp had been offered shelter in some other farm which he tried, there would not at least have been this particular fire, and had not the first farmer come home weary from a poor market he might have been more generous; and so we might take the story back through the whole history of the farmer and the tramp and beyond them to their ancestors and all who had dealings with them in any way. Indeed there seems to be no point at which we can stop; the laws of physics, our psychological make up, the whole system of things in short, seem to be involved in some way in a relatively trivial occurrence. There seems thus to be a case for saying that what we pick out as *the* cause of some occurrence depends on our interest at the time. In the case of the fire and the tramp our interest is centred especially on the sort of thing, from the vast network of the inter-relations of events, which we can avert or alter. We cannot change the composition of hay or the dependence of fire on oxygen. But we can do something about tramps and the access of other potential smokers to haystacks.

All this is much too vast a subject to be pursued further now. It is enough to show that, once we get beyond very rough and ready purposes, it is not by any means a simple matter to assign *a* cause to each event, and this is itself a matter which Descartes seems not to heed sufficiently at any point. He seems content with insisting that every event must have a cause, and he takes this to be a much more simple and self-evident matter than further reflection discloses it to be.

A further question, and one more important for our purpose, is where the element of necessity comes in when we say that every event *must* have a cause. We find that there are in fact regularities and the most consistent concomitant variations in nature—a flame is always hot, water boils or freezes at various temperatures and so on. But *has* this to be? Could it be merely something fortunate which we have consistently found to be the case hitherto in our own experience and that of others? That may seem to be an odd supposition, but on what grounds do we reject it? Some have maintained that the necessity in causal relations is merely psychological, that is that the regularities we have in fact observed hitherto have set up a very firm expectation of a certain sequence of events, we cannot but count on things happening in a certain way, we cannot bring ourselves to doubt whether the flame will burn us and so on; but there is, so some hold, no objective or rational justification for this. We have been fortunate hitherto, but for all we have good reason to believe the world of nature may suddenly become altogether chaotic. Something like this was the position put forward with great ingenuity by the philosopher David Hume a century later than Descartes.

This topic and the question of the justification of our normal expectations and the predictions we make day by day and in science form what is usually known as the problem of induction. It is one of the basic problems in logic and the theory of knowledge. It has proved extremely difficult to find a satisfactory justification of induction, as almost all students of the subject, including those who hold fairly firm views about it, would agree. My own view is that we cannot give a satisfactory account of the element of necessity in causal relations, that is that water is bound to boil in certain conditions and so on, without going beyond the context in which the question is usually treated. The necessity, in distinction from observed regularities, comes in, I believe, as a reflection of our basic conviction that nothing can ultimately be fortuitous and due to chance, that is it is the appearance on a secular plane of a principle which is essentially, in the way outlined already, a religious one. The principle of cause and effect has its root in the domain of religion.

But if this is sound we here find Descartes laying down as a basic and simple secular principle a notion of which no full and adequate account can be given without reference to religion. A principle which thus purports to be a finite and secular starting-point of an argument that is to take us from the finite to the infinite has accordingly the implication of the infinite in it from the start, and the argument only gets under weigh by the importation into its seemingly secular start of notions that concern mainly, in the last resort, the conclusion; in other words something of the basic conviction of there having to be God is imported or read back into the initial premiss of the argument by which the existence of God is to be established.

This is much more patently true when we pass from the general affirmation of the principle of cause and effect to more precise specifications of it. We discover, for example, that a cause is understood to be an 'efficient cause', in the sense that it is an active agent which strictly produces the effect and must account for everything in it. The notion of an efficient cause in this sense, in distinction from a regular or necessary precondition of some event, may owe something to our experience of ourselves as agents, but it certainly does not arise directly from our observation of the world; all that we are led to anticipate there are the sequences we in fact observe. And, in my view, the main reason why we are also apt to assume that a cause must strictly produce the effect and account for it is the sense that somewhere every event must have such a source; and so here again, in the tendency to think of ordinary causes as efficient causes, we have an importation into a principle of the natural world of something that has its proper significance in the relation of the finite world to its transcendent source.

A much more remarkable feature of Descartes' notion of causality is the further one which is closely connected with the idea of efficient causality, namely that a cause must contain in itself all the reality of the effect, or, as we might be more disposed to put it, that there can be nothing in the effect which is not already present in the cause. This seems far removed from anything we would normally be inclined to think from reflection on causes and effects as we find them in the world around us. Striking a match may be said to cause a flame, but there is nothing to suggest to us that the flame is in some way already present in the match or in the process of striking it, we are not releasing the flame out of something that contained it. The multiple accident on a motorway is not contained in the icy condition of the roads or the fog that occasioned it. That would only be said in a highly figurative and not very helpful turn of speech. No one seriously thinks of the effect as somehow lurking in earlier conditions out of which it is released.

Yet Descartes not only believed this, he took it to be practically self-evident, a simple elementary axiom which had only to be stated for everyone to agree on its soundness. How did this happen? Part of the answer is that Descartes was more under the influence of the scholastic medieval thinkers whom he claimed to have repudiated than he realized. But why did they think in this curious way, and why did it not occur to Descartes to question the doctrine he had imbibed from them? I submit that this again is due to the fact that, while nothing in causal relations as we learn about them in experience could suggest or support the present doctrine, yet there is a sense in which there can be nothing in the world which is alien to the Being of God or not contained in God in the sense that He has absolute mastery over it; and it would not be improper or even odd to say in this sense that all things are already in God, or in the mind of God as some would prefer to say, as their ultimate transcendent source; there can be nothing in the world which falls outside the absolute control of God.

But here again we have a religious principle in the purported secular notions which are to lead us to religion.

For the record we must add that Descartes did not hold that a cause had to hand on all its reality to the effect. Otherwise God could only have created God.

The use of the term 'reality' also calls for comment. We tend to equate reality with existence. But I have already noted the tendency of scholastic thinkers to assume that there can be degrees of being and that an entity is more real in proportion to the qualities or 'perfections' it has. That notion is also reflected in Descartes' procedure and, as I have already hinted, this is also a case where the way it is appropriate to think about God is extended improperly into other contexts.

Let me now state the principle of causation as Descartes understands it. He affirms, to use his own terms, that 'Everything that exists must have a total or efficient cause and this cause must contain in itself all the reality or perfection contained in the effect'.

The next step is to assert that the effect may be contained in the cause in more than one way.

(a) The effect is *formally* in the cause when it is strictly the same sort of thing as the cause, that is when it literally possesses the quality which it hands on to the effect. The seal imprinted on the wax gives the wax its own shape. But it would be difficult to apply this to God as Creator of the material world. God is a spiritual and not a material reality. How then are the qualities of physical things contained in God? The scholastics had said that matter is contained *eminently*, or in some superior way, in the mind of God. An analogy here would be the way in which a picture may be said to be contained in the mind of the artist. There is no canvas or pigment in the mind of the artist, but there would still be a sense in which the picture comes out of the mind of the artist, his skill and insight and so forth produce it. We must not press the analogy too closely, for God is Creator in an absolute way that has no strict parallel in our own activities and the exercise of the gifts bestowed upon us. But we can now see what Descartes had in mind in following the scholastics in the reference to (b) *eminent* causality. God is the formal cause of absolute perfection, the eminent cause of everything else.

We move now to yet another stage in the argument. It is to affirm that 'cause-and-effect' applies to the ideas in our minds, and that this happens in two ways. These depend on two sorts of reality which an idea is alleged to have — *formal* and *objective* reality. The formal reality of an idea is the reality it has as a psychological event, as something which is occurring now for example in my own mind. The formal reality of all ideas is the same, be it the idea of a speck of dust or the idea of God — all that is involved is that I should have the idea; and in this sense the cause of an idea presents no special difficulty. The idea depends on my continuing to exist, and thereby on my past history and so on. This offers no special way of passing from the idea of God to the existence of God. I may be said to be myself the formal cause of my idea of God. But an idea has reality in another way. It is an idea *of* something, of some real or imaginary object, and when we form the idea we think of the object as possessing certain qualities. The objective reality of an idea is the qualities we think of the idea as possessing. The objective reality of the idea of an orange includes the round shape, the yellow colour and so on which we think an orange must have. The state of my mind, when I think of an orange, is not round or yellow but the objective reality of the idea contains such qualities.

This will seem to us a strained and unusual way of talking, even if there is nothing of substance that we may wish to query in it. But I am sure that it will seem particularly odd to readers of today to find Descartes applying the principle of causation to the objective reality of ideas. It is natural to ask what is the cause of some thought I may have in the sense of seeking to discover how in fact I came to have this thought. But cause-and-effect seems rather out of place when we consider the alleged objective reality of ideas.

That however does not daunt Descartes, and he moves to the closing stages of his argument by insisting that we must look for the cause of the objective reality of the idea of God which we have in our minds. The idea of God is the idea of a supremely perfect Being, or, as Descartes would put it, a

Being who has every perfection. He considers a possible objection, namely that the idea of God may have been obtained only by thinking away the limitations of finite things; it would thus be a somewhat negative idea and not have positive content. But he replies, very properly, that this would be the idea of the indefinite, not of the true infinite. The latter is not obtained by leaving out the limits of finite things. It is rather the idea of the absolutely Perfect which does not admit of any limits. It is logically prior to the idea of a finite thing. In knowing our own limitations we have the notion of a Being who does not admit of any.

In respect of its formal reality this idea is on a level with any other and may be accounted for on the basis of my own existence and history. But objective reality is another matter, and when we apply the principle of causality to it we find we must presuppose as its ultimate cause some reality which contains all that this idea contains, that is all perfections. But such a reality is obviously God himself, and thus only God's existence can account for my having in my mind the idea of God.

If this argument were valid it would mean that Descartes could have stemmed the stream of his doubt by starting with God's existence rather than the certainty of his own existence as established in the *Cogito*. He admits this but declares that the most immediately effective way of counteracting the doubt was to start with his own existence.

This then is Descartes' first proof, and it will be evident that it makes a number of highly unusual assumptions. Perhaps the most remarkable of these is the one I have just been noting, namely that causality can be applied to the objective reality of ideas. It would not occur to us to say this in any normal study of cause and effect as we find it in the world. What lies behind it, it seems to me, is the conviction that everything of which we can think opens out to ultimate Reality as its source, the conviction being torn from its proper setting and allowed to invest our ideas of temporal things as such.

Granted this and other assumptions on which Descartes proceeds at each stage, the argument is certainly conclusive.

If a cause must contain the reality of its effect, and if this can be applied to the objective reality of ideas, then God must exist as the cause of my having the idea of God. On the other hand the argument only succeeds because at all its stages the premisses have been filled out with assumptions which have their proper significance only in relation to the conclusion to be established. This is exceptionally evident in the elaborate argument under review and it makes Descartes' procedure unusually interesting and significant. It is so in two ways.

Firstly it shows the strait to which we are reduced when determined to find a clear irrefutable argument by which to pass from finite or secular premisses to conclusions about a transcendent reality. The hopelessness of the enterprise is high-lighted in the assumptions, in themselves so odd and implausible, that Descartes has to make, especially those which concern the way a cause must contain the reality of the effect and the application of this to ideas and their objective reality. On the other hand, the fact that these assumptions could be made and presented in a way that carries some sort of conviction suggests that they have significance in some context, and this, as I understand it, exhibits the depth and the range of our insight into there having to be God and the impact of this on various other features of our thought. It is noteworthy how often, in many contexts, Descartes insists on the certainty and clarity with which we see that there has to be one Being whose essence and existence are one. The insight we have in religion into the Being of God, as presented in Chapter Fourteen, was, I submit, a very constant one for Descartes. His mistake was to fail to realize that it was just one insight which presented the infinite as involved in the being of everything else, and this led him, understandably, to try to dress out this insight in the form of an argument, proceeding exactly like other arguments, from unquestionable finite premisses to a conclusion about God. The lure of this procedure is plain, especially for a rationalist like Descartes. It would enable us to answer the atheist in a firm and final way; clear-minded people could not be atheists. But Descartes should in fact have realized that the position is not so simple and that his task was not in fact that of providing a foolproof demonstration of the existence of God but to elicit the insight into the inevitability of there being God as this arises in those contexts and features of experience which force our thought most sharply to the point where the unlimited is seen to be involved in limited finite being. The positive implications of Descartes' procedure are no less significant than its obvious inadequacies in the form of the demonstration he claimed it to be.

FURTHER READING

Descartes, by S. V. Keeling (Ernest Benn) is a very good study of Descartes' position as a whole, including his treatment of religious questions. Some of the works listed at the end of Chapter Two will have relevance here also, and to these may be added *Descartes' Discourse on Method*, by Leon Roth (Oxford). The student should also consult some of the relevant passages in Descartes' own writings in books like *Descartes — Philosophical Writings*, a selection made by Elizabeth Anscombe and Peter Thomas Geach. The last book has a valuable introduction by Alexandre Koyre and a good bibliography.

CHAPTER SEVENTEEN

THE ARGUMENT FROM DESIGN AND
THE MORAL ARGUMENT

I turn now to somewhat different types of argument for the existence of God; the student of religion needs to be familiar with these as well as with the arguments already noted.

Firstly the Argument from Design, or the Teleological Argument—from the Greek word *telos*, an end. Mention of this argument has been made already. In essentials it is an argument from the alleged evidence of order or pattern in the world, including the suitability or adaptation of certain things to various ends, to the existence of a Supreme Intelligence who has made the world in this way and sustains it. The main discussions of this argument are those of Hume and Kant, and although both these thinkers found the argument unsatisfactory for not dissimilar reasons, they also both expressed themselves impressed with it in certain ways.

Hume for example declares:

A purpose, an intention, a design strikes everywhere the most careless, the most stupid thinker; and no man can be so hardened in absurd systems as at all times to reject it ... all the sciences almost lead us insensibly to acknowledge a first Author.

Kant likewise writes:

This proof always deserves to be mentioned with respect. It is the oldest, the clearest and the most accordant with the common reason of mankind. It enlivens the study of nature, just as it itself derives its existence and gains every new vigour from that source. It suggests ends and purposes, where our observation would not have detected them by itself, and extends our knowledge of nature by means of the guiding concept of a special unity, the principle of which is outside nature. This knowledge ... so strengthens the belief in a supreme author of nature that the belief acquires the force of an irresistible conviction.

In its more downright form the argument found a famous presentation in the work of William Paley and it is a common theme in the work of the Cambridge Platonist Henry More and in the Bridgewater Treatises. Many nineteenth-century writers were impressed by it, and perhaps the most subtle and sustained presentation of the kind of approach to religion which the argument from design typifies is that of F. R. Tennant in his *Philosophical Theology*. In Paley's work we have the well-known comparison of the watch. If I came across a watch for the first time by the seashore and had never seen one before, I should be strongly disposed to conclude, even if I did not discover properly what its use was, that the intricate machinery had been assembled for some purpose by an intelligent being; I would not think that it had just happened to be shaped in this way in the natural course of things. But in fact we do find much in nature which is not due to human contrivance and yet appears to have been assembled to serve a purpose. The human body, the delicate structure of eye, ear, the internal organs, the nervous system, the brain and so on strongly suggest that human bodies have been designed in some way to enable us to live, see, and move about in the world as we do. Must we not then presuppose a supreme intelligence to account for all this?

One common objection to this procedure today is directed against the very idea of an order of the world of nature or of our experience as a whole. The idea itself is vapid or pointless, for, whatever the world were like, we would be bound to impose some order upon it in trying to think of it or understand it at all. Mr. Thomas Macpherson puts the point in these terms[1]: 'Whether or not you see order in something depends on how you look at it. If there are a lot of blobs of many colours on a piece of paper, the crimson, orange, and scarlet blobs in which form together a rough kind of square, while the blobs of other colours are arranged anyhow, are we to say that the colours exhibit order or not? That depends on how you look at it. You can probably find order in anything, if you consider it in one of the ways in which it may be considered. And you can probably find "disorder" in anything if you

1. *Philosophy*, July 1957, p. 226.

consider it in other ways.' Order appears thus to be relative and when we think of the universe as a whole it tends, so the argument goes, to have no significance at all. Macpherson puts the point thus: 'What does it mean to say that the universe is ordered? As I asked earlier, what would it be like if it were not ordered? It really seems that by saying that the universe is ordered we are saying no more than that the universe is as it is. And there would seem to be no way of making the idea more precise.'

These objections owe much to the influence of Wittgenstein and the current fashion of making allegedly metaphysical notions pointless or bogus. They do not seem to me to succeed at all. It is true that we can see various things as exhibiting order or disorder according to what we are looking for, but we could not do this unless the entities in question did have a certain shape or order in certain limited respects. There is a difference between blobs which form a rough kind of square and those which do not. And when we are asked the more fundamental, and seemingly devastating, question of what the universe would be like if it were not ordered, the answer seems to be plain enough. It would be a universe in which things changed at random, without rhyme or reason as we say. Flames would be hot one moment, cold another, water would freeze in the fire and melt there next time, nothing would retain its weight or solidity but vary and fluctuate beyond the wildest of delirious dreams. Nothing could be counted on, there would be one chaotic whirl of change. This, it may be argued, would not give us a world at all, certainly not the world in which we could live and function as we do now. But that is surely beside the point. The point is that we are alive and intelligent, and that the world has to have a certain measure of stability and system for this to be possible at all. The only sense in which the alternative is not conceivable is the irrelevant one (at this point) that we could not in fact exist as we do now in such a world and form the conception of it or observe it.

I do not think in fact that it can be questioned at all that there is remarkable order in the world as we find it. We have first of all the causal continuity of things. Even if this should not command all our confidence, it has at the very least the sort of consistency and exactitude of concomitant variation which induces us to persist in seeking an explanation of the most bewildering events and make the most elaborate predictions with assurance. Even if there should be an element of indeterminacy in nature,[1] and the matter is certainly much in debate, the extent of it is too slight to influence our normal anticipation of the course of things. Within this general system of nature we find moreover that things so arrange themselves that extremely distinctive patterns occur, ranging from basic molecular structures to the organization of human bodies, the changing seasons and myriad other conditions of the sort of existence we are thus enabled to have. As a constant feature of this, much neglected by those who underestimate the order of the world around us but a source of perpetual wonder to others, is the unfailing dovetailing of our perceptual experiences through all the infinite gradations of perspectival and kindred variations. So perfect is the order here that most persons live their lives through without ever stopping to ponder it or to become aware of the problem of perception and all that is involved in it.

There is thus a remarkable and impressive order in the world we inhabit. Within our own activities and in the relationships of conscious processes to the material ones with which they are integrated, all this is continued in ways that can hardly fail to bring words of astonishment and wonder to the lips of all who allow themselves to ponder it with alert and reflective minds. On all these counts (and I shall not seek to elaborate them further here) the eloquent tributes of Hume and Kant seem to call for our fullest endorsement.

The real trouble arises just where Hume and Kant thought that it did, namely when we ask what exactly follows from the order and the adaptation to estimable ends which we undoubtedly find in the world. It is here that Paley's analogy causes misgiving. We assume that the watch has had a maker because it is a particular entity in a system of things within

1. Usually known as the Heisenberg principle. For a short discussion of this principle and its general implications for philosophy see *The Foundations of Ethics* by W. D. Ross, p. 217-218.

which we seek to find the proper explanation for everything. But to seek an explanation for particular things or events, in terms of their relations to other things or events, is one thing; it is another, even when all allowances are made for the complexities and variations in types of explanation, to seek in the same way a kindred explanation of the system of nature itself as a total system. Do the resemblances and analogies hold here?

It is by no means certain that they do. But even if they did, the argument would not take us as far as many have supposed. It would not give us an absolute Lord and Creator of nature or the world, but, as Kant put it, an architect or designer able to arrange materials in certain ways but also limited by them; we would not have an ultimate author or source of the world such that the very nature of the materials themselves depended entirely upon Him. To get this we have to go beyond the argument from design itself and invoke the more radical consideration of some more absolute source of the world involved in there being a world whatever its nature—that is, we are back with the insight which lies behind the cosmological argument.

The argument from design, taken strictly, yields us thus much less than religious people usually require; and as I have noted, it is by no means certain that it yields us anything at all. The facts leave us wondering, but do they after all resemble sufficiently closely the sort of phenomena which we normally ascribe to the work of intelligent agencies? There is certainly much that can be explained in other ways, by natural selection and other features of the long process of evolution and so forth; and where explanations of the sort hitherto available fail us, is it not the proper course to go on looking for the same sort of explanation in principle as science usually supplies? This could involve the agency of intelligent beings very much abler than ourselves, or of one such being. We may well find evidence of intelligent beings in other parts of the universe some day, and they may be much more finely endowed than we are and manifest themselves differently. But it would still be some specific evidence that would establish this, there would be distinctive operations of such agencies. But the adaptations we find in nature in general and the causal continuity on which these depend seem to be of a different order, and if we had nothing to go upon besides normal modes of explanation we might either leave the matter open or say more boldly that the system within which explanation is possible cannot itself admit of explanation in the same terms.

What lends plausibility to the argument from design is that here again there often lurks within it the very different and more radical insight into the necessity of an explanation in some sense of all there is. This is why some have said that the teleological argument presupposes the cosmological argument. This is not strictly true but it is near the truth. But when we think of God as a truly transcendent reality we do not take the specific features of things or the course of events as a direct clue to His nature. God's perfection is not inferred from peculiarities of the kind of world we find He has made, it is absolute and bound up with His having to be, whatever the world is like.

On the other hand the sort of intelligibility we find in the world around us and in our own lives helps us beyond measure in coming to appreciate the need for the sort of explanation which passes beyond the normal intelligibility of things; and it is not surprising therefore that the features of the world of nature which exhibit the most impressive patterns lead the mind on most easily to the point where we see it as the reflection of a Reality which surpasses it in every way and is the mysterious condition of it. Small wonder that the psalmist should say: 'The heavens declare the glory of God; and the firmament showeth his handiwork.' What really comes home to us in words like these and the moods they reflect is not the notion of some master mind keeping the stars to their courses and making them lovely, but rather the sense of a mystery and splendour which is hidden as much as it is disclosed in the natural beauty and symmetry of things, a holiness that shines unseen in the shining light of the stars. We could have boundless admiration of a master mind, and we might cower in fear of him, but we would feel none of the sort of awe and sense of the holy of which the psalms are redolent.

It is thus by the assimilation of some features of it into a more radical and disturbing insight that the argument from design truly appeals to us. If it is not understood in that way it moves at far too human a level, and this means not only that it fails to echo the truly religious response to the magnificence and wonder of the world we inhabit, it also fails altogether of its purpose. The inferences in which it claims then to consist are not warranted and do not seem to come even near justification. There are moreover special difficulties which it meets in the facts of evil and waste which are also a feature of the world. Much of these we may be able to rationalize, in the sense of showing that they are incidental to achievements which compensate for them. But, as I shall contend again, there is much evil in the world, some forms of suffering especially, which cannot be subsumed plausibly in this way under overriding ends which we can comprehend even in principle. This is a very grave difficulty for religion and a constant source of tension within it, but it is not an insuperable obstacle if we see religion aright, as I shall also try to show later. But it would present an insuperable difficulty if we were proceeding along the lines of the teleological argument taken strictly. The most that we could maintain would be that there is behind the world of our experience some mind very much greater than our own, but also limited in power and making the most of the recalcitrant material at its disposal.

Many thinkers, impressed by the problem of evil, have been attracted to this notion of 'a finite God'. An indication of some of their writings will be found below. For my own part I find it little in accordance with what the religious consciousness generally seems to have been like, and I find little in the course of nature or in human history which could lead to anything as precise as the notion of a supreme designer or manipulator of things as we find them on the whole, although I do find abundant indication of a mystery which altogether eludes my understanding and which is written into the substance of all there is. Nor would I find the needs which religion especially meets satisfied in the notion of an architect or designer of the world. It is in the everlasting arms and everlasting mercy that sinner and saint find eventual rest. But more of that later.

Perhaps I should add that those who advance the teleological argument will be strongly tempted, if not strictly required, to find some overall pattern in the general course of history as well as in the world of nature. Such views are sometimes advanced on very general or *a priori* grounds, as when T. H. Green tries to prove that an 'Eternal Spiritual Principle' is steadily 'reproducing' itself in the course of nature and history. But theories of this sort usually depend on very strained and questionable arguments—as is certainly true in the case of Green. It is a rather desperate expedient to try to prove anything about the course of history without inspection of the historical facts themselves. But when we look at the facts we have somewhat mixed impressions. There certainly seems to have been a general upward trend in the course of history and there is striking progress in some regards. But the upward trend, even if we can be quite confident about it (and many would doubt that), is certainly a very erratic one; there have been many backslidings and dark ages and the almost total destruction of great civilizations and lapses into barbarism; the cost where there has been gain has sometimes been enormous. All this much weakens at any rate the notion of a guiding hand discernible in the general course of history and human development. The problem of evil becomes very grave, and many would say insoluble, if we have nothing on which to go other than our general observation of the course of history.

Some have indeed felt this so strongly that they have posited, not merely recalcitrant material which the divine manipulator is not wholly able to subdue to His purpose, but an independent active power of evil in the universe—or perhaps many such powers. One famous form of this doctrine is the Manichaeism which developed out of some features of Persian religion.[1] The world is presented here as the battleground of warring forces of good and evil, although it is generally held that good will triumph in the end. There do not seem to me to be adequate grounds for postulating a power of evil in this way; we may let our imagination play over the

1. See *History of Zoroastrianism* by M. N. Dhalla. Cf. Charles Gore *The Philosophy of the Good Life*, Chapter VIII.

waywardness and ironies of things or present our own temptations as the work of some Screwtape[1] or other. But there seems to be little in the facts to warrant more than picturesque metaphor. The evidence would need to be much more precise than it is before we could do more than note the facts of evil. Paranormal psychology might perhaps take us further, but I much doubt whether there is available as yet any evidence, from this field or any other, which could begin to point firmly to the reality of demons, much less to one dominant power of evil at war with the good.[2]

Even so, the facts of evil present a very grave obstacle to any religious view that is directly based on observations of what the world is like and on inferences from this, unsupported by more radical considerations, to some ultimate controlling agency. Nor, as I have hinted, are these the basic ways in which the religious consciousness functions. How, on some other view of religion, the facts of evil must be handled will be indicated later.

The idea of design has obvious affinities with the idea of worth or goodness. Contrivance must be for some end, and this would be pointless if the end had no value. Extensive appeal to some realization of goodness in the course of things is thus usually involved in the argument from design. But value may be understood in various ways. It may be thought to be merely subjective, that is it may reside entirely in the appeal some end makes to me or to someone else as a matter of fact. This would suffice to provide a justification for purposive action. But we also tend to think of worth as being more independent or objective than that, and we speak in this way of standards of worth and behaviour, of ideals, norms, rights, duties or, as it is sometimes put, a moral order of things; and when we think in this way that, in turn, is sometimes made the basis of a further and more direct transition from the idea of worth, and especially of the moral

---

1. C. S. Lewis. *Screwtape Letters.*
2. It is interesting that demonology in various religions tends to centre in the belief in one dominant power of evil. See *Buddhism and the Mythology of Evil* by Dr Trevor King.

worth of our own actions, to the idea of God. This is commonly described as the argument from ethics to religion.

This argument was brought into special prominence by Immanuel Kant. Kant was particularly impressed by the objectivity of the moral law and the absolute intrinsic worth of the good will. He stressed the way we seem to be confronted by an absolute moral demand, or, as he put it, a categorical imperative, an 'ought' that is not in any way dependent on what we feel inclined to do. A duty is something which 'calls' us whether we like it or not. But it is impossible, so Kant argued, to think of duty in this way without logically invoking also the idea of God.

In Kant's own system this submission took a very peculiar form. He held that we could not, in the strict sense, have knowledge of God. For, on his view, knowledge is confined to a world which is relative to the sort of minds we have; and this, as he understood it, is a world of which we learn through the senses and the structure which such experience must have. But this would suggest to us all the same a world that has not the limitations of the world of our experience, and while, *ex hypothesi*, we cannot know such a world the door is 'left open' for some other sort of contact with it. This comes to us through faith. But faith, as Kant understood it, is not quite so distinctively religious a concept as we usually suppose it to be. It does not involve some special religious insight or a divine disclosure, it is not bound up with any particular religious events. It consists solely in certain presuppositions of our having moral convictions and being subject to the moral law, in Kant's terminology it is 'a postulate of Practical Reason'. Our reason, in its 'practical' or moral exercise, makes us aware of our duties and even prescribes their content, mainly through the notion (a mistaken one, I am sure) that, as a duty is not what someone happens to want, it must be the same for all. But when we think of duty in this absolute way, and grasp its implications, it seems that we must also think of God.

This is because we perceive a requirement in the moral order of things if I may so put it, that virtue should earn the reward of happiness. Justice, it might be said, calls for the union of virtue and happiness, it is wrong that virtue should go unrewarded. On the other hand we must not seek to encompass this directly in our own moral actions. For we are not acting for the sake of duty if we have our minds on the reward, our motives must be pure and free from self-seeking. Nor will it do if the result is accidentally achieved; and in fact there is much in the natural order of things to frustrate it, whether we think of the reward as pleasure or in some more idealized way as the fulfilment of our basic or more rational or moral aims. There must thus be some ultimate guarantee of the eventual union of virtue and happiness, and we must thus presuppose a Supreme Being to encompass this end.

This will seem to many a rather artificial way of invoking the existence of God. He is made to figure in a somewhat remote way, a glorified *deus ex machina*, to adjust the ends of morality to the actual fulfilment of our aims. But the same principle may perhaps be put more plausibly and detached from matters incidental to Kant's system if we say, as some of Kant's followers have done, that a genuine system of morality requires a Moral Governor of the Universe. The main difficulty here is to see how precisely this argument works.

For some people it works in this way. They maintain that genuine morality requires that standards of worth and duty be objective; they must not be our own creatures, there must be a genuine right and wrong in the nature of things, as we might say. But, it is also argued, we cannot have this objectivity except in the form of some upholding of the moral law by God. It is only a divinely imposed morality that is objective.

This argument is a very common one, and it has been restated many times of late by writers of standing. It is one of the main themes of Professor Leonard Hodgson in his Gifford Lectures *For Faith and Freedom*. But I must confess that, when the argument is clearly presented and not obscured, as it often has been, by cloudy metaphor, I find it most unconvincing.

For some the plausibility of the argument turns on a false analogy with the law of the land or some similar positive law. The law of my country has to be imposed (or at least maintained) by some authority. But the moral law is not strictly a law in this sense. We see that we ought to behave in certain ways, there is not normally in ethics itself a reference to some imponent, it is only by metaphor that we speak of a moral duty as imposed. Moreover, if moral duty required to be set or imposed like the law of the land, this would not prove that it was so imposed. In the absence of further considerations we might reject the notion of a distinctive moral duty or question its claim to objectivity in the form required by the argument. We certainly cannot have it both ways, we cannot say, as I would, that moral objectivity is certain in itself *and also* that it is altogeher uncertain without religion. That would be very confused procedure.

Furthermore, the plain fact seems to be that we expect all to recognize their duty, at least in some form, whether or not they are religious believers. We do not tell the atheist: 'You clearly do not believe in telling the truth or being kind when it is no gain to you or regard it as a duty or moral good, you have no understanding of right and wrong in the moral sense, you know nothing of guilt, remorse and so on.' We put the unbeliever in the same class as everyone else here, we do not exempt him and we reason with him about an ethical matter in the same way as with anyone else; we expect him to appreciate good things in the same way as we do. It would be absurd to hold that unbelievers do not appreciate right and wrong, good and bad, in the same way as we do. Such difficulties as they encounter are difficulties we share with them. Nor is there any reason to suppose that, when they recognize duty and right, they must do so in some quite different way from religious people, that duty, for example, cannot be objective for them as for others.

Indeed, do we not all know some extremely high-minded and idealistic atheists, people who concern themselves much about moral principle and social good without this having any religious implication for them? Was not Gilbert Murray a notable example in his own day? Was his concern for peace and social good tainted in some way or confused because he was not a Christian? It would indeed be perverse to say that. Moreover, some of the best philosophical defences of the notion of moral objectivity have come from clear-sighted agnostics like G. E. Moore, or C. D. Broad, and from other writers who, even though they are religious, make no reference to religion in this context. There is only the slightest casual allusion to religion in W. D. Ross' *Foundations of Ethics* or in the relevant ethical parts of the writings of authors like A. C. Ewing or Brand Blanshard. But it is here that the case for objectivity, and against relativism, has its stoutest defenders today.

There are, of course, atheists who do not believe in moral objectivity; indeed such belief is much out of fashion among philosophers at present. But the debate with them is not conducted in religious terms, but in terms of the sort of arguments we find in the works of Ross, Ewing and Blanshard. It is not absurd to hope to convert the relativist without at the same time making him religious. The religious person may wish to do both, but he need not despair of attaining the one end without the other.

Ethics, in short, is on all fours with other matters so far as the present issue is concerned. No one need be religious to grasp some ordinary matter of fact. To convince you that there is a tree outside my window I just ask you to look at it, I make no mention of God; nor do I need to know anything about your religion. One does not need to be religious to count or to solve some advanced mathematical problems. We teach geography, chemistry, physics, without explicit reference to the Bible. Some Christian apologists, in desperation, have indeed maintained that there is a Christian mathematics, a Christian chemistry and so on. But I have no conception what this could be. If the scientist is wrong he must be proved wrong by the relevant evidence. A Christian scholar or scientist may have a certain attitude to his work, but this does not affect directly what he discovers or teaches. Nor will he always be the better teacher. Religion is not expressly relevant to what is true in spheres like those instanced, and brilliant discoveries are made all the time by atheists and agnostics. We do not question their findings or impugn their theories because they are not religious people. Nor would this be just impracticable in the largely secular society of today, it would be absurd in itself.

But is ethics any different? Why should it be? True, it is at the very centre of our lives, but directly it concerns what we deem of worth and what we find obligatory in the present world. Even if we had no religious faith, would we not still deem it plainly wrong, inherently wrong, to cause needless suffering or to torment someone who happens to be at our mercy? Is there any inconsistency in believing this and not believing in God? There may be, I firmly believe there is, an ultimate dependence of all things on God, and this goes for mathematics and ethics as for anything else. But it does not hold of ethics in some way which is not true of other things, and one does not have to see the inevitability of an ultimate Ground of all there is before one can have normal understanding of the world around us. We do not have to see everything in a religious light before it makes sense, and this goes for ethics as for other truths. The more we can bring the atheist to see the truth about God, if our religion is sound, the better; but until this end is reached, or if we fail altogether to reach it with him, there remains much ground that is common as a matter of ordinary understanding and enlightenment; and there is no reason why idealistic atheists should not work alongside with Christians for social and ethical ends they have in common. Nor need the Christians suppose that the atheist is here being curiously inconsistent; the latter is only falling short of something further which the Christian claims. These further claims may be of the most overwhelming importance in themselves, and they may have ramifications that extend widely into other spheres. But they can hardly be thought to be indispensable conditions of good sense in all regards at other levels.

This does not mean that ethics is not of a central importance for religion. Nor does it mean that religion has had little to do with the process of moral enlightenment. I shall return to both these questions and to kindred issues later. It has also been contended earlier that the sense in which we find God to be the ultimate transcendent source of all there is involves His absolute perfection, although in some way which eludes our direct understanding. Our sense of the good finds expression in this way at the heart of things, and this, which we also found to be in some way behind the ontological argument, is one reason for the persistence of the view, so plainly untenable in itself, that we can have no proper understanding of goodness without also being aware of God. Indeed, if the notion of goodness made no sense for us in itself what point would there be in talking about the goodness or perfection of God? We must not, in short, expect all truth to be directly an extension of religious truth. But that moral truth has a great deal to do with the central concerns of religion is equally plain to me, and the way in which this has to be understood will be considered in due course when certain other matters, indispensable to a sound understanding of the relations of morality to religion, have been set out. For the moment it must suffice to insist that there is no strict argument from moral objectivity to religion or any similar explicit dependence of ethics as such on religion. This is not the whole picture. But the reader must be patient and wait till the picture can be made more complete in due course.

FURTHER READING

In addition to the works mentioned in the text the following books will be found relevant.

The Philosophical Bases of Theism, by S. Dawes Hicks, has a very lucid account of the argument from design. *The Idea of God,* by Pringle-Pattison (Oxford), *Moral Values and the Idea of God,* by W. R. Soreley (Cambridge), *The Faith of a Moralist,* by A. E. Taylor (London), and *God and Nature,* by G. F. Stout (Cambridge) all contain well-known variations on 'the moral argument'. My own favourites among these are the books of Pringle-Pattison and Stout.

A short and very lucid recent defence of theism in which subtle recourse is had to the notion of design and to the moral argument is that of H. P. Owen in *The Moral Argument for Christian Theism* (Allen and Unwin). This book makes a very plausible case for positions which many philosophers of today, including those sympathetic to religion, had thought to have been finally discredited. It would be a good exercise to consider how far this book escapes the strictures of Thomas Macpherson or of Ronald Hepburn in *Christianity and Paradox,* c.f. also the Further Reading for Chapter XXII.

CHAPTER EIGHTEEN

MYSTICISM

We are now in a position to turn to a more positive side of our subject. The main problem hitherto has been — how are we to think of God and what must be understood by saying that God is absolute or transcendent? And we have seen that, as God is not a part of the finite world but a Reality in some way beyond it, we cannot know God as He is in Himself; He is essentially mysterious and beyond our comprehension. But if the mystery of God is as complete as it appears to be, have we not a very serious problem on our hands, namely that we seem also, in some religions especially, to make some very bold assertions about God and claim much intimate fellowship with Him? We address God as a person, we pray to Him, we say that we know His 'mind', that He has been active in history and even that He has appeared in the world in the form of a man. How are assertions of this sort possible? How can we in any way fill out our knowledge of God if God is as elusive and mysterious as we have seen Him to be? Must we not be content just to recognize Him, perhaps in humility and reverent awe, and say no more.

This problem is a much more acute one for some religions than for others, as some religions, the Christian perhaps more than any, make much firmer and fuller affirmations about God than others. But it is hard to see how any religion can avoid this problem altogether.

Those who come nearest to avoiding it are of two sorts. On the one hand we might have religions with a 'finite God' or some 'absolute', like that of much nineteenth-century idealism, which is continuous with our own nature. But this is rarely, if ever, to be found in actual or live religion. On the other hand we may have the religions whose devotees simply stand in awed silence before the mystery and majesty of God. In practice this is again an ideal that is rarely realized. It is hard not to have some specific thought about the object of worship, and the religions which, in theory, show the most caution here tend in fact in their day-to-day life to assume much more determinate forms and have more precise and colourful practices than seems necessary for them.

One of the closest approaches to the 'way of silence', if I may so call it, is that which claims that, in the last analysis, the distinction between us and God disappears. We become God or are absorbed in the being of God, or we realize that, rightly understood, the distinction between finite beings and God is an illusion. God is strictly all in all, and what seems to be the independent life and history of other things, the variety and colour and the entire passing show of the life of this world, is an illusion, a fantasy, a dream without any substance. This is no doubt a very difficult view to maintain with consistency. A dream, and the dreamer, have after all some reality, and the notion of the present world as a total illusion, or even as a mere dream, has come in for some severe censure of late even among some leaders of the religions where such notions have prominence. I shall note this again. It must suffice now to add that in the religions where God is everything, or where all things are in some way identified with God, the aim of religion tends to be to enable us to realize the illusory character of our separate existence, and of the ills thought to be attendant upon our involvement in that illusion, and to pass in this or some other way beyond the world of finitude and be identified with the one Eternal reality—or, it may be, realize our identity with it at all times.

There are many forms of this view and varying degrees of strictness with which it is held. It presents us with one form of mysticism. The word 'mysticism' is a rather ambiguous one, and like the word 'religion' it is often used very loosely. Some are apt to describe any form of spiritual experience as a mystical one. This is a grave mistake. 'Mysticism', in its serious usage, has a fairly precise meaning. It is derived from a word, *muō*, which has affinity with our words 'mute' and 'mum', and reflects the silence of the worshipper before the incomprehensible mystery of God and the incommunicable character of an experience of God. More strictly it stands today for union with God. But not all union with God is a mystical one. What characterizes mystical experience is the alleged directness or immediacy of our union with God, and it is the claim to realize this union which characterizes mystical experience and the disciplines which are thought to make it possible. In one of its major forms this claim is thought to involve the annulment of our finite status; there is nothing between us and God because we are (or become) strictly one with God in a way which makes all separation and division unreal. As it is sometimes put, there is not a 'many' but only 'the One', the Eternal which is all-pervasive.

Not all the views which identify finite beings with God are, however, of the mystical variety. I have referred already to nineteenth century idealism. This is undoubtedly a form of monism, that is of the view that there is only one Reality and that all else is a part of it. But, in the usual forms of this idealism, finite things do have their place as phases or elements of the being of God. Their reality is not wholly impugned, but only their distinctness; they have their place in the one system of being, although much in the form they take for us is 'mere appearance'. But there are forms of monism which deal more harshly with finite being. They annul it and claim that there is, in the last analysis, only the One undifferentiated whole of Being. It is this form of the claim to strict identification with God that is usually thought of as a mystical one. Some forms of recent idealism, and especially the work of the greatest figure this movement produced, namely F. H. Bradley, tend towards mysticism. Indeed, the so-called 'supra-rational' features of Bradley's thought are a form of mysticism—and an impressive one. Bradley's very famous *Appearance and Reality* could not be improperly described as a sustained philosophy of mysticism.

It is in Hindu religion that we find the most consistent affirmation of our literal union with God. But Hinduism is a very diversified religion and has had a long and colourful history. In some of its forms it approximates more to the sort of monism we find in recent idealism. But the more typical form of Hinduism, especially in its sophisticated expressions, is the more severe kind of monism in which diversity, and the world of change and of 'the many', is in some way annulled or superseded in the undifferentiated unity of the Whole. In between these varieties of monism, in Hindu religion and writings, there are many intermediate positions which accord varying prestige and status to finite reality. In many forms of Buddhism also the aim is to pass altogether beyond the imperfect reality of our present existence, but in this case the 'passing hence', although incomprehensible to finite thought, is not so explicitly an identification with some One Ultimate Reality. In practice, I believe, the 'goal' of the Buddhist is closer to the union with transcendent reality than has commonly been thought—and I hope to touch on this matter also a little in another chapter.

A particularly interesting and significant form of the alleged identity with God is that which we find in Sufi mysticism. This is a development of Islamic religion, and the movement of thought which leads from traditional or Orthodox Muslim religion to the ideas and practices of the Sufis is extremely revealing. In its normal and original form Islam is much closer to Hebrew and Christian traditions than to Indian religions, and it centres upon the absolute distinction between man as a created being (and all other creatures of course) and his transcendent Creator. Nowhere does 'the gulf' between man and God receive greater stress than in orthodox Islam. One of the main reasons for the tension between Islam and Christianity has been that the Muslim could not find any doctrine of incarnation compatible with the majesty and transcendent power of God; it has seemed to him an inescapably idolatrous doctrine. Human and divine reality are altogether different, and nothing must be done to question the transcendent glory of God. God is absolute Lord and we are dependent in every way upon Him. But unless we are extremely careful this emphasis can only too easily lead to the view that all that we ourselves are and do is directly encompassed by God Himself. If there is nothing that is not expressly encompassed by God, if my dependence on God is such that I only breathe and move through Him, then we come very close to saying that my own actions are the actions of God Himself in me. This is one of the main sources of the doctrine of predestination in Christianity as well as in Islam, and it also took the form in Islam of severe fatalism, that is of a belief in irresistible external determination. But once this step is taken we have almost made God all in all in our own actions. There appears to be no room for freedom and we can easily come in this way to the view that all that we are and do ourselves is an extension or manifestation of the activity of God; and at this point the emphasis on the transcendence of God and the difference between Him and His creatures tends to pass, by one of the most curious and instructive paradoxes, to the very opposite affirmation of an identity of man and God.

There are other aspects of Sufi mysticism, including the scope it offered for the more emotional and individualistic features of religious life—and the debasement of this in some distortions of the ecstatic excitation of the feelings and the senses, a common danger for all religions when the emotional side is strong. But my concern now is with the ease of transition from the emphasis on God's transcendence and otherness, if this is not very carefully handled, to the opposite extreme of the identification of all finite reality with God.

Orthodox Islam set its face firmly against this development. When one of the most notable and influential Islamic mystics, namely Hallaj, taught that man was God incarnate he was denounced and eventually put to death. At his execution he uttered words of prayer very reminiscent of the words of Jesus on the cross. Earlier he had written in verse the words:

> If thou seest me, thou seest Him,
> And if thou seest Him, thou seest us both.

This is not however the only form of mysticism. There is also the mysticism which claims, not that we are strictly identified with God, but that, without becoming God, we have direct or immediate contact with Him. This is not the same as the intuition of the being of God. It is immediate contact with the reality of God. Those who claim this experience naturally find it impossible to describe it properly. They speak in metaphors or 'slantwise' as Evelyn Underhill put it

The experience itself is incommunicable. But the metaphors which are meant to give us some impression of it stress the direct unmediated character of the experience. Some mystics speak of 'touching' God, even 'tasting' Him.

There is no reason why an experience should not be incommunicable. Some experiences are certainly very difficult to communicate; and we almost certainly have some experiences which we cannot properly communicate to others. Nor are these all of a religious nature. A person born totally blind could not be made to understand properly what we mean by colour. He could take it from us that it is pleasant to see colours, and he could learn which of the many objects he handles have this or that colour. But we could not tell him properly what colour itself was. He would have to see it. Nor could we tell anyone what physical pain was if he should be some fortunate creature who had never experienced any. It is probable that some of the paranormal experiences which are being widely studied today are of so radically different a nature from ordinary experience that many of us can have no conception at all what they are like in themselves.

This naturally makes us cautious, and we need some strong independent evidence before we allow that it is likely that some experiences are as different from normal experience as is sometimes alleged. But caution is one thing, out and out scepticism another. I shall not go now into the sort of independent evidence which would impress us here.[1] But there could be evidence firm enough to warrant a strong presumption, and, on the other hand, we could certainly not rule out on principle the possibility of an experience not directly communicable to others. That would be sheer dogmatism.

When therefore a claim is made to have a direct experience of God we cannot rule this out just because we do not have this experience ourselves and can form little conception of what it would be like. If we did so we would, moreover, be putting ourselves in an odd position *vis-à-vis* those who say they have no sort of religious awareness. But there could be other reasons for disallowing the claim. It might be found to

1. I have discussed this question in Chapters XIV and XV of my *Our Experience of God*.

be an inherently impossible claim, and this objection could not be ruled out on the grounds that we can pass no sort of judgement on an experience we have not had in any way ourselves. It will not do to say—'who are you to question what the mystic alleges? You have had no mystical experience yourself'. If anyone told me that he had found a square-circle in my garden I would deny this straight away. I might be curious enough to see what sort of object, if any, could have been described in these preposterous terms. But I certainly would not step into the garden on the off-chance that, as I had not seen this object myself, it might after all, for all I knew, turn out to be a square-circle. I know at once that it cannot be, just because there cannot be such an object.

This holds, it seems to me, of the claim to have an immediate contact with God. It is not just that there is strong evidence against this, that the prophets, for example, usually declare that the God they have come to know is also a God who 'hides himself', it is not that we have not had this sort of experience ourselves and need to be cautious in admitting the likelihood of a very remarkable claim. We know from the outset that there could be no immediate contact with God. For this would surely imply that we knew expressly what it was like to be God. We would be aware of God as He is— in His essence. But one of the things we need to stress most about God is that He is transcendent in a way that precludes this. The way we recognize His existence involves His being a Reality of that kind. To claim to know God directly, in the strict sense, is like claiming to have found a square-circle.

Does that mean that the claim the mystic makes here is altogether bogus? By no means. It certainly does not follow that mystics are insincere or fraudulent persons who are seeking to impose on us. There are no doubt poseurs and impostors who call themselves mystics, and in a field which goes so far beyond normal experience, and where we often find much eccentricity, the imposition may not always be easy to detect and expose. We may have to give the benefit of the doubt when we would normally withhold it. But it would be very hard to doubt the sincerity of the more famous mystics. Many of them were notably saintly persons, modest in their claims and outlook and very little anxious to make any display of their own attainments, sometimes according them a quite subordinate place. But to be sincere is one thing, to be sound another; and while I would not wish to deny that the mystics had remarkable experiences of some sort, I would not agree that they have described them correctly when they claim to have known God directly, to have 'touched' and 'tasted' the Divine nature in this sense.

This does not mean that there cannot be extremely intimate experiences of God. I shall stress later that there can be, but I shall also hold that they must be indirect. Their importance is not, in my view, in the least impaired in that way. After all, our experience of one another is also mediated. We do not know the mind of another as we do our own, but we can have a richly intimate fellowship all the same. My impression is that the great mystics did have a peculiarly close relation to God and that, in their concern and enthusiasm, they misdescribed this as an unmediated contact with God. This would be more likely to happen if, as seems probable, they had modes of awareness and further accompaniments of their experience which went beyond the sort of experience we normally have.

In some of its forms the claim put forward by the mystics involves a repudiation of the distinction between subject and object. If this were merely a striking way of saying how completely we may forget ourselves in the absorption of our attention in some object that holds it, there could be no objection to it. If the actors at the theatre know their business and have a fascinating play to perform, we soon forget our own role of spectators, we identify ourselves with the actors. But however absorbing the performance and however oblivious of ourselves we may become, we never strictly cease to be spectators. There remains a valid and basic distinction to be drawn between the onlooker and that which he contemplates. I do not see how this distinction can be superseded; it is true that God cannot be one finite thing among others, but He is a Reality other than ourselves of which we claim in religion to be aware, and however we may become lost to ourselves and the world in such an experience we are none the less having an experience of a Reality which is not ourselves.

We are reminded in this context of what was said earlier about the idea of encounter with God, and the alleged I-Thou relation. Prophetic mystical writers of today, Martin Buber in particular, claim that the subject-object relation is superseded in all forms of the I-Thou relation. This is thought possible because of a relation which involves no sort of 'knowledge about'. But this submission, whether advanced by Buber or by more 'existentialist' writers, is quite bewildering to me. As observed earlier, I have no notion what sort of contentless experience this could be. We do find, however, in recent allusions to mysticism and in appraisals of it, frequent recourse to the perplexing notion of a relationship with other persons which involves no knowledge about them — or which goes altogether beyond such knowledge. It seems to me plain that in any experience, other than experience of our own states, the distinction of subject and object is unavoidable, however unobtrusive it may also be.

This brings me back to the first form of mysticism noted above, that which claims not direct contact with God but identification with Him or absorption in some way into His Reality. This does not give us a contentless relation, for there is here no relation between us and God — we are God. But there are other objections to this supposition, and they seem to me overwhelming. A finite creature could be eliminated or annulled, but it is hard to see what it could mean for it to become literally part of God. It would have ceased to be as a finite being, and what, in that case, is our affirmation *about*? There are in any case very grave difficulties in the notion of a merging of persons at any level. I shall contend later that persons, although destructible, have an indivisible nature which precludes any strict absorption of one in another. And how, if I were absorbed in the being of God, would I be benefited or redeemed or saved in any other way? I would just cease to be; there would only be God. My neighbour would cease to be also; there could be no Kingdom of Heaven.

It does not follow that there is nothing to be extracted from the affirmations, mainly in Oriental religions, that we eventually become one with the being of God. For here again there is much misdescription of genuine and profound experience and a remarkable testimony to the sense of the ultimate and absolute nature of God. There are also many accompaniments, some more and some less incidental, of this sort of mystical religion which are of great worth and interest. It has provided a corrective to crass worldliness and an incentive to living a deeply spiritual life. There are also many dangers involved, the dangers of escapism and neglect of our responsibilities here and now, the sort of other-worldliness which has been thought, often with justification, to make religious people very poor citizens of this world. There is also the danger of unhealthy preoccupation with 'inner' experience and personal sanctity which makes some forms of mysticism a perversion of genuine religion. It is on these grounds that Aurobindo and others have sought to modify Hindu religion.

In Christian countries mysticism has usually been highly regarded, and some of the most notable Christian saints were eminent mystics.[1] But in the Christian religion the mystic has rarely claimed strict identification with God. The emphasis was usually on direct *contact with* God. Even the more extreme type of Christian mystic, like Meister Eckhart, would be found insisting that, even in the most intense mystical experience, 'soul is soul and God is God'. Orthodox Christianity would certainly require this, and so do all religions which involve a deep understanding of the notion of 'Creation'.

A further feature of mysticism has considerable interest. It is the disciplines by which mystical experience is usually attained. These have sometimes involved much asceticism and mortification of the body, and this raises many problems, including ethical ones. The more specifically mental and spiritual disciplines are of great interest, and there is probably much to be learned from them for other forms of religion. Connected with this are the various stages through which the mystic passes before the ultimate union with 'Supreme Being' is thought to be attained. There is a remarkable similarity in the forms these have taken in different cultures at times when these could have influenced one another very little, if at all. Another problem of considerable interest today is the relevance of paranormal psychology, and of

1. As may be learnt from the books listed at the end of the chapter.

states of mind induced by drugs like mescalin, to mysticism and to the ecstatic states which it sometimes involves—and to the accompaniments of these. But these are matters which I cannot effectively discuss in the space at my disposal now. The reader must be referred to what I have said about them elsewhere and to the selection from the vast and colourful literature of the subject appended to this chapter.

I must refer, however, to one recent attempt to provide a philosophical justification of the more extreme type of mysticism. This is found in a notable and much admired book by Professor W. T. Stace, entitled *Mysticism and Philosophy*. Stace is a well-known philosopher and a very lucid writer, whether he is dealing with the more severely technical problems of philosophy or with questions of more general concern. In this book he has done the subject of mysticism the very great service of raising sharply the more distinctly philosophical questions it presents. No one has done this so effectively before, most writers on the subject being content to describe it in rather general terms. Professor Stace's own position does not seem to me however one that can be sustained.

He rejects the sort of mysticism which simply identifies God and the world—a view that would perhaps be better described as pantheism. This seems to Stace to be just a 'silly view' and he takes Professor Hampshire to task for ascribing it to Spinoza. We must maintain instead the curiously paradoxical position that

(a) The world is identical with God
and
(b) The world is not identical with God

This gives Professor Stace the opportunity to come to terms with common sense and avoid denying that there is any sense in which 'the many' are real. But his success depends on its being possible to say two quite opposite things. The many are real, they are also not real. There is not, for Stace, to be any mitigation of this paradox. He is very firm on that point. The paradox is not a rhetorical one designed to make us stop and think. It is not just a literary device. Nor is it a case of misdescription of their experience by the mystics themselves.

Nor are we to say that reality is in one respect many, one in the other, the 'double location' theory. Nor is the claim meant to be ambiguous. 'There is no ambiguity', we are told, 'in the claim that I cease to be this individual, and yet I remain this individual.' We have to take the contradiction in its most downright and literal sense. We must be quite bold about it.

But what is wrong with contradiction? Everything, we would be inclined to say. A downright contradiction is not even false, it is meaningless. If I say that my book is blue and also, in respect of the same part of its surface, not the shade of blue alleged for it, then I have just not said anything. I cannot mean this contradiction, I am uttering words but not entertaining a thought.

This is what Stace questions, and for so gifted and shrewd a thinker the arguments by which he seeks to justify so odd a theory are exceptionally strained. He proceeds thus, for example, in one place: 'If "A is B" is a meaningful statement and if "A is not B" is also meaningful, it is impossible that the connective "and" placed between them should render the conjunction of the two meaningful statements meaningless.' But surely everything turns here on the connective. The meaning of the statement is in the whole of it. As a whole it is nonsense even if parts, by themselves, are quite meaningful.

Stace also seeks to fortify his position by a 'delimitation of the areas of logic and non-logic'. Logic applies to 'any world in which there exists multiplicity', but while 'the many is the sphere of logic, the One (is) not so'. This seems to me dangerous doctrine. If we give up the sheet-anchor of logic there is no telling where we may drift. We must, however, say that in some sense God is beyond the world as we find it and that there must therefore be some Reality which goes beyond the categories of our thought and reason. But to say that God is 'beyond' or 'above' is one thing. It leaves it a mystery how God exists and what is His relation to the world. It does not require us to identify God with the world or to call logic as such into question at all—as if reality could be, though it happens not to be, illogical. 'Supra-rational' and 'supralogical' are very open notions. The trouble with Stace's position is that he does not reckon with this, he is very sensitive to the mystery and transcendence of God but he also wants to 'scale' this down 'to the logical plane of the intellect'; and this is what we cannot do without the highly questionable and dangerous doctrine that 'the logic and the illogic occupy different territories of experience'. We must not commit ourselves to that doctrine but rather disclaim the attempt to make sense of what is alleged to go beyond the way we make sense of things. If God is truly transcendent we do not know how he is related to other things, that must remain an unfathomable mystery to us; and this is what the doctrine of Creation preserves and accentuates for us. But if we try to rationalize the mystery our presumption recoils upon us in the form of questionable paradox and dangerous impugning of logic, to say nothing of being committed to saying that there is at least one sense, and that the most radical, in which finite things are not real. That they are real seems to me beyond question, and the plurality of them is real. We need not impugn this if we also say that they are rooted in some Reality which is altogether different—provided we are content not to say more and do not slide off the very narrow edge along which we must walk when we speak of the transcendent. That, I fear, is what Professor Stace, with all his sense of the mystery of God and his familiarity with mystical writings, has been apt to do at crucial points in his own thesis.

It should be noted that Professor Stace also claims that the Western mystics, who usually reject the notions of strict identification with God in favour of some kind of dualism, were largely under pressure from established authorities, like the Church or orthodox Islam. There seems to be in fact very little, if any, evidence for this. My own view is that the dualistic mystics were offering a better account than others of experiences of an exceptionally close relation to God which they shared in many ways, but not in all ways, with Eastern mystics. In neither case is the description offered altogether adequate. Why should it be? We do not expect that of the day-to-day accounts we give of normal experience.

There is in fact much further work to be done on the

problems presented by mysticism. We shall be much helped in this by recent studies in paranormal psychology and by investigations of the role of symbol and image in literature and experience. Such distinctions as that between 'introvert' and 'extrovert' types of mysticism, as this is drawn by Professor Stace, should also much advance the subject. I cannot, however, pursue these issues further here and must be content to observe, in leaving this subject, that whatever the judgement we finally pass on the claims made by the mystics themselves, there is undoubtedly, in the reports of their experiences, a very rich mine to be quarried by those who would seek a profound understanding of religion.

FURTHER READING

Mysticism, by Evelyn Underhill (Methuen) is a well-known and valuable work, Chapter IV of which contains an instructive account of the main characteristics of mysticism. Another well-known work is *Christian Mysticism,* by W. R. Inge (Methuen). The works of Rufus Jones, an influential figure in American life as well as a notable scholar, include standard studies of mysticism. His *Studies in Mystical Religion* and his articles on mysticism in Hastings' *Encyclopedia of Religion and Ethics* can be much commended. Among more recent works are Cuthbert Butler's *Western Mysticism* (Arrow Books) and *The English Mystical Tradition,* by David Knowles (Burns and Oates).

Mysticism Sacred and Profane, by R. C. Zaehner contains a wealth of interesting new material and much careful analysis of major problems.

The student is strongly urged also to examine some of the writings of famous mystics at first hand. There are admirable recent editions of the works of St. John of the Cross and St. Theresa. A guide to the thought of these persons will be found in Volume 1 of *Studies of the Spanish Mystics,* by E. Allison Peers (S.P.C.K.).

Mention was made in the text of W. T. Stace's *Mysticism and Philosophy* (Lippincot). This book is notable for its bold and precise presentation of the more strictly philosophical questions raised by the subject of mysticism. Few books have ever been more successful in that regard, whether we accept the author's solutions or not. It should not be missed by philosophical students of mysticism. A long review of Stace's book by H. H. Price appeared in *The Journal of the Society for Psychical Research,* June 1962.

Closely related to the problems of mystical experience are the problems raised by paranormal phenomena. I have discussed these as they bear on religion in Chapters XIV and XV of *Our Experience of God.*

CHAPTER NINETEEN

ANALOGY AND NATURAL THEOLOGY

We have seen that there are very grave difficulties in the claims usually advanced by mystics (or on behalf of them) if these are taken at all strictly. But even if these could be sustained that would leave major questions unanswered for many religions. For the claim that is usually made in religion is that here and now, in our present state and with all its limitations, we can learn certain things about God and come to know Him. The normal mode of knowing God could not be that of mystical union, in the senses we have been noting. In some of these senses at least the problem just could not arise. We somehow get altogether beyond the sphere of 'knowledge about'. But in many religions the claim to know something here and now about God is central—and this is especially true of Christianity.

There are mystics who have claimed that, in the course of their mystical experience, they have had the substance of specific doctrines, like the doctrine of the Trinity, made clear to them. But it is very hard to see how this could come about independently of the considerations normally thought relevant, such as the witness to the work and person of Christ in the Bible. Could the doctrine of the Trinity have become meaningful to Christian mystics independently of what was normally available to them about it? I much doubt this, but even if it could, there would still be a problem of how, being finite and limited creatures, we could, even at the height of mystical experience and the greatest luminosity, affirm meaningfully certain things about a Reality whose essential being or essence we could never grasp. Mysticism, whatever else may be said about its claims, offers no way in which a religion like Christianity could by-pass the problem of the specific affirmations made about God. I turn now to some ways of dealing with that problem.

One of these is Natural Theology. There are many forms of this, and I shall only indicate here some of the main ones. Normally, and in its most traditional form, there are two distinct stages of natural theology. The first of these is concerned with the existence of God and it offers variations on the themes already extensively discussed in this book, such as the traditional arguments for the existence of God and whatever may be thought to lie behind them. Assurance is thought to be obtained in this way about God as a transcendent or eternal Reality which exists by the necessity of its own nature and on which everything else is dependent. At a second stage, in one of its major forms, natural theology tries to elicit from what is thought about the being of God and our dependence on Him certain further truths about God. This takes a form known as the doctrine of analogy.

To understand this doctrine we have to note various ways in which the idea of analogy may be understood; and to grasp the meaning of these we must begin with the distinction between the way a term may be used in the same sense, in various applications of it, and certain variations in the use of a term. In the first case, a term is said to be used 'univocally'. In this sense we might say both of a salmon and a trout that each is a fish, and we might speak of a fishy smell both in a cavern by the sea and in a fisherman's basket. We mean the same thing when we use 'fish' and 'fishy' here. But we sometimes use the same word in senses that have nothing in common—that is equivocally. In the amusing example provided by Dr. Mascall we read of the lads in a village cricket team who asked the Vicar if they could borrow one of the bats of which the sexton had said he had plenty in the belfry. It is not however easy to provide good instances of the wholly equivocal use of terms. For even when terms have several sharply different meanings these have usually a subtle common factor somewhere, as in the case when we speak of a tree growing in the garden and of putting a tree in a shoe to hold its shape, or of serving sauce in a 'boat' in which no one could think of sailing. In these latter cases the senses of the terms in question are not wholly different although they are certainly not the same. When a committee leaves a resolution 'on the table' they do not literally leave anything behind when they go away. An example which takes us closer to the theological doctrine of analogy is that in which we say of a holiday resort and of a person that both are 'healthy'. We do not mean that the resort enjoys good health in the sense in which a person is physically fit. We mean that it is a place where people are likely to be healthy and so on. In this sense the description is an analogical one.

There are, moreover, two main forms of the analogical uses of terms. We may find the common factor in a relation which two terms hold to a third, as when, in a standard example, we speak of a place being healthy and of a person having a healthy complexion. The different meanings are derived here from a relation to a 'prime analogate', really a healthy person. It is he who is strictly or formally healthy. But it cannot be in this sense that terms are applied analogically to God. For there is no being antecedent to God to whom the predicate can apply more formally than it does to Him. In religion then we have to do with analogy in another sense which is founded on a relation which one thing bears to another. Of this there are again, in the traditional doctrine, two main forms. One is called the analogy of 'proportion' or of 'attribution'. Here the property belongs formally to one thing and derivatively to the other, as when health is found formally in a person and derivatively in the complexion which is a sign of his health. In the case of God and his creatures the basic relation is that of dependence on God's creative power, and we thus come to the conclusion that we can speak of God being good, for example, in whatever way is necessary if He is to be able to produce goodness in His creatures. There can obviously be no objection to this conclusion. But the question at once arises whether any substantial advance has been made—or any advance at all. It is certainly a very general and vague assertion to say that God must be good or wise in whatever way is necessary for Him to be the author of these qualities in finite beings. Have we learnt anything here which we would not know already in knowing that God is the ultimate 'ground' or 'source' of all that is? That seems unlikely, especially when we remember that the insight we have into the necessary being of God involves regarding Him as being in every way perfect. If His ultimacy involves perfection in this way have we learnt anything further in concluding that He must be good in whatever way is needed to be the transcendent cause of goodness? All this certainly leaves it very mysterious how various attributes belong to God.

A further difficulty is this. If the argument is given any substance and we are asked to recognize some explicit identity between God as a transcendent Being and the attributes of the beings He creates, must not this apply to all attributes of finite things, including evil? Would we not have to say that God must be evil in whatever way is necessary for Him to be the source of evil in the created world? This is much more embarrassing than the normal form of the problem of evil. There will always be a very considerable difficulty about evil for any view which considers God to be the absolute and ultimate source of all things, and I shall return to this question later. But it is all the same one thing to ask how there can be evil in a world created by a perfect Being, it is another to pass directly from the evil we find in the world to an attribute of evil in God in the same sense as that in which goodness is ascribed to Him. The former perplexity is severe enough, the latter seems to rule out at once all possibility of easement; we would be pronouncing God to be in some sense evil in Himself.

There have of course been some thinkers who have not shunned the ascription of some evil propensity to God, subsisting along with His goodness in the same nature. This is not to be confused with the view of those who hold that there are two ultimate powers of good and evil at war with one another in the universe—another view we shall note briefly later. The view in question now is that there is evil inherent in the nature of God Himself. But when this view is held[1] we also find that the notion of God involved is a very vague one, and it is hardly a view that can be entertained at all by anyone who claims the sort of insight into the distinct transcendent reality of God with which we have been concerned

1. As it is by Jung, for example, see *Jung and the Problem of Evil*, by H. L. Philp.

and which is strictly adhered to by those who advance the doctrine of analogy.

The commonest line taken by advocates of the doctrine of analogy when they feel embarrassed by the present difficulty is to take a very bold view about evil, namely to say that evil is not positive but only a 'privation' or absence of goodness. This seems to me a very difficult view to apply to major forms of evil—indeed I do not think it can be true of anything that is properly evil. But ingenious arguments have sometimes been used in the desperate attempt to represent all evil as essentially some form or limitation of goodness. In my view they are doomed to failure from the start.

I suspect also that the doctrine of analogy, as reproduced here, involves a subtle retention of the notion that there must be a community of nature between cause and effect. This is a curious notion, as I have hinted already. It would not occur to us in normal reflection on cause and effect, and the retention of it has been a source of much needless difficulty—in dealing with mind and body, for example. In a transcendent reference we can see a little better what makes it plausible. For there can be nothing which is truly alien to God or outside His control as the unconditioned source of things. But it is very misleading to present this peculiar truth about the ultimate relation of God to His creatures in the form of a general principle about an alleged community of nature of cause and effect. That is a distortion which can cause much avoidable difficulty.

It remains to note one attempt to give a little more body to the doctrine of analogy. This involves reference to the notion of 'the analogy of proportionality' by which the same attribute is thought to belong to different things in different modes according to the type of beings they are. The distinctive thing about God's being here is that it is self-existent, and in ascribing goodness to God, initially by the analogy of attribution, we find that we can also, in combining with the former analogy the analogy of attribution, come to the conclusion that the goodness of God must be self-existent. The logical apparatus by which this argument is advanced is much too subtle and elaborate to be described properly here. But it is again a moot point how much is accomplished. Few would claim more than a very mild reduction of the ultimate mystery of God, and those who are confident, as I am not, that an advance has been made without jeopardy of the truth about God's transcendence, would also be the first to insist that the doctrine of analogy, even in its boldest reach, leaves us very far short of the specific claims about God and His dealings with us made in the religion, namely Christianity, within which the doctrine arose. There is little diminution of the need for a separate supplementary theory of revelation.

Let me now give a brief indication of a position that closely resembles the doctrine of analogy, although the resemblance has not often been noticed. It is that of Otto in the account that he gives of what he calls the schematization of the idea of the holy. We have observed already that for Otto the sense of the holy is the sense of an object of worship which is altogether transcendent and thus beyond the grasp of reason. But this does not mean for him that reason has no place in religion—least of all that we can surrender to unreason. The progress of religion gives increasingly greater place to reason, not in the sense that the supra-rational element is dulled—that must never happen if religion is to be true to itself—but in the sense that an increasingly prominent place must also be found for reason. How does this come about?

It comes about because the holy can be schematized. This is an unusual term. It is derived from Kant. According to Kant we can only have knowledge of objects as they appear in a world that is relative to the mode of consciousness we have. There are thus certain 'pure concepts of the understanding', as Kant calls them, which have to be translated, or made to work as it were, within the sort of experience which is possible for us and applied thus *a priori*, that is without specific empirical justification, to the objects of the world that we apprehend. The ideas of cause or thinghood (substance) are thus given a form by which they are significant and indispensable modes of the unification of the world of our experience—without them the world would simply be a chaotic and unintelligible confusion. Kant thought he had drawn up a complete list of *a priori* notions that are relevant here.

Otto provides nothing quite so elaborate in his account of the schematization of the idea of the holy, and he may have misled his readers by suggesting too close an affinity between his own position and that of Kant. He has certainly been much criticized on that score. All that he wishes to hold is that we may characterize the essentially elusive idea of the holy, and give it more particularity and relevance to us, on the basis of certain 'felt analogies' of the experience of the holy or the numinous with some other experiences we have in the normal course of things as finite beings. Two central features of the numinous consciousness are reflected in the Latin words which describe it—*mysterium tremendum et fascinans*. The holy attracts and repels. It is in this way like some object we fear and also admire. Fear and admiration are fairly familiar emotions for us all. They involve no reference 'beyond' and are not essentially mysterious. We all know what they are like as human reactions in the present world. But they can also serve as pointers to the peculiar sort of awe we feel in religion and to the special way we 'glorify the Lord'—the praise which is the complement of 'fear of the Lord'. There is no strict identity between fear and awe in these senses and the ordinary modes of them; for the former derive their specific character from the distinctive experience of the transcendent which prompts them. The difference is not just one of degree. All the same, the finite emotions provide some clue, by a felt analogy, to the nature of our sense of the holy and help us to pick out the distinctive strands of the latter and see where it touches our present experience most closely.

Among further 'felt analogies' which function in this way are those which lead us in due course to ascribe to God such attributes as Spirit, Purpose, Reason, Good Will, Supreme Power, Unity, Selfhood. Particular importance attaches to the sense of transcendent worth in our experience of the holy, for this provides a link at the very centre with moral ideas as we find them in normal experience. This is one of the main ways in which admirers of Otto defend him against critics, like John Oman, who accuse him of neglecting the moral factor in religion or sacrificing it to the sense of awe and dread in the presence of God. Otto is fully convinced of the very close link between the sense of God's mystery and the attributes which enlightened religion ascribes to God and which determine the place which religion should have in our lives as a whole.

The rational is not therefore just something added to the supra-rational, or existing alongside of it. There is an essential relation between the two, and Otto is very anxious to maintain this link and to justify in that way the work which theology undertakes in helping us to understand God and all that He requires of us. We have still to talk about God in highly symbolic ways. Nothing that is said of Him is to be taken at its face value. For although we speak of God in terms of 'power' and 'purpose' and so on and understand these terms in religion as we normally use them, yet they have an application which goes altogether beyond our understanding. God, as Eternal Being, is not 'spirit' or 'power' in the way in which we manifest or exercise these, but we have none the less a justification for speaking of God in these terms and ascribing to that the utmost importance. Religion is not left without content or discipline.

I think Otto is quite correct in holding that when we use particular terms of God, or ascribe attributes to Him, we do so in a symbolic way as already indicated. In his emphasis on this, as in other ways, Otto has done a great service to religion. But I am not happy about the way he establishes his link between the transcendent and the particular terms in which we refer to it. There is not, in my view, any objection to the notion of 'felt analogues'. These should prove a very helpful guide to the sense of the numinous and a way of evoking it. But I also wonder just how far they take us. Do they help to give us more than a firm grasp of what the consciousness of God as ultimate and transcendent Being involves? Must we not go deeper into what religious experience as a whole is like to understand what justifies the more specific ways in which we speak of God? Even if Otto has really advanced the subject here, are we not still moving at the level of considerable abstraction and far removed from specific affirmations like those of the Christian faith or other claims to a sense of God dealing with us in the substance of day-to-day experience? Are we not, in this regard, in essentially the same position as the advocates of the traditional doctrine of analogy? I suspect that we are, although I also think that Otto, in centering attention on religious experience and its accompaniments, points us much more effectively to the way a genuine advance may be made in the understanding of the more specific features of religion.

There remains yet one other form of natural theology—a most important one. But it need not detain us much here. For, in essentials, it has already been discussed in another context, in Chapters Five and Seventeen. Account has been given especially in Chapter Seventeen of the way certain thinkers sought to establish the existence of God from consideration of what the world is like, including above all the indication of design or system or worth in the life of men or in nature. If this attempt were successful it would not only show that God existed but also tell us a great deal about Him. The argument, as has already been indicated, would be similar in substance to the arguments by which we establish the existence of finite things. That, it was implied, is the main objection to it. But when we call in some finite entity to account for certain other things we require it to be of a certain nature.   It can only account for something else by being the sort of thing it is, even though much about it may remain obscure—as often happens in science. If God then were posited in the same way, in principle, as we posit certain finite entities to account for others, we would have distinctive indications of His nature in those features of reality with which the argument begins.

There have been many attempts to determine the nature of God in this way. In some of them there is confusion between the present teleological procedures and the way God is said to be involved, as a transcendent and unconditioned Ground, in the being of anything. But it should be evident now that the two positions are radically different, even though the term 'transcendent' may be found quite often in the context of teleological religious thought. It should also be plain why I consider the enterprises in question to be doomed to failure from the start. I have said as much as is possible within the limits of this book on that score already. None the less, natural theology in the form of speculations about the nature of God based on distinctive features of finite things, has played so important a part in much religious thought and theology that some further indication of its nature must be given. We have also to remember that, even when this kind of thinking fails in its ultimate purpose, it manages to disclose much that is important in itself and which can also have vital importance for religious understanding in other ways.

Let me then note two main forms of natural theology in the present sense:

(*a*) Natural theology and idealism. Note has already been taken of the view that the universe is a systematic whole in which whole and part very closely imply one another. Much of this was learnt from Plato, although his final view of the universe went beyond it. In dialogues like the *Theaetetus* and the *Sophist* he set himself especially to stress the interdependence of whole and part and its importance for rational processes. In the nineteenth century many followers of Hegel became extremely confident about the possibility of determining the ultimate nature of the universe on the basis of the principle that 'the Real' must be rational through and through and that it thus contained nothing which could not in the last resort be understood through its having to exist by its place in the one system of rational necessity in which the universe consisted. Some idealists, notably the greatest, F. H. Bradley, broke away from this tradition and recognized features of experience which gave the ultimate nature of the universe a supra-rational character. But even they were predisposed to think so much in terms of one all-inclusive system that they failed to see how an ultimate transcendent reality is consistent with the distinctness of finite beings as preserved in sound understanding of the doctrine of creation. Others were even bolder in regarding all things as elements in one system which could be exhaustively grasped by our reason. We might fail *in fact*, since our reason is limited, and much would continue to remain obscure *to us*. But in principle the universe could be understood through and through, and the main features of it as one system could be discerned in the understanding we have of those features of it which we do comprehend.

This is what some implied by saying, with Tennyson, that if we understood all about 'the flower in the crannied wall' we would 'know all about God and man'. But others objected to this way of thinking. G. F. Stout, for example, urged that it would obscure the fact that no part of the whole taken in isolation from others is an adequate or reliable clue.

The clues which idealists took to be important for their purpose varied a great deal. For some evolution was the key notion. For others the main clue was found in certain views about mind and matter. Both these approaches are admirably illustrated in Samuel Alexander's well-known work, *Space, Time and Deity*—more admired from afar than read today, I suspect. G. F. Stout also holds that mind and matter are co-extensive[1] and he arrives in this way at the notion of a universal mind which pervades the world of nature and human experience. We have also in Stout's *God and Nature* one of the clearest affirmations of the idea of value as a major meta-physical clue. He argues that, as value is objective, it must belong 'to the constitution of the universe' and this is held to imply that 'finite good cannot be what it is — cannot be good at all — unless it belongs to the self-complete unity of a universal good'. If, he continues, this 'self-complete good is not to be at the mercy of alien circumstances ... its power must be commensurate with its authority. It must have might as it has right. It must be the controlling and all-pervasive scheme of the universe as a whole, including all finite beings, all temporal process, past, present and future.'[2] This, in turn, is thought to require the God of theism as 'an actual agency' which ensures for the complete good its eternal fulfilment within the universe as a whole.[3]

Variations on similar themes are found in other impressive philosophical works at the close of the nineteenth century and early in this one. Some of these are already listed at the end of Chapter Nineteen. It would be a great mistake to suppose that,

1. See his *Mind and Matter*, Book II, Chapters IV, V, VI, and VII.
2. *God and Nature*, p. 309.
3. op. cit., p. 317.

if we find idealism in its general principle inadequate, there is little to be learnt from the major philosophical works it produced. Closer heed of such books would be very helpful and salutary at the present time.

(b) 'Empiricist' teleology. I have put the word 'empiricist' in inverted commas. It is a title claimed by some of the thinkers I have in mind here. But they could not of course be strict empiricists if they claimed any knowledge of a reality other than that which is expressly disclosed to our senses. In fact they assert much that is boldly non-empirical in the proper sense of that term. But what impels them to describe themselves as empiricists is that they are impatient with the rather abstract *a priori* starting point of much speculative idealism. They wish to begin with 'the facts', as these are found in nature and human experience, and to show that these lead eventually to a theistic view. In practice their procedures are often very similar to those of their idealist contemporaries, but they exhibit a caution, in dealing with finite personality especially, which some idealists were apt to neglect.

The most impressive representative of this school of religious thought is F. R. Tennant. His outstanding work is the two volumes of his *Philosophical Theology*. But all of Tennant's writings repay careful study. In his main work he presents a sustained account of the self as a subject or, in a technical term, a Pure Ego, which seems to me of the utmost importance. I hope, indeed, that its significance will be rediscovered soon and that the author's works will be widely read again. Tennant is also most emphatic in describing himself as an empiricist. This is unfortunate, for a Pure Ego is certainly far removed from what we normally understand by empiricism. But the intention is to show how this and kindred notions arise from reflection on what we find experience to be like, and this is meant to lead to the view that 'Belief in God becomes reasonable if the idea of God be found as indispensable for explanation of the totality of our scientific knowledge about the world and man as is the idea of the soul for explanation of the totality of our knowledge about the individual mind'.[1] This also yields in due course the idea of

1. *Philosophical Theology*, Vol. 2, p. 254.

God 'as a father of spirits who respects the rights and privacies of other and humbler persons'.[1]

In the last contention we see very clearly the concern about the facts of experience and of human personality noted earlier. A related feature of natural theology, most of all in recent forms is also well illustrated in the work of Tennant, namely the tendency for it to make itself comprehensive, to be all in all in religious thought and thus require no supplementation from revealed theology. Tennant, for example, regards Christ as 'the unique revealer of God' because He 'possessed in the fullest measure insight into the divine purpose in the world and for man', and in the light of this 'Christianity may be said to be the climax of the historical development of natural religion, and the crown of natural theology. "Revealed" religion, in other words, becomes the final phase of natural religion.'[2]

The distinction between natural theology and revealed truth about God becomes at least rather blurred in these ways. Is revealed truth merely a refinement of what we learn from 'natural' reflection upon the world and experience? Advocates of natural theology differ in their answer to this question, and on the whole their answers are apt to be uncertain. But, if we do recognize some distinctive revealed truth about God, may it not be that this is present in some measure in all particular knowledge of God? In other words, if we reject strictly natural theology at certain points, must we not reject it throughout for all determinate religious affirmations. I think that we must; and I have earlier given an indication of the reasons for the essential inadequacy of the procedures of strictly natural theology. But this does not prevent the work of writers on natural theology from providing us with many of the ingredients of a sound view of revealed truth or of the nature of man and the world as true religion requires us to understand them. I think in fact that they do this, and that this is very true of some of the writers I have mentioned and especially of F. R. Tennant whose books I much commend for that reason.

1. op. cit., p. 258.
2. op. cit., p. 240.

FURTHER READING

Existence and Analogy. E. L. Mascall (Longmans).
The Nature of Metaphysical Thinking. Dorothy Emmet (Macmillan).
The first of these books contains the most direct account of the traditional doctrine, together with vindications of its relevance today. The second work contains some wide-ranging suggestions for the application of the doctrine to our problems.

For Otto's idea of the schematization of the holy the reader should first consult the relevant parts of *The Idea of the Holy*. He could then read a critical account of this in Chapter IX of *The Modern Predicament*, by H. J. Paton, and the defence of Otto against criticisms like those of John Oman and Paton in C. A. Campbell's *Selfhood and Godhood*, Chapter XVI.

CHAPTER TWENTY

REVELATION AND AUTHORITY

The idea of revelation is the idea of something which is being shown—more strictly, unveiled or unfolded. This is usually thought to happen in religion by the initiative of some agent who makes himself known in this way. In revelation then God shows us what He is like and what He requires of us. But He does not do this by showing us what it is like to be God. As we have seen, that is not possible; and this is the point of the famous story of God hiding Moses in a cleft rock so that he might see the glory of God without seeing His face—Moses could not see the face of God and live. God then takes the initiative in giving signs or hints of Himself within modes of experience which are familiar to us and in terms which we can understand. The reference is to a mystery which we cannot fathom but the counters or notation, as it were, are not elusive or strange; they are drawn from the content of common experience. God thus makes Himself known within the world or within the lives of men. Even if the media He adopts are unusual ones, they have still to be within our reach as finite beings, and even where there is abnormality this appears mostly in some accompaniment of the divine disclosure, not in the substance of it. Intimations of God seem to be, in principle, well within the reach of all, however disturbing or startling they may appear to be in other ways. Indeed there is a remarkable homeliness about much that purports to be divine revelation. The mystery is more in the origin than in the substance of the communication, the words are often words of love and justice and mercy; and although these may take some unusual forms in God's commendation of them they are in themselves notions we reckon with all our lives and meet in the most familiar situations.

This does not mean that we find God's revelations easy to accept, they may drastically upset our ways of thinking about ourselves and our neighbours. But this is a disturbance at the finite level. It demands some reorientation of our own attitudes, and we may sometimes find it perplexing that some things should be required of us; but that is not the major problem at the intellectual or philosophical level. The hard problem here, and to my mind much the hardest problem in religious thought, is to justify the reference beyond in what is commended to us and communicated to us about God. We may know tolerably well what it means to 'love mercy' but what does it mean to say that *God* loves mercy and how do we know that the words which purport to tell us this are genuinely the words of God? What is the warrant for divine disclosure, what assurance have we that it is God and not man who is speaking, or if it is in the first place the word of a man what enables us to say that God speaks to us through him? How do we know when we have a vision of God, how does a word become 'the Word of God'? This is our crucial problem.

The problem is harder because there is no strictly direct disclosure of God; if there were, if we could see Him strictly as He is, then there could be no doubt about it, the revelation would carry an absolute guarantee in itself—it could only be a revelation of God. But this is what is ruled out by the nature of the case, it is inherently impossible; and if God has thus to communicate with us in terms of what we understand as finite beings, if He has to make Himself known within the human situation, how are men able to recognize the ways in which He does this, how does an occasion which is in substance a finite one carry with it some reference or overtone which is more than finite? It is not very hard to see how we can understand God if He speaks to us, as it were, in our own language. But how then do we know that it is God who speaks?

The claim that God does make Himself known or speaks from within the experience we have as men is sometimes put as the view that God is immanent. The main idea here is that we do not have to choose between saying that God is beyond and saying that He is within. He is both. But this is a rather ambiguous notion as it stands. If it means, as it has sometimes done, that God is in some way part of the world or to be identified with some process in the world, then it is in my view very mistaken. God is altogether distinct from the world, and the form of immanentism which leaves this uncertain borders at least on pantheism which treats all there is as some part of God. The latter position has at least the merit of being unambiguous. Some allusions to the alleged 'image of God in man' share the ambiguity of the notion of immanence. There is an important sense in which man has been made 'in the image of God' and we can also quite properly speak, as many sacred scriptures do, of the 'indwelling' of God in man. But however these terms are to be understood, they must not be taken to mean that we ourselves are in some way divine beings or some extension of the being of God. God may dwell among men or within them but certainly not in the sense that God Himself or some part of Him becomes a part of us. If the doctrine of the Holy Spirit, in the Christian religion, meant that God is to be identified in some respect with His creatures, it would contradict what is basic in the Christian doctrine of God.

Part of the difficulty here comes about, I suspect, because men have sometimes tended to think of the relation of God to the material universe as, at any rate, similar to the way our bodies belong to us. But even in our case, as I shall stress later, there is a sharp distinction to be drawn between mind and body. It is certainly a mistake to suppose that the world of nature is the body of God in a way not unlike our having a body. We may quite properly speak of the indwelling of God in nature. But if we do we must remember that we speak in highly metaphorical terms. God is the Lord of creation and in no way limited by it. He is in no sense a material being; nor is He any other part of finite reality.

This may seem to create special difficulties for any doctrine of incarnation, and most of all for the Christian. But I do not think anyone can begin to understand the Christian doctrine of the Incarnation who does not first take the fullest measure of its difficulties—and the very remarkable character of the claim that is made. It is a doctrine that is very ill-served by assimilation to other ways in which God may be said to be 'in' the world. It has little indeed in common with doctrines which incline to some kind of pantheism. It is in the rejection of all the latter forms of union of God and man that we can begin to see what is involved in the Christian doctrine of Incarnation and the way it is seen to be true.

We must be careful then not to identify God with nature or with any human voice or deed. If God speaks to us within the world it is not in the sense that He is part of the world. That is ruled out from the start. But how then do we come to recognize what is specifically of God in the world, where is His voice to be heard, what are the modes of His manifestation, 'the signs of His Presence'? In one sense He is everywhere, nothing could be without Him. But we are now concerned with the sense in which He is in particular times and places and speaks to us the particular word. How do we know that this is the word of God?

On some accounts there is no need to answer this question. For if, in revelation, we have a case, not of our finding God, but of God by His own initiative making Himself known to us, how can there be any question about it? It is for God to choose the media in which He discloses Himself—according to a curious view of Karl Barth He could have disclosed Himself equally well to stones and to men. Indeed, is it not presumption to ask for a justification of revelation? Are we not putting God in the dock and asking Him to justify Himself? Should not our attitude be one of grateful acceptance and unquestioning obedience?

There seems however to be much wrong with this position. It is of course true that if revelation is known to be such it cannot be questioned. That would be like asking, 'Why should I do my duty?' or 'Why should I believe the truth?'. If something is my duty, then this means that I should do it, and if something is taken to be true then we obviously do believe it. But we are often uncertain what are our duties and what is the truth; and even when we are not, there is still point in asking what it is for something to be true or a duty. There are likewise questions to ask about revelation. There are many to whom it is not clear that God has revealed Himself, and even those to whom it is thought that God has expressly revealed Himself are sometimes in doubt about it themselves.

There is much fluctuation of faith even among the most devout. There are two sides to revelation. It involves man as well as God and I do not see what a revelation could be like that does not involve the use of the faculties with which we are endowed as human beings. If, on Karl Barth's extraordinary supposition, stones became recipients of revelation they would have become something very different from stones. In what way then are our faculties involved in revelation? What form of certainty does it give, and how is doubt dispelled?

If we stress the personal character of our fellowship with God, and thereby, as in Christianity, highlight the worth of persons, it will be more evident how much our minds, and the full reach of our minds, will be involved in this fellowship. The questions normally appropriate to belief and the distinction of true and false will have correspondingly more significance. God will not be dealing with us as merely passive recipients of truth, whatever that might be, but as creatures with a role of their own to play in attainment of the truth, even the more expressly God-given truth.

These are matters much overlooked in one very familiar view of revelation, namely the one which I shall call for the present 'the appeal to authority'. The commonest form of this view is that which regards some pronouncement or a body of sacred scripture as expressly given by God in exactly the form in which we have it, almost as if God had dictated or written it for us. The words themselves in this way carry the divine imprimatur. This is the view which is held by Christian 'fundamentalists' (or literalists as they are also described) towards the Bible. It means that every word of the Bible is literally inerrant, every verse must be taken in the plainest sense and never questioned. Orthodox Muslims take the same view of the Koran and the Mormons have the same view of the Book of Mormon, allegedly disclosed to Joseph Smith by an angel and miraculously deciphered by him from an otherwise unknown script on gold plates, subsequently taken back to heaven.

It is surprising that intelligent people should still adhere to this position, as some seem to do. Perhaps the student of religion could gain much from asking how that comes about. It is a position exceptionally fraught with difficulties. What are we to say for example of competing claims to revelation of this sort? There are some things common to the Bible, the Koran and the Book of Mormon, but there are also many differences. The Muslim does not consider anything to be revealed besides what was given to Muhammad and collected in the Koran. A secondary authority belongs to other sayings of Muhammad, his more personal pronouncements—'off the record', as we might put it—and to tradition. But all strict revelation is contained in the Koran, and that is beyond all question. But much in the Koran, including versions of stories we find in the Old Testament, is at odds with the Bible—and, as a further complication, we find that Islam itself holds the Bible to be in *some* way inerrant. How shall we judge between such claims when every form of judgement seems to be ruled out from the start? Can we say nothing for our preference for one form of sacred scripture, except that we believe it—*in toto* and almost blindly we might add?

There are also internal difficulties. It is not just that the contents of various scriptures are at odds with each other, but that individual scriptures are far from consistent. We have more than one version of some events described in the Bible, and these are sometimes contradictory. The substance of the teaching offered in one part is also at odds with what we read elsewhere, and although Jesus said that He came to fulfil and not to destroy 'the law', His teaching, and that of the prophets before Him, correct much that was said 'of old'. There seems to be progress and correction within the same scriptures. Moreover much is affirmed in the scriptures I have noted which is altogether at variance with matters we feel compelled on other grounds to believe. The story of creation and of the sin of Adam and Eve in the Garden of Eden can hardly be taken at its face value by anyone with even the most elementary knowledge today of world history and anthropology. There is likewise much in the Bible which is so inherently implausible that, even if it cannot be strictly disproved, it can hardly be taken seriously as it stands, whether or not we believe in miracles.

It might be argued that difficulties of this kind appear on any view of revelation. For if there is a divine disclosure there can be no question about it. But we may reply that the problem is at any rate not so acute if the revelation is thought to make use of erring human faculties. There seems to be no way of coping with it at all if we are thinking of some literal inerrancy.

Nor do these difficulties apply merely to questions of fact. We read of God in parts of the Bible and in other scriptures as instigating men to actions which are most repugnant to our own consciences, actions which it seems thus impossible to ascribe to the initiative of a supreme and perfect Being. When we say this we are in some fashion judging the Bible; and however presumptuous that may appear, it is very hard to avoid it in the present form. And surely, when we take some scripture to be the Word of God to us, we are having regard to the quality or content of what it contains. We would not want to take the Bible as sacred scripture *whatever* it taught.

A further form of the appeal to authority is that which vests the authority in some institution, such as the Church. To do this we have to be clear what is the Church, for in one obvious sense at least there is no Church but only churches. Even if these are in some further sense all part of *the Church*, we have still to reckon with discordant voices and competing authorities. But even if it were clear which was the appropriate authority, we would still need some reason for accepting it. This does not mean that we cannot take anything on the authority of other persons. We are all the time doing this, for we cannot test everything for ourselves. We ask the way of complete strangers and put very implicit trust in time-tables which we could not check without immense labour. We believe the accepted findings of science just because this is what 'the scientists say'. But again we do none of this blindly. We have good reasons for supposing that scientists are likely to be right, time-tables reliable and a willing stranger likely to be helpful. We do not choose these authorities at random. Nor is it unreasonable to accept the guidance of people more expert or more experienced than ourselves in literary, aesthetic, or even moral matters. Here also there are many ways in which others are likely to 'know better'. It does not follow that we always accept their verdict. But there could be even a hard personal moral problem about which the opinion of someone else, someone wiser and more experienced, could count more for us than our own reflections on the problem. And, in similar ways, there can be much room for deference to wise and experienced people or to institutions in religion. But we do not take this course without prior independent grounds for accepting our authority, in whatever measure we may do so. An authority must produce its credentials. We do not accept it at random, nor in the same way in all regards.

Were this not the case, we would have no answer to those who say: 'We accept the authority of Hitler or the Nazi Party,' or 'We put our trust in the Communist party'. If we regard some religious body or institution as our authority in religion we surely do not do so irrespective of what they are like. We must have justification at some stage for our choice. In that case the original problem is still with us.

It is with us also when we turn to subtler forms of the appeal to authority, like much that we find in dogmatic theology. By dogmatic theology I understand here the affirmation of a set of doctrines abstracted from the context which first gave them significance and presented as if they were meaningful in this way and final in themselves. Rarely has consistency counted so little as in this kind of theology. This is the sort of context in which we are assured that we are 'free, but not free to do good', or that 'if I feel I *ought* to do right, it is a sign that I cannot do it',[1] or that 'the divinely present Word cannot be tied to a correct doctrine'[2] but also 'demands obedience which can never take place without correct theological doctrine'.[3] The tortuousness by which it is sought to defend these flatly contradictory positions is only matched in the writings where they appear by the boldness with which reason is defied and indeed brought under condemnation as the sign of a proud and unregenerate nature which seeks to subdue to its own

1. Emil Brunner. *Divine Imperative*, p. 74.
2. op. cit. p. 145.
3. op. cit. p. 154.

understanding the matters which go beyond its grasp and can only be received in a spirit of unquestioning obedience. Contradiction is given the more dignified name of 'paradox', and the fact that we deal in religion with a mystery which is transcendent and irreducible is made the cover for irresponsible play with extravagant paradox in matters where difficulties and seeming contradiction can be dispelled by clear thinking. It is as though, in dealing with transcendent reality, anything goes, unreason being itself the sign of the properly transcendent reference of our thought.

The only serious concern which this kind of theology shows is for the presentation of certain traditional doctrines taken in their most explicit sense. There is little attempt at imaginative reconstruction of the situations and experiences which prompted the pronouncements on which the doctrines are based. A cool and superficial rationalization of inspired and highly figurative utterances is given, by one of the oddest paradoxes in the history of mental aberration, the cover of an alleged divine sanction for unreason and is set aflame with religious passion. The results are often very sinister, for not only is the impression conveyed that there is no proper place for reason in religion—that revelation and reason are poles apart—but also there is the proliferation of ideas, like those of man's total depravity and the futility of all effort at social and moral improvement, which give a gloomy and distorted picture of man's lot in the world and an impression of his nature and aptitudes little consistent with the role which true religion requires him to play.

This type of theology has flourished much of late. That may seem strange in an age of progress and enlightenment, but it must be considered in part as a reaction against a too facile liberalism in much religious thought at the turn of the century. It is also not unconnected with the general resurgence of unreason in the modern world, as we find it in politics and cultural matters as well as in religion. This is a phenomenon which I have myself ventured to examine and criticize in some of my books, directing my comments especially against the depreciation of elementary ethical convictions which the denigration of human aptitudes in recent theology has involved. This will concern us in the next chapter too.

An appeal to some kind of dogma, as the ultimate truth in religion, is encouraged also by the predicament in which many find themselves as the result of extreme Biblical scepticism. If the conclusion is reached that no reliance can be placed at any point on Biblical accounts of alleged historical events, it becomes hard to see how the specific affirmations made about the work and person of Jesus can be justified. That the scepticism, in its extreme forms, is not warranted seems to me also plain. Much of it comes about through confusion about the nature of historical judgements and the method of validating them. But for those who are led, in Biblical studies, to extreme historical scepticism the distinctive Christian affirmations are very hard to sustain. I do not think myself that they can be sustained if the quest of the historical Jesus is like seeking a will o' the wisp. But some have sought to redeem the situation here by distinguishing sharply between the Jesus of History and the Christ of Faith. The latter is known by some inner assurance or in the God-given experience of the Church and in turn it gives us some kind of warrant for the subsequent identification of the Christ of Faith with the Historical Jesus. But this seems to me a very strange and desperate course. Its supporters are apt to be impatient of argument at crucial stages, in spite of being open to the point of almost cultivated scepticism on historical questions. One cannot reason, in the last resort, with a claim to direct and personal assurance, but in the present respect the situation is one to which famous words may apply, namely that it 'admits of no refutation but produces no conviction'.

This does not mean that there is no important place for dogma in religion. I think there is. But dogma (or doctrine) is derivative. It does not carry its authority expressly in itself. One can quite properly ask how a dogma is vindicated, and there are also very pertinent questions about the meaning of various dogmas and the order of priority in which they stand. The proper commendation of religion should not thus take the form of confronting people with a set of doctrinal or credal affirmations to be accepted neat, as it were, and in their entirety. This gives a very wrong impression of what dogmas are. On the contrary we must go beyond the dogmas to some reality which gives them their significance and consider very carefully how the latter is to be understood. In the last resort, however wedded to their particular creed, most intelligent people, I suspect, come to feel at some point the need to offer some justification for 'the faith that is in them'. They do not accept or commend it blind. If they did, if inquiry and criticism of all sorts are ruled out, allegiance could be given, in principle, to any sort of dogma, however absurd or repugnant to us—it would be just 'given to be believed'.

There are indeed people so desperate, in their affirmation of a religious faith, that they consider the absurdity of a dogma to be a merit. For this they lift out of their context such Biblical references as those which speak of 'confounding the wise', of the Gospel being 'foolishness to the Greeks' and so on. This is most unwarranted, for whatever these difficult utterances mean, and if we take them in their proper context they are not as strange and perplexing as they seem, they certainly do not mean that a Christian can believe things in an intellectually irresponsible way and without bringing his God-given faculties in their full and proper exercise to the assimilation of the truth given by God. Crude rationalizations are no doubt to be avoided, and truth in religion as in art and other matters, is often subtle and strange. But to protest against misleading simplifications is one thing. To glory in absurdity is quite another, and it can hardly serve the cause of true religion.

Impressed by the difficulty of making revelation central and authoritative in religion while also retaining respect for reason in its proper place, some have had further recourse to ideas we have mentioned in another context, namely the ideas of encounter and meeting and of some relation with God which has no specific content. The important thing, it is held, is not to 'know about' God but to 'meet' Him. The fellowship we have with God is a live and personal one, and in the Christian religion what we have is the supreme encounter of man with God. But here again we must point out that there is no mere meeting which does not involve some 'knowledge about'. There is indeed a rough distinction to be drawn between 'knowing people' and just 'knowing about' them. I know much about people whom I have never met or known, although our language is not always a clear guide here. I may come to know some people well by correspondence without ever meeting them, as those words are normally used. But that there is a distinction to be drawn between extensive knowledge about people and the insights we have in the warm give and take of intimate relationships is also plain, and I myself have no doubt that we must stress this for the right understanding of the relationships of God and man which are claimed in the Christian religion. There is, for this reason, a prominent place to be given also to our own obedience and responsiveness. It is, I think, encounter that we do have with God, and I much welcome the prominence given to this notion in recent religious thought. But it does not, on the other hand, relieve us at all of the hard task of giving some account of this encounter. There is 'knowing about' in all knowing. I could not meet or encounter anyone except on the basis of what I take him to be and what I observe him to be doing or judge him to be thinking. Nor could we encounter God except in finding that God makes Himself known to us in certain ways and has various ways of dealing with us and eliciting or requiring a certain response from us. The notion of encounter thus affords no way of avoiding the very hard question of how we know that some things are true about God and His dealings with us. Epistemology, to use the technical term, cannot be kept out of religious understanding at any point, not even the central and intimate one of divine disclosure.

At this point some are disposed to fall back on pragmatism. This is a philosophical attitude which was very fashionable at the close of the last century. It had very gifted and eminent exponents in William James and F. C. S. Schiller. It is not so fashionable today, notwithstanding that some disciples of William James are still very active. But in one way or another the pragmatist approach to truth tends to be sharply revived whenever the difficulties become insistent—in philosophy and religious thought alike. It has reinforcement today, in some quarters, through misconceptions of the way truth is established in a field where spectacular achievements continue to impress us, namely science. What then is pragmatism? The answer may be well conveyed in the title of one of William James' most famous books, namely *The Will to Believe*. We resolve to believe because we must act in certain situations, and the vindication of our belief comes when we find that it 'works'. There are two main elements here, and they are not always well distinguished. There is, in the first place, the notion that we can somehow make up our minds to believe, an idea which is much endorsed in commitment theories of truth in philosophy and theology today. I have shown already why I consider this unsatisfactory. Secondly, there is the notion that a belief can be somehow justified by the consequences of adopting it. It 'works' in this sense in practice. A belief is true, it might be said, when it is good for us to believe it. But this seems to me a peculiarly odd view of truth, and some of the oddities of it were well displayed by Plato in his criticisms of the early and impressive presentation of it by Protagoras. There may be ways in which it is good for us to believe something whether or not it is true. If I were due to be tortured it might be best for me not to know this and believe the opposite. The fact that good results follow from adopting some view is very far from proving that the view is a sound one. It might be that the good results were achieved by some 'useful illusion'. I admit that an initial case is made for a belief, especially in vital religious matters, which leads people to live noble lives and raises the tone of a community. But this is not the final argument. A belief must be known to be true on its own account; and, in fact, although it would be strange if very mistaken beliefs continued to prompt men to do good, it is possible for grave error to have good results 'in practice'—as we say. The unbeliever will certainly not be content with glowing accounts of the lives of the saints or the good the Church has accomplished. For even if the record were not as stained as it is, the atheist could argue that this was just a fortunate consequence of being subject to certain errors and illusions. He might even go so far as to add that the illusion should be encouraged, although I much doubt this—for it could be maintained that error is itself a gravely bad thing and that in the long run, most of all once questions and doubts are raised, the illusions may prove more harmful than useful. But whatever might be said on that score, the belief itself could not become a sound belief merely because its adoption had good effects.

For this reason, it can only be in a qualified way that exhibition of the good lives and noble work of religious believers can have place in religious apologetics. They have a place. But the final appeal is not to them. Belief must be shown to be sound in itself as well as in some consequence of holding it.

I mentioned a confusion due to the way we speak about truth in science. We sometimes say that a theory is true if it 'works'. But this is ambiguous. It may mean simply that the theory works if it is in accordance with the facts and explains them. On the other hand it may mean that it has useful applications, that it 'works' more in the sense in which a device works. The former meaning is the relevant one where establishing the truth is concerned, but this can be obscured by our use of the same terms in the two cases. We must avoid a similar confusion in religion.

If then we are not to appeal to authority or have some unwarranted recourse to the ideas of encounter, commitment or of what it is useful to believe, how shall we proceed?

I shall now indicate, in the next chapter, what seem to me the main clues for our solution of this question and then offer a further short account of the way I approach the subject myself.

FURTHER READING

Few discussions of the principle of authority in religion have surpassed that of S. T. Coleridge in his *Confessions of an Enquiring Spirit*. Although written early in the last century it is highly relevant to the controversies which have been started by recent Biblical criticism and to kindred problems of our time. I can think of no better book to recommend to anyone attracted to some kind of fundamentalism. A recent edition with a helpful introduction and notes has been provided by H. St. John Hart. It could be followed by study of:

The Authority of the Bible. C. H. Dodd (London).

History and Christian Apologetics. T. A. Roberts (S.P.C.K.).

The second of these books has a helpful outline of the different attitudes adopted towards the question of the historicity of the Gospels by representative and influential scholars.

Further discussions of the general notion of authority in religion may be found in two books already mentioned:

The Modern Predicament. H. J. Paton, Chapter II.

Selfhood and Godhood. C. A. Campbell, Chapters I and II.

In *The Religious Revolt Against Reason*, H. de Wolf presents a searching and incisive critical treatment of authoritarian types of recent theology.

On the subject of pragmatism mentioned at the close of the chapter the following works may be consulted:

Present Philosophical Tendencies. R. B. Perry, Chapter IV (on 'Pragmatism') and the appendix on William James. A more recent but rather difficult book is *American Pragmatism*. Edward C. Moore (Columbia University Press).

Pragmatism. William James.

Logic for use. F. C. S. Schiller (London).

CHAPTER TWENTY-ONE

REVELATION AND EXPERIENCE

I think we find one of our main clues to the problem with which we have just been concerned in the proper sense in which something is said to be true if it works, namely if it follows from the appropriate evidence. There can be no evidence, in the strict sense, for the existence of God. But where further truth about God is concerned it is on evidence of a certain kind that we must, in my opinion, rely. But what sort of evidence is relevant here? We have already seen that we cannot rely on any wholly secular considerations. There is no way of building a bridge from these to some Reality beyond them. What evidence, then, can there be for divine disclosure, what are the signs of God's intervention in the lives of men and how are these recognized, can we say more than that 'the vision approves itself to men of genuine insight'?[1]

There are various considerations that will help us here. One is the analogy with our knowledge of one another. This, I repeat, has no application to our knowledge of the *Being* of God. But it is very relevant to the way God discloses Himself. We do not, if I am right, know one another's minds directly but only through the intervention of each of us in the world as each of us apprehends it, mainly in perception. Our bodies are especially involved in this mode of communication. God has no distinct body in the same way. None the less we must learn to recognize in the course of events and experience peculiar intimations of the presence and activity of God.

A further clue may be found in what Richard Bell tells us in a particularly illuminating discussion[2] of the way the mind of God was thought to be given to Muhammad. According to tradition the message was brought in some way by the angel

1. *For Faith and Freedom*, Leonard Hodgson, p. 100.
2. *Introduction to the Qur'ān*, pp. 29–36.

Gabriel. But Gabriel is only mentioned twice in the Koran, and in both cases the reference is to the stage of Muhammad's life at Medina which was much later than his call at Mecca and the early and more formative of the revelations he is thought to have received. In any case no claim is made that Gabriel appeared in visible form. Bell thinks the reference to the angel is 'a later interpretation of something which Muhammad had at first understood otherwise'; and he adds that the commonest account in the Koran is that Allah may 'suggest' something or send a messenger to suggest. The Arabian word *awḥā* has now come to be used for revelations communicated to Muhammad through Gabriel, but originally, as its use in the Koran itself indicates, it stood more for something flashing into one's mind in a moment of inspiration. It could thus be fallible, and it is not unlikely that Muhammad himself believed that he had on one occasion at least (in sanctioning the role of certain pagan deities) been prompted by Satan in what purported to come from God. In this way then the prophet could be regarded, not as the wholly passive recipient of a finally formed message, but as a human being to whom the truth came in the form of suggestion or inspiration.

This brings us close to the sphere of poetry and artistic creation, and this I present as a further clue. It is no accident that art has had such a prominent place in religion. Much prophecy took its shape in the highly figurative language of poetry; and many who have dealt with the subject of revelation, especially in recent years, have stressed the close affinity of poetry and prophecy. Of such writers few have written more helpfully than Dr. Austin Farrer. He underlines the role of images in the process of revelation—images in the sense of figurative notions like the 'divine king', the 'good shepherd', 'the ever merciful father', the 'lamb that is slain', and so on. Sacred literatures abound in images of this kind. Farrer also shows, in what is perhaps his most distinctive contribution to the subject, that such images have a life of their own, in the sense that accretions of meaning are acquired by them in their progress from one situation or context to another or in the transmission to a new culture. No one who wishes to investigate this subject today can afford to neglect what Dr.

Farrer has to say about it in readable books like *The Glass of Vision*. In such writings we see how the image which develops, as a theme develops and takes shape in general literature, the work of fertile, profound imagination, has thus a prominent place in the right understanding of revelation.

To do this justice we must also note two further things about art. Firstly it is never a merely emotional matter. Emotion is certainly there, but it presupposes a peculiar illumination of the world around us and of distinctive situations. There is no art without insight. But, in the second place, this insight cannot be analysed or distilled into independent affirmations. What a poet says is bound up with the way he says it and it cannot be translated[1] or interpreted without parody or distortion into other terms. There is that finality about artistic symbolism.

These are further clues. But we are not home yet. For religion is not art, not even the most illuminating art. Where does the main difference lie? I have here some quarrel with Dr. Farrer. For he thinks that one distinctive difference is that poetry deals with general notions, religion with the particular. I think it is the particular that poetry also illumines, but *qua* poetry it need not be concerned with more than secular reality. How then does an image become distinctively religious? I must here join issue again with Dr. Farrer. For he thinks the image is divinely given as such. 'The Bible-reader will immerse himself in the simple image on the page before him, and find life giving power in it, taken as it stands.' This comes dangerously near the appeal to authority again, and Dr. Farrer has been taken severely to task for this by Helen Gardner in *The Limits of Literary Criticism* and by several others. But in that case we have still with us the problem of how the imaginative prophetic vision authenticates itself.

I shall now go beyond the indication of what seem to me the main clues to the problem of revelation and sketch my own

1. It can, of course, be translated in the literal sense of being rendered into another language, although this also presents many problems. How far, for example, is the translation of poetry a new artistic creation? Some of the problems of the translator are instructively discussed by Idris Bell in his long and fascinating introduction to his *Dafydd ap Gwilym—Fifty Poems* Y Cymmrodor, Vol. XLVIII.

position. As I do not wish to give this undue prominence and would prefer to see the reader, in the first instance especially, follow up the clues in his own way, and as I have presented my position at length in my book, *Our Experience of God*, I shall confine myself here to the barest outline.

There seem to me, then, to be certain distinctive occasions or experiences in which a sharp and insistent consciousness of the being of God becomes closely associated with certain other features of the situation in which it occurs, most of all by making us more alert to what is most distinctive in the situation and giving us a sounder perspective in which to view it. I have sometimes described this as a certain toning of the situation as a whole in such a way that our understanding of it, in normal or finite ways, is deepened and enhanced. The substance of what we apprehend in this way is finite or secular, that is it concerns the world around us and the way we should live in it, but the insight is obtained through the difference made to our insights and perceptions by the impact upon them of a profound and disturbing sense of the involvement of God in all things and the mystery and majesty of His Being. This affects especially the moral aspect of our lives, and we thus find that the content of what the prophet tells us has no peculiar mystery or bafflement in it, beyond the novelty of surprising ethical insights as such, but that it is also charged with a significance which is not of the order of the moral insight itself and pervades the whole of it. What is shown us and required of us can, in principle, be grasped by all alike; it is to do justice, to love mercy, and so on. But it is prefaced by the words: 'Thus saith the Lord.' That is what especially distinguishes prophecy—that these are the things which God pre-eminently requires, that they are highlighted and deepened in our experience in our intensified consciousness of God and carry within them in this way the stamp of His particular concern about them; this is where God seems to count most of all, and we feel warranted in this way in ascribing these particular insights to His exceptional impact upon us.

There are many situations in the Bible which illustrate this. The most famous is the account of Moses at the burning bush to which allusion has already been made. On this occasion

Moses had not only a remarkably clear understanding of the transcendence and mystery of God but also, in close association with this, an indication of his own mission and how to undertake it, how to deal with his people in the plight in which they found themselves and how to give them the assurance and stability they needed. He was enabled in similar ways to shape for them in due course the basic laws and the attitudes which were formative in their subsequent history. In all this the exercise of ordinary wisdom and insight receives a special authenticity and character through the infusion into them, in subtle ways not perceptible in detachment, of Moses' sense of a Beyond which pervades all the present. The stories of the patriarchs before him convey the same impression. Their consciences were sharpened and informed in the exigencies of situations in which they were also profoundly conscious of God. This is what reaches more sublime heights, although still often imperfect, in the psalms and prophecy.

Nor are these situations confined to cases of informing and correcting our moral consciousness. Take the well-known story of Jacob at Bethel. Here was a man who, by his meanness and treachery, had made himself hateful to his own family and was tasting for the first time the bitterness of the lonely outcast. He carried in his heart, however jauntily he may have conducted himself earlier, an obviously heavy burden of guilt, he had gone against all which his upbringing would induce him to treat with the utmost respect. He would not, by normal expectation, find God near him in this state, he had cut himself away and brought on himself despair and destitution of which the account gives unmistakable signs. The loneliness of his surroundings reflected a lonely and despairing state. Yet it was in just this situation that Jacob had his most vivid consciousness of God as a living Reality having an unbounded concern for an unworthy person like himself. In stories of this kind, and there is more than one significant instance in the story of Jacob, we find the beginning of the consciousness of God as one who seeks, a Reconciler of infinite mercy, which became in due course the high theme of prophecy and the Gospels.

It is important to stress that situations of the kind instanced do not occur in isolation from others, they have ramifications in our lives as a whole and there are recurrences and patterns of them which strengthen the association of the finite factors involved with the sense of God and give the process as a whole an extended and developing content. Nor is this extension and strengthening a merely psychological matter. The logical link becomes stronger too in the continuities and varieties of such religious experiences, much as our confidence in one another and mutual understanding are extended in varied situations of fellowship and encounter in the world. The study of the details of this process constitutes, to my mind, a very important part of the task of theology.

A further feature of the process I have noted is its linkage with the life and history of a people as a whole. This is notably the case in Jewish history. The Jews have no monopoly of revelation. Situations like the ones I have been noting appear in parts of the Koran and in the accounts of the life of Buddha and in Hindu scriptures. The 'enlightenment' of Buddha and its preliminaries amply repay investigation along the lines I have noted, and it will be a very fine exercise for the student of religion to compare instances of profound and formative religious experiences as they are found in very different cultures. But there is one feature of these which he will not find apparent to anything like the same extent in the religions just mentioned as in the Hebrew-Christian tradition. That is the peculiar intertwining of the developing religious awareness and the shaping of a people's destiny. The patterning of religious experience becomes a very distinctive strand in Jewish history and the impact of the elements within it on one another gives a distinctive range and depth to the process of God's disclosure of Himself as a seeking and reconciling God. The enactments of God on the stage of men's own lives and problems stand out sharply here and begin, in the quality of the illumination involved and in the closer linkage with formative events, to have a 'once for all' character.

It is this which comes to its culmination in the events narrated in the Gospels. It is claimed by the Christian that Jesus, when seen against the background of all that had gone before, acquires that distinctiveness, in the blend of moral and spiritual teaching and of both with their immediate and remarkable instantiation, which sets Him apart, as more than a further term in the process of divine disclosure. He sums up the process as a whole in His own person. His reactions surprise us and yet, in an array of challenging situations, seem unerringly right. This impression, extended and refined by committed imaginative pondering on the events recorded, brings the Christian to the point where he finds, as even Martin Buber to his bewilderment found, that Jesus cannot be classified and this ripens into the view that Jesus can only be thought of, in the light of all the evidence, as God Himself, under the limitations of human existence, bringing his work of reconciliation to fulfilment. There can be no exhaustive explanation of so remarkable an occurrence. The Christian does not claim, and is not bound to do so, to understand properly how the same person can thus be God and man, or how God could be God under such limitation. He can only declare that this is what must have come about, and he declares it, not blindly or defiantly, but as the only thing that can be said adequate to the events as he reconstructs them.

It is for Christian theology and apologetics to amplify and exhibit this impression of the person of Jesus effectively. All we can attempt in this book is to set it in its place in our understanding of what revelation is like. But it will be evident that if the distinctive Christian claim is sustained it will provide a unique focus for our understanding of the work of God in the world at all other times and places. It will be pre-eminent and final. But it should be added that the individual does not come to apprehension of this in detachment from his fellows. His reason takes into itself the impact made by Jesus, not only on the more immediate witnesses but on the community whose life He shortly began to inspire and on the continuing experience, with all its vicissitudes and errors, of the Christian Church in all ages. By these means also, and in the assimilation by each of us into the varieties of his own experience of the corpus of the Christian witness in others, the significance of a final event is enabled to extend itself beyond its once for all character and afford continuing enrichment of experience and ever new disclosures of God unremittingly at work in the world and in the lives of men. Revelation, for the Christian, is final in Christ, but did not end with His own temporal history.

I shall not go further in this book into the special claims advanced by Christians. These involve, at the centre, the beliefs held about the divinity of Jesus, and it must suffice to give a general indication of the way that belief is formed. What is further held can be seen to take its place in relation to the basic notion of the Incarnation. But there are two other matters to be noted about the way revelation takes shape and develops. The first is that the distinctive features of the divine disclosure brought about in this way are given precision and an abiding lodgement in the thoughts and hearts of men through impressive and moving images, that is by figurative expressions. These sum up the main import of what comes to be known about God and they should be considered, not in detachment, but in relation to the live and developing experience of God which gave them birth. Some of them will have much significance on their own account, in literature for example or in music, and we might in any case be tempted to consider them at their face value as simple comparisons. A true understanding of the way symbolism functions in art should help us to avoid the latter peril. But the main point is that figurative terms in religion, whatever their form, take their true religious significance from their place in a developing process to which they are organic, that is the process gives them birth, in their religious suitability, and they themselves help to extend and give shape to the process on which they depend. To understand the language of religious imagination we must have insight into the shaping of religion as a live and developing experience.

It is here that Dr. Farrer's account of the life of images is so helpful, and it is here also that it could be misleading if it should be assumed, as he sometimes suggests, that the images can be detached from the experience they illumine and given an authority of their own.

The images which help to focus and develop and to sustain and renew the life of religion are of many kinds. The most obvious are those we find in speech or writing, but along with these go other expressions of religion in architecture, music, art and so forth. Our performances in acts of worship function in the same way, although that is not their only purpose. Examination of the many ways in which such images have a place in religion is a fascinating subject and one which the student will find very rewarding today. I can now give no more than a hint of the way to approach it.

The student should be warned however of the many uses of the word 'symbolism' which he may often meet in this connection. In one of these meanings symbolism stands for precise and accepted meanings given to certain terms or symbolic objects, as when a boat became a symbol of the Church carrying the faithful to salvation and a fish, in a more artificial way due to the peculiarities of certain Greek terms, became a symbol for Jesus as saviour. What matters more is that these and other more familiar symbols should also be functioning in more subtle integration with the words, insights and aspirations of men in the many-sided experience which adopts these symbols or expressly produces its own for its own creative purpose. It is symbolism in this sense that has importance in religion.

I must add that there is also a sense in which the initial ingredients of religious understanding, namely the patterned content of men's awareness of God in His dealings with them, are themselves symbolical. For they do not tell us directly what God is like but only afford the clues from which His will towards us is known. But on the relations between the various senses in which we may speak of symbolism in religion, as I understand the subject, I must again beg the reader to refer to what I have written at some length on the subject as indicated in the reading list at the end of this chapter.

The matter remaining to be mentioned is the function of creed and doctrine in relation to the processes noted already. These credal affirmations come about when it is felt that the main elements in the course of God's disclosure of Himself to us need to be brought into prominence and guarded against various perversions of them or opposition to them. What is attempted here is as explicit a formalization of the truth as the nature of the case allows. That it is important to do this, and to continue to review our attempts at the task, is amply shown in the history of the Christian religion. If this religion is sound there is something of the utmost importance to be preserved within a continuing distinctive process in which certain outstanding historical events are germinative. The distinctiveness of what has to be preserved in this way may easily be lost or distorted in the many vicissitudes to which a religion is subject over many years and in circumstances which change extensively. It has undoubtedly been very important for Christianity to have certain definite formulations of its main principles. But we have also to remember that the formulation of such principles is not final and that creeds have to be considered in relation to the events and insights which give them significance.

This does not mean that we have always to be changing our creeds or calling them in question. Far from it. We should be chary how we modify pronouncements into which much of the experience and wisdom of the past has with difficulty been distilled. Even in patently erroneous statements there is often some insight to be preserved in another way. But, whether we find much or little to alter, we can never afford to forget that the significance of the doctrinal affirmation is not to be found by considering it by itself in detachment from live experience but only by taking it in close and vital relation to the events which originally led to its being formed.

The perils, the almost certain disasters, of interpreting doctrines in any other way are many. Highly figurative expressions have sometimes been lifted out of their context in sacred scriptures and given in this way a shallow and on occasion most objectionable interpretation in doctrinal statements and in subsequent theological elaborations of these. That in turn can encourage and shelter further perversion of true religion. But the fact that doctrine is open to manifest and grave abuse in this way is no reason for dispensing with it or according it an unimportant place in religion. As elsewhere we find that religion here challenges us to the exercise of the utmost vigilance and alertness. It is a battle in which there is no laying down of arms; and the work of committed inspired scholars, conscious of the dangers of pedantry and of the isolation of religious thought from live religion, is a service of which religion stands increasingly in need with the advance of culture.

Nor is this a matter of concern merely in a Christian context. The significance of doctrine and the question of how figurative terms in religion are to be understood is becoming increasingly important in the eyes of enlightened representatives of other religions. These are major topics of discussion in the most suggestive and helpful writings of the Indian philosopher and scholar of our own day, Sri Aurobindo. This gives us again an outstanding point of comparison between the great religions.

The way God makes Himself known to us involves, I have maintained, the exercise of our own alerted faculties, He speaks to us as the creatures He has made us; but our faculties are imperfect, especially at immature stages in the development of the individual or the race. For that reason there may come about also distortions of the truth even in situations where it also seems certain that God is speaking to us. This helps us to understand much that would otherwise be utterly perplexing in sacred scriptures. But this is a theme that is best unfolded in the general consideration of a further topic which is quite central for the philosophy of religion, namely the relation of ethics to religion. That is the topic which calls for attention next.

FURTHER READING

I have followed fairly closely in this chapter the views advanced in my *Our Experience of God*. The reader may like to compare my position with that of Leonard Hodgson in *For Faith and Freedom* (Blackwell). On the question of the way we know other persons from within our own experience an article by H. H. Price, 'Our evidence for the existence of other minds', in *Philosophy* for 1938 is very illuminating. On the subject of the relation of poetry to religion I suggest, out of the very vast material available:

Metaphor and Symbol. Edited L. C. Knights. (Proceedings of the Colston Research Society.)

Studies of Type-Images in Poetry, Religion and Philosophy. Maud Bodkin (Oxford).

The Glass of Vision. Austin Farrer (Dacre Press).

Thinking and Experience. H. H. Price, Chapter VIII on 'Image Thinking' (Hutchinsons).

The Limits of Literary Criticism. Helen Gardner (Riddell Lectures: Oxford).

Poetry for You. C. D. Lewis (Blackwell).

The Life Divine. Sri Aurobindo (Dutton & Co.).

CHAPTER TWENTY-TWO

RELIGION AND ETHICS

The relation of ethics to religion is a very difficult subject, and it is also one about which a great variety of opinions have been held. These fall into three main classes. Firstly, there are the views of those who think religion has, in some ways, been harmful to ethics; then we have the view that religion has had little to do with ethics; and finally it can be held that religion and ethics are of great importance for one another. I hold the last view, but let us consider the others first.

There are two main ways in which it might be thought that religion has been harmful to ethics. It may be held that religion is *essentially* out of accord with sound ethical thought and practice. Secondly, it may be held that *some* religions, or some features of certain religions, are inimical to ethics. These two possibilities are not always distinguished. Many violent denunciations of religion have depended mainly on profound dissatisfaction with some particular religious teaching or practice. It is certainly not hard to find much, in the long and varied history of religion, to which the gravest objection may be taken. But it does not follow from this alone that religion must be condemned. We might as well condemn morality also on the ground that there have been vicious forms of it—or politics on account of unjust and despotic régimes. Most good things may be abused, and the particular excellence of some things makes them exceptionally open to abuse. But nothing is properly judged on the score of the abuses to which it is liable.

Among the main complaints made, on ethical grounds, against religion is that it encourages the sort of other-worldly preoccupation which hinders people from taking a proper and responsible part in the life of this world; it makes us bad citizens, as it has sometimes been put. This is the gist of Rousseau's celebrated complaint against Christians—they would make poor soldiers and have little heed of their rights and political privileges. There seems to me to be little substance in this complaint. Christianity, rightly understood, has a great deal to do with the way we live in this world. But there have, no doubt, been some forms of Christianity which have involved the sort of withdrawal from the world which does not accord properly with due heed to our present obligations — or indeed our rights. It is however in Oriental religions that we find most ground for the present accusation. For the more prone we become to regard our present existence as an unreal or illusory one the more likely are we to set our minds mainly on release or some kindred escape from the ills of our present lot; we shall not set ourselves to combat evil but to rise above it to some realm where it does not matter. Some forms of Buddhism would encourage this, although we should not forget the powerful emphasis on compassion in the Buddhist religion. It is Hinduism perhaps that lends itself most easily to a morally inhibiting indifference to the claims of the present life, and it may be worth noting again the grave concern of some progressively minded Hindus with this side of their religion. Sri Aurobindo wrote:

The principle of negation prevails over the principle of affirmation and becomes universal and absolute. Thence arise the great world-negating religions and philosophies; thence too a recoil of the life-motive from itself and a seeking after a life elsewhere flawless and eternal or a will to annul life itself in an immobile reality or an original non-existence.[1]

Aurobindo complains that the 'mighty shadow' of this kind of philosophy 'broods everywhere' in India.

This may be an exaggeration, and it must not be forgotten that there are many sides to Hinduism — and many forms of it. Much in the practice of it turns on a sense of justice in the universe at large which determines the lot of men in successive lives according to their merits; and any sophisticated form of Hindu monism would claim to have a proper place for high moral conduct within the scheme of things within which we function in some way as we do now. There is impressive

1. *The Life Divine*, p. 374.

ethical teaching in what many regard as the main Hindu scripture, *The Bhagavad-Gita*. But it can also be seen how easily a monistic religion could lead to an attitude of apathy and indifference to our own lot or that of others in this world, and that has certainly happened in some forms of Eastern religion.

It is, in the main, a somewhat different hazard that the Christian religion has to run. This comes about when certain doctrines are formulated in detachment from the relevant experience and literary context. Among such doctrines are various forms of the doctrine of 'the Fall' and Original Sin. These imply that men, in virtue of their corrupt and sinful state, are incapable of doing good. They cannot even recognize the good, for this is where they inevitably 'hold down the truth in unrighteousness'. Christian ideals become in this way 'impossible ideals' intended to bring our lives under condemnation and expose our need of redeeming grace. Exponents of these views appear little daunted by the unreasonableness of holding us guilty for failure to comply with standards which we could not recognize—we sin in ignorance and sin is unavoidable. The confusion which this engenders in our ethical thinking is atrocious, and although many of the prophets of these gloomy and reactionary doctrines belie much of their own teaching in their own lives and persons, there can be little doubt of the generally mischievous effects of their doctrines. Not the least of these is to make Christianity repellent to enlightened people. The same result follows from much that is taught about divine punishment, including at least most forms of the notion of vicarious punishment.

There is little doubt then that religious teaching can be morally harmful. The institutional life of religion has also sheltered, and sometimes actively encouraged, grievous practices of which persecution is an outstanding example. But we should always consider these in relation to the other sides of the picture. It is not enough to throw up one's hands in horror at the folly and wickedness to be found in various religions. We must pay heed also to the remarkable good which religion has done. Above all, the wise student will consider how it comes about that religion which, on the face of it, we should expect to be always on the side of goodness has in fact had features we deplore so much. How is it that it is possible at all to speak the words of the famous Latin line—*tantum religio potuit suadere malorum*?

Before dealing with this question we must note the position of those who think that religion is morally indifferent. Not many hold this position, and of those who do the majority are those who think that religion has very little substance and has played a negligible part in history on its own account; it is thought to be an accompaniment of processes which continue mainly by their own momentum. Some of those who hold that the course of history is wholly or largely determined by material factors would hold the present view of religion. But their position is an extremely implausible one. In one way or another religion has been a dominant factor in men's lives in the past; and if its claims have any substance we should expect it to continue to influence our conduct in radical and far-reaching ways.

We have seen that the influence of religion has not always been a good one. Opponents of religion will have their own explanations of this. If religion is false it is not surprising that men should be misled by it and that progressive thinking about moral and social questions should be hindered by religion—as implied in the view of religion as the 'opiate of the people'. But if religion is true we should expect religion and ethics to have much importance for one another; and if we can discover what is the proper relation between the two we can perhaps understand better how, in certain situations, they appear to be much estranged. Let us then proceed to the view that, in some way, religion and ethics have much importance for one another. This is the natural view to take, and it is by far the commonest view among those who have any regard for religion. It is indeed odd, to say the least, to suppose that religion and ethics do not go together. But what then more precisely is the relation between them?

On some views the answer is very simple. Religion is itself nothing but ethics—or ethics with relatively incidental accompaniments. This, as we have seen, is the position of Professor Braithwaite, and many influential theologians come very close to it today. The reader will not however expect me to comment further on these views. They have been considered already in another context. It will be more helpful to consider the place of morality in a less exiguous view of religion.

This brings me to a position which is very widely held, namely that ethics depends directly and wholly on religion. What is right, it is argued, is what God has ordained, and if religion is without substance then ethics, in any proper sense, must be found wanting also. Of this again there are two forms. It may be held that the distinctions we normally draw between good and bad, right and wrong and so forth, have no meaning or justification apart from religion. It may also be held that, without the help of religion, it is impossible for us to do what morality requires. These two positions often go together. They are also much confused, both by those who hold them and by others. A good example of the first position may be found in the work of Professor Leonard Hodgson. He takes a generally liberal view of theological questions, but he can none the less write as follows:

If this space-time universe, this developing process, be the whole of reality, I do not see how we can ever get beyond the acknowledging of it as a brute fact. Change follows change, and it so happens that among the products of the process are we human beings, with our capacity to observe and think about what is going on, and to make moral and aesthetic judgements. I can see that in such circumstances our observations of matters of fact, and generalizations based on them concerning the way in which things are likely to go on happening, might achieve a certain degree of objectivity. But I do not see how our judgements of value could ever be more than the expressions of our own subjective tastes; and those the tastes of finite creatures conditioned, during the brief span of their existence, by the outlook of our time and place. In theory, the last word would rest with the existentialist; in practice, with the dictator.[1]

I find it hard to understand how Professor Hodgson can write in these terms. I am sure that if he lost his religious faith he would not in fact side with the dictator or regard questions

1. *For Faith and Freedom*, p. 130.

of good and bad as matters of mere subjective taste. The question is not one we can discuss exhaustively here, for that would require us to go carefully into the problem of objectivity in ethics. But this is one of the points where disciplines obviously overlap, and the student is urged to consider here some of the arguments about ethical objectivity as they appear in more severely ethical writings. Some suggestions have already been made at the end of Chapter Two and a prominent place among these, as a further introduction to the problem, should be given to A. C. Ewing's *Teach Yourself Ethics*. In the meantime I add the following observations.

One should distinguish carefully between various senses in which good and bad (and other basic ethical notions) could be thought to be relative. It is plain, for example, that ethical requirements vary with the circumstances in which we find ourselves. There is normally nothing more innocent than drinking a tumblerful of water. But if I were in an open boat at sea, with a limited supply of water to last the whole company till land or help was reached, it would be exceptionally wicked of me to slake my thirst at will surreptitiously whenever I could do so. The duty of a doctor present at an accident is different from the duty of the ordinary man. But there is nothing to disconcert us here, and I should have no reluctance in allowing that every moral rule we can think of must admit of exceptions in some extraordinary circumstances. Nothing is absolute in ethics in the sense of holding irrespective of the facts of the situation in which we find ourselves.

What the advocate of objectivity needs to hold is that, granted the circumstances, there is something required of us in them irrespective of our own attitudes or decisions, something which is 'right in itself' as we say. Some might go further and hold that there are certain basic rules to which no exception is allowed. But this is an extremely difficult view to sustain, and it is in no way necessary for the 'objectivist' to try to do so. Among the factors relevant to a decision, moreover, are the opinions of people other than the agent who has a particular duty to perform. Compromises are required and deference, at some stage at least, to the views of others. We must also take account of social institutions, including political ones. The fact that some action is legally required of me is obviously a very important factor in deciding whether it is also ethically my duty. The question of how far we should compromise on matters of this kind is a complicated one and the reader should consider what various writers have said about it. It must suffice now to note that the inherent or objective character of moral obligation, and of the ethical notions that go with it, is not impugned by admitting the need for adjustment and compromises in the senses indicated.

The main point for us in this book is whether the case for ethical objectivity is affected by whether or not we hold some religious view. It seems plain to me that it is not. A strong consideration in support of this is the fact that some of the most careful and persuasive defences of ethical objectivity make no explicit reference to religion and are, in some instances, the work of agnostics and atheists. There is little mention of religion, for example, in Sir David Ross' notable *The Foundations of Ethics* or in A. C. Ewing's *The Definition of Good*, although both are religious people. G. E. Moore and C. D. Broad are pre-eminent advocates of ethical objectivity, Moore's *Principia Ethica* being perhaps the most famous of all statements of an objectivist view. But to neither of these did religion commend itself. Their arguments on ethical questions lose none of their force on that account, and I know of no way in which the case for the objectivity of ethics could be defended except by arguments like those used by the thinkers I have mentioned or by Brand Blanshard in a severely ethical discussion of the same question in his *Reason and Goodness*.

There is also a certain grave consequence of affirming a direct dependence of ethics on religion, namely that we should be committed to denying the right to speak in terms of good and bad, right and wrong, in any strict and proper sense, to all non-believers; and we should have thereby also to release them from all proper accountability. They would not be entitled to their judgements, it would not make sense from their point of view to recognize a moral obligation. But no one would seriously take that attitude. If an atheist does someone an injury we do not say that, as an atheist, he could not know better. We expect people, independently of their being religious, to recognize obvious duties in the same way as everyone else. Moreover, it seems beyond doubt that many unbelievers, including those just mentioned, have shown exceptional sensitivity to ethical questions, and some, like Gilbert Murray for example, have been extremely active in support of high ethical and social causes. Are we to say that it was inconsistent of them to do this, that, as they did not believe in God, there was no point in their working for the noble causes they served? Do we not all in fact know many unbelievers whose conduct is not merely beyond reproach but outstandingly praiseworthy? It is plain that we do, and no theory which denies that can begin to make sense.

Let me put the point in another way. Suppose we were convinced that there was no God or any life besides the present one, would we straightway conclude that we could do as we pleased, that if it appealed to us to hurt someone we had at our mercy we might as well do so, that there would be nothing wrong in leaving the needy and destitute to their fate, that the words 'cowardice', 'cruelty', 'boorishness' and so on would lose all significance? Obviously not. Pain is bad as pain, and not to relieve it when we can is in itself morally contemptible. We only need to exercise our normal faculties in finite situations to recognize some obligations and distinctions of worth.

Yes, it may be said, we would certainly recognize obligations of some sort even in a Godless world, but they would not be properly ethical, least of all objective. They would be matters of enlightened self-interest or personal predilection, there would be no inherent justification for such attitudes. Now there are many who say that ethics is a matter of enlightened self-regard or emotional attitudes or personal commitment, and we cannot examine their views closely now. There are also various ways in which objectivity in ethics has been understood. But it seems also plain that the way we normally understand good and bad, as distinctions we draw in ordinary finite contexts, is not affected by expressly religious notions, and that whatever we find to be involved in recognizing such distinctions holds on its own account.

This does not preclude our holding, if we wish, that ethical ideas have some religious implication. One of the most resolute advocates of moral autonomy, to use the technical term for the view that ethical notions hold on their own account, is Dr. A. C. Ewing; but he is also disposed to think that there may be an argument from ethics to religion. I do not quite agree with him, but it is not out of accord with his defence of moral autonomy to hold this further view about religion and ethics. It would not require him to accuse the atheist of inconsistency or folly but only of failure to see the truth of something further which Dr. Ewing holds about morality.

My own view is that we neither argue from ethical objectivity, or from ethics as understood in some other way, to the existence of God nor require God as some kind of support for the moral order. I claim that we can see that there must be God without inspecting particular features of the finite world, there could not be a world at all without God. But the insight through which this happens is an insight into there having to be a Reality which is complete and perfect in every way, and we can thus affirm that all there is is ultimately dependent on a Reality which is good through and through. In this sense, ethics like everything else is dependent on God, but this is a dependence whose exact nature we cannot understand and it is not peculiar to ethics, it is equally true of mathematics or of any matter of fact — or of all science; and it has nothing directly to do with the understanding of these matters in themselves.

He would be bold indeed who held that we could make sense of nothing without also seeing the truth of religion. We do not refute a scientific claim on religious grounds, any more than we bring religion into day-to-day affirmations, such as 'the sun is shining' or 'this table is hard'. The irreligious person is as well placed as any other to appreciate these things. If I am to show that the table is not hard I do not open the Bible or remind you of the Creed, I induce you to touch it. If your calculations in arithemetic are wrong I point out the error. There have indeed been people who have, in desperation, urged that there is a Christian mathematics, Christian chemistry, and so on. But this seems to me to be as implausible as any view can be. How would a Christian analysis of some substance in the laboratory differ from a non-Christian one? What would the Christian teacher of chemistry say that would be different from the teaching given by a non-Christian one? Are great advances in science made solely by Christians? Plainly not, and if the secular scientist is in error, he must be shown to be so on properly scientific grounds, not on religious ones. But why should ethics be in a different case?

It seems certain that it is not. We do not normally refer to religion to convince someone that an action is wrong. It is enough to say, 'it will cause so much pain' and so on. This does not mean that the moral qualities follow strictly from the facts of various situations. There can be much debate as to what is the linkage between fact and value, and the place to consider this closely is in a book on ethics. I myself believe that some specific ethical insight or intuition is involved at some point. But what concerns us now is that, however we understand ethical judgements as such, we make them and agree about them at the secular level in the same way as we do in other matters. Even when our ethical ideas have taken shape in a very religious setting religion does not come extensively into the existence of these ideas. We can share them with our secular friends and talk about them in common terms.

There is thus no dependence of ethics on religion which is radically different from the way other things lead to religion. Indeed, if we did not have some understanding of goodness as a finite concept it is hard to see how we could talk meaningfully of God as a supremely good or perfect Being. When, therefore, certain people fail to agree with us about God, it does not follow that we cannot agree with them about other things, or that we must suspect them of radical inconsistency. It is a pity that we cannot induce them to see the truth, as it seems to us, about God, and we may hope to convince them some day. But we should be pleased when we find that we stand on common ground in the promotion of certain ethical purposes.

Is this, then, the entire story? By no means. The topic has a further positive side which I must now briefly indicate.

FURTHER READING

References have already been supplied in Chapter Two on the general questions of ethical objectivity and responsibility. These may be supplemented now as follows:

Attacks on religion from an ethical standpoint may be found in several essays in *Objections to Humanism*, edited by H. J. Blackham (Constable). The very different view that ethics depends on religion is well exemplified in works like Emil Brunner's *Revelation and Reason* (S.C.M. Press) and Reinhold Niebuhr's *The Children of Light and the Children of Darkness* (Nisbet). Discussions of these positions will be found in my own *Morals and Revelation*. There is an excellent discussion of the view that ethics depends on religion in 'The Autonomy of Ethics', by A. C. Ewing (*Prospect for Metaphysics*, as above); and in the same volume D. A. Rees attempts a cautious statement of the view that ethics has some essential relation to religion. The general question at issue here is discussed from various points of view in a symposium on the autonomy of ethics published in the *Hibbert Journal*, Vols. XLVII and XLVI; there is a similar symposium, to which the contributors were R. Holland and myself, in the *Proceedings of the Aristotelian Society*, Supplementary Volume XXII.

An extremely penetrating recent study of the problems presented by the relations of ethics to religion is *The Theological Frontier of Ethics*, by W. G. Maclagan (Allen and Unwin). A liberal treatment of the same problems, in their Biblical and doctrinal context, is found in F. R. Tennant's *The Concept of Sin* (Cambridge), now a minor classic, and in *Religious Philosophy*, by H. A. Wolfson (Harvard Press). A study of some standard work on Christian Ethics, like *Basic Christian Ethics* by Paul Ramsey, will be very rewarding to the student at this stage.

For a comprehensive survey of ethical questions as they appear in a Christian context, I very much commend *Personality and the good* by Peter A. Bertocci and Richard M. Millard (Mckay).

CHAPTER TWENTY-THREE

THE VOICE OF GOD AND THE VOICE OF CONSCIENCE

It must now be stressed that religion is not just superimposed upon ethics or some concern we merely happen to have concurrently with being moral. It will be plain already from what was said earlier that the sense of God's perfection and holiness lends its additional sanction to judgements of worth and duty. But we have now to add also that it is within our ethical understanding that God works pre-eminently to disclose Himself. I have outlined already how we must think of revelation; it involves a deepening and refining of moral insight in a way which is to be assigned expressly to God and which we come to recognize as His dealing with us. It is in ethics that God comes nearest to us, and the link between ethics and religion is therefore very close. The voice of God is above all the voice of conscience, but not in the sense that it is nothing but one's conscience; it is a divine refinement of the working of conscience. But this presupposes in turn that conscience itself is operative, as a human endowment, on its own account. It could not otherwise be a medium for divine disclosure *to us*; it is not absorbed into religion, and we fall into grievous error if we suppose that it is—as many theologians have unfortunately done.

This makes the relation of ethics to religion a much more intimate one than if we merely postulate God as some kind of support for otherwise untenable ethical notions. The linkage is closest at the point where, as in central Christian notions, God is thought to come into intimate personal relations with men. It is in moral contexts more than any other that the fellowship we have with God takes shape.

These are matters which some critics of religion much overlook. Some humanist writers have attacked Christianity recently on the ground that it is authoritarian and despotic where moral issues are concerned. The assumption underlying this criticism is that the Christian claims to be given by God a set of principles which, in having explicit divine sanction, are invariable and infallible. It is as if God took us behind the scenes, as it were, and showed us the truth as it is for Him. But I have argued that we do not come to know the 'mind' of God in this way. We learn about Him from ways in which He is recognizably at work in some operations of the human aptitudes with which He endowed us, and as those gifts are imperfect we may be in error even when we are also convinced that God is helping and directing our thoughts.

Divine guidance, in short, is not something that comes to us 'out of the blue' or when, as some have recently taught, we empty our minds of everything else. God does not put His saints in a privileged position, nor does He speak to them as if, in some respect, they were also God—the mistaken supposition of some Barthian theologians who suppose that our ordinary faculties are so depraved that God can only speak to God within us. He speaks to us in ways we can understand as men and through the faculties which He has given us. This means that religious people have to live in the same world of strains and tensions as other human beings, they are not lifted above the level of agonizing moral perplexities. On questions of fact, as these bear on ethical decisions, there is no reason to expect a religious person to have invariably a sounder understanding than his secular neighbour, he may sometimes be badly out on his facts. But his moral insights are also fallible, and thus although the influence of religion in ethics is one of refining and correcting, it may be operative in a situation where in other ways we are gravely in error; and this is one of the reasons why men have sometimes felt convinced that God was instructing them to do things which we would consider atrocious today. We must not suppose that God was not at work at all in situations where men did barbarous things in His name. But for that very reason we must not cease our vigilance in trying to understand how the course of revelation has involved much correction of what was said 'of old' and in grasping properly what God has to say to us in the complexities of the situation in which we find ourselves today. There is no 'short way' for the Christian in these matters, nor any 'laying down of arms'.

It can of course be conceded to humanist critics that in practice religious communities have often been intolerant and harsh. The institutionalizing of religion carries with it that peril. When one speaks in the name of God one is apt to become arrogant and dogmatic, and the firmness of prophetic conviction tends to become the rigidity of conservative habit made more unyielding by vested interest. Few things are plainer in the history of religion than the constancy of this sort of temptation. It *is* all the same a temptation and one against which we are increasingly warned in the ripening of religious consciousness. In the refinement of religion we are led to appreciate better that God does not guide us by absolute rules imposed altogether from without but by patiently bringing us, in ever more intimate fellowship with Himself, to more mature and discerning ethical insights. These we are entitled to express with firmness but not in any spirit of arrogance and intolerance. Nothing is further removed from authoritarianism than the teaching and example of Jesus.

It is in similar ways that ethical factors function in the more rounded insight by which the Christian claims to recognize the work and person of Christ. Here also God speaks to us as the creatures He has made us, and, even when we come to the point of acknowledging the teaching of Jesus as the teaching of a person who is also God incarnate, the assimilation of this teaching into our own experience and the application of it to new and changing situations involve the alert and subtle exercise of our own quickened ethical sensitivity.

This must not however lead, as it has often done of late, to a sense of complete uncertainty and imprecision in ethics. To abjure infallibility is not to say we have no sort of compass. The conscience within which God speaks is truly conscience. There is nothing in the inwardness and flexibility of genuinely religious ethics to warrant a lax and fumbling ethical attitude, least of all on matters where even elementary ethical principles at their own level are precise and certain. When the voice of God is heard within the voice of conscience it is not the voice of easy accommodation but that of a deepening of all that we already associate with conscience and with the accumulation of ethical wisdom in the past. It is genuine conscience, not an ostentatious accommodation with prevailing fashion, that is to be sanctified in the service of religion.

Religious conviction will, moreover, bring with it additional religious duties. To become aware of God is to have a new relationship which requires to be sustained and cultivated in certain ways, and this will have ramifications throughout the range of our other duties. God is a Being to be worshipped, and while worship is the natural response of any person who is profoundly aware of God this may also impose strains and exactions which have to be met in various ways. Religious sensitivity brings its own temptations and its own opportunities for special service, and there is also the need to persist when faith becomes uncertain and weak. Religious observances are often described as religious duties, but it is not merely in outward observance but in many other more subtle ways that religion summons its votaries to performances and cultivation of attitudes of mind which have no relevance in a secular context.

There remains now a somewhat different problem. For in ethics we have not only to consider how we determine what is good or right, but also to ask how we come to do right. The root problem here is that of freedom. It seems absurd to tell someone that he ought to do something unless we believe that he can do it. But what sort of 'can' is this? Is it enough that we have the mental or physical power to carry out what we propose? Some would say that we must also be free in adopting our purposes, there must be a basic freedom of choice. Thus arises one of the most persistent and perplexing of all philosophical problems — the problem of free will. This is again much too vast a problem to be considered carefully in this book, and I must again urge the reader to extend his understanding of the subject by making full use of writings like the ones listed at the end of the chapter. It will be very hard to make headway with some religious questions without having a very clear understanding of what is involved in the problem of freedom and responsibility as an ethical problem. Ethics and religion impinge very closely on one another here.

Those who deny that we have free will are usually called determinists, those in the opposite camp are called libertarians. But the issue is not always as clear as this. For there are many forms of determinism and many ways in which the libertarian position may be understood. Some hold that everything we do is entirely determined by certain states of our bodies. This is the more extreme form of determinism. Others allow that mental processes are effective on their own account, subject of course to certain physical conditions, but hold that our actions are none the less determined by the sort of persons we are at the time, that being in turn determined by heredity, environment and so on. Some of those who think this argue that we can still be considered accountable for what we do, for, they insist, the determination takes place through our own natures and understanding, it is 'self-determination'. This kind of determinism thus claims to have room for free will, and there can thus be a confusing overlap of positions which are said to be determinist or libertarian. The strict libertarian holds that self-determination is not enough. To be fully responsible, on his account, I must be free in a way that is not determined at all, it must be possible to say that I could have acted otherwise even though everything else remained the same.

A stock objection to the strict libertarian position consists in pointing out that there is an obvious continuity of character and conduct. We are able within limits to anticipate one another's conduct, we rely on one another in various ways. This would hardly be possible if, as it has been put, 'any action could come from any man at any time'. The libertarian counters by urging that we only exercise absolute freedom of choice within certain limits, usually those provided by the opposition of what we most want to do at some time and what we think we ought to do. For much of our lives duty and interest, as it is put, coincide; we want to do on the whole what we feel we should do. The libertarian can thus allow for the normal and extensive continuity of conduct and character.

The determinist who feels that his position has room for

accountability and freedom will not find it hard to maintain that, while we are accountable creatures and capable of sinful actions, all that we do is in the last analysis determined by God. The providence of God, it will be said, is operative everywhere; and it may also be urged that when we do right this is solely through the help of God or by the influence of His grace upon us. This, however, will not satisfy the strict libertarian. He will argue that, however the act is determined, it cannot be subject to moral praise or blame unless the responsibility for it rests on the agent himself. It will be stressed that, if our good actions are ascribed to God, then God must in the last resort be the author of our evil actions as well.

This is the point where many thinkers find certain religious affirmations highly objectionable on ethical grounds. The notion of inevitable sin, of a sin that we inherit or share with others, of sin that comes about through the way God Himself hardens our hearts, is thought by many religious people, as well as by critics of religion, to be morally repugnant and out of accord with what we think in other regards about God. I fully share such misgivings, even when it is said that the sin is made inevitable through the alleged 'Fall' of man and his rebelliousness. The traditional doctrine of the 'Fall' seems to me full of confusions and out of accord with some of the plainest deliverances of our moral consciousness. I go further and agree with the strict libertarian that if we are properly accountable for our actions we must be unambiguously free in choosing to do or not to do our duties. But this does not mean that I would brush aside wholly the scriptural references and kindred considerations which suggest the determinist views to which I object. There is something of importance to be learnt from the sense men have had that God had Himself hardened their hearts or blinded them so that 'they could not see' the course to be followed. But it is in contexts of this kind that we need the probing and imaginative reconstruction mentioned earlier. We may then discard certain notions altogether as undiluted error, in others we may find much truth which has been distorted or misrepresented by taking certain religious affirmations, especially highly figurative ones, at their face value or by failing to realize that what is said in the intensity of some religious mood may only uncover certain sides of a rounded religious experience.

Nowhere is the need for imaginative study of religion greater than in respect to the points where religion impinges most closely on questions of freedom and accountability as these present themselves in ethical thought. The topic is a central one for the philosophy of religion and it throws into sharp relief certain features of current theological controversy which call specially for patient philosophical examination. I cannot pursue the matter further here, but I shall be referring to it again (in Chapter Twenty-five) and giving some indication of the way in which I approach the subject myself.

FURTHER READING

Conscience and its Problems by K. E. Kirk (Longmans)

Christ and Conscience by N. H. G. Robinson (Nisbet)

Conscience and Christ by H. Rashdall (Duckworth)

Conscience in the New Testament by C. A. Pierce (S.C.M. Press)

I deal with the theme of the present chapter in two papers in the *Congregational Quarterly*, 'Crisis and the Christian' (Jan. 1950) and 'Religion and Mystery' (Jan. 1952).

CHAPTER TWENTY-FOUR

THE SOUL

This book has been mainly about God and the way we know Him. No other course would have been appropriate, least of all as I understand the subject. God is the chief concern of religion, and my guiding purpose has been to give a fair impression of the way we must think about God and His place in human experience. But there are two sides to religion — the side of God and the side of man. In saying what I have said about God I have said some things, and implied others, about man. These admit of much further study, and a sound appreciation of the God-man relation requires a proper understanding also of the nature of man and his capacities. In this chapter I offer a very brief outline of the matters most to be heeded here.

Importance has already been ascribed to the distinctness of persons and it has been shown how much this is overlooked or belied in various forms of monism, that is in systems of thought or religions which treat the individual as a phase or element in some one whole of being. No more need be said on that topic now. But the battle for the soul of the individual has to be fought on more than one front. One of these is the theological one. Indication has already been given of the tendency of some theological doctrines to absorb the individual, metaphorically speaking, in some alleged corporate entity which is no person in particular, and of this again nothing further can be said at present. But it is necessary to indicate one very important contemporary context in which the notion of the individual soul, as Western religion at least has normally thought of it, is gravely imperilled. This arises from the direction taken by recent philosophy, for just as traditional monism implied a metaphysical threat to the usual idea of the soul, so we find a different but complementary anti-metaphysical trend closing like the other arm of a pincer movement on the heavily beleaguered citadel of the idea of the soul. He who would defend 'the soul' today must be flexible and resourceful and willing to deploy his forces in more than one direction.

To leave metaphor, I am referring of course to current empiricism and its accompaniments. As we have seen, no consistent empiricist can allow for any reality which is not entirely comprehensible in terms of the reports of our senses. We have seen in a fairly extensive way how this bears on the idea of God. But it is no less fatal to the idea of the soul as some reality distinct from the body and capable of outlasting it. Indeed it could well be said that the idea of the soul provides in some ways a more formidable and inescapable challenge to empiricism than the idea of God. The latter might seem to be the more ponderous challenge, since it involves a more preeminently spiritual and transcendent Being. But the idea of at least a self or person of some kind is more difficult to escape. The empiricist can say that he will dispense with the idea of God; if he is an unbeliever the idea of God need not disturb his empiricism. But no one can with any plausibility deny that he must refer in some way to himself and to other persons. We cannot avoid the language of 'I' and 'thou' and 'him' and 'me' and 'they', though we can in actual fact, whatever the impoverishment involved, eschew religious language. An account of some kind must thus be given of what is meant by a self or person, and the empiricist is forced thus to essay what seems a very difficult task, namely to account for all that we mean by the idea of a person in terms of what we can publicly observe.

This makes the doctrine of the soul a very decisive crux in contemporary thought. We have seen already that it is crucial in other theological and metaphysical ways. But by its place at the centre of philosophical controversy today it may well prove to be the pivotal point which will determine what shifts of emphasis the future will see and what course will be given to culture in its many forms.

There have been empiricists who have not shrunk from the implications of this theory, for the notion of personality, in its fullest rigour. Of such, to his credit, was David Hume. He sought to reduce the self to a series of fleeting impressions and ideas, eliminating thus not only the reference to some more abiding physical reality but also all recognition of any permanent reality on the inner side of the flow of sensory events. The feeling we have that the self is more substantial than this is ascribed by Hume to certain relations and resemblances between our perceptions, especially the way they influence one another through memory in the form of association of ideas. Hume is convinced that an explanation in these terms is unavoidable, for he is certain that he discovers nothing in himself besides 'a bundle or collection of different perceptions'. As he puts it in oft quoted words:

For my part, when I enter most intimately into what I call *myself*, I always stumble on some particular perception or other, of heat or cold, light or shade, love or hatred, pain or pleasure. I never catch myself at any time without a perception, and never can observe anything but the perception. . . . The mind is a kind of theatre, where several perceptions successively make their appearance; pass, glide away, and mingle in an infinite variety of postures and situations. . . . The comparison of the theatre must not mislead us. They are the successive perceptions only, that constitute the mind; nor have we the most distant notion of the place, where these scenes are represented, or of the materials, of which it is composed.

Those who wish to look closely into the subsequent history of the subject, and the student is here as elsewhere advised to do this if he can, must consider Kant's claim to have answered Hume at this point, as elsewhere in his theory of mind and knowledge, on the basis of the unity of our experience. To grasp relations between various items in the 'world of objects' we apprehend we must be distinct from each of them. There must be some centre or focus to which the impressions are referred or a subject which holds them together. But at the moment we can do little more than note how sharply the controversy has flared up again in our time. Hume had the consistency to see that, if empiricism is true, no account of the self as some abiding entity can be sound; and with the vigorous revival of his kind of philosophy today the dissolution of the soul, as some kind of spiritual entity, is again at hand and the task is renewed of giving some account of the way we normally think of ourselves without invoking any reality that is not observable and capable of being described in empiricist terms.

There have been many notable attempts to do this. A typical instance, and one that has perhaps been more discussed than any other, is that of Professor Gilbert Ryle as we find it especially in *The Concept of Mind*. Professor Ryle appears to have two main aims. The first is to exhibit the absurdity, as he sees it, of what he calls the 'official view', namely the view of the soul as some unobservable inner entity. The second is to offer an alternative account of the way we must understand the mind or the self. In pursuing the first aim Professor Ryle declares that he intends to proceed 'with deliberate abusiveness', and I think that in this at least he undoubtedly succeeds. Whether that strengthens his case or inspires confidence and a sense of his conducting an impartial philosophical inquiry, the reader must judge for himself.

The main butt of Professor Ryle's attack is Descartes and his notion of the soul as a substance or distinct reality interacting with another substance, the body. The word substance may not be the best one for us to use here, it suggests some kind of solid stuff; and it was certainly not Descartes' intention to give that impression of the mind. He meant mainly that a mind was a distinct entity (*res* or 'thing' is another term he uses) and he was following here the traditional use of the Latin terms. The mind is not reducible to the body, nor the body to the mind, nor can a mind be conflated with another mind. But mind and body influence one another, or interact, and the relation between them is peculiar and intimate. The mind is not strictly *in* the body, as a pilot is in a vessel, to use Descartes' own comparison. Indeed, the mind is not *in* anything, since it is not a spatial entity; the essence of mind is thought, the essence of body is extension. But in spite of being so radically different these two are in a peculiarly close relation through the influence of one on the other.

An admirable statement of the position which Descartes represents and to which he gave classic expression is provided by Professor R. J. Hirst. He writes:

The essential notions seem to be; first that there are two distinct orders of being or substances, the mental and the material. Mind or mental substance is neither perceptible by the senses nor extended in space; it is intelligent and purposive and its essential characteristic is thought, or rather consciousness. The body on the other hand is part of material substance, perceptible and extended, it lacks purpose and consciousness and, at the macroscopic level at least, is governed by rigid laws of cause and effect. Secondly, the person or self is strictly to be identified with mind and to be regarded as a mental substance; each one of us is primarily and in reality a mind or soul, though in some ways associated with a body. Hence one can legitimately speak of the mind as the entity that experiences, wills and thinks.[1]

Professor Hirst does not accept this view and I shall note some of his objections to it shortly. But in the meantime let us return to Professor Ryle. In his presentation of 'the official doctrine', also described as 'Descartes' myth', he writes:

Some would prefer to say that every human being is both a body and a mind. His body and his mind are ordinarily harnessed together, but after the death of the body his mind may continue to exist and function.

The term 'harnessed' as used here is significant. It is hard to avoid using some metaphor in describing the relation of mind and body. But it is revealing that, at the very outset, Professor Ryle should be using a metaphor which suggests very strongly that he is thinking of mental processes, as envisaged in a Cartesian position, as closely analogous to material ones or, as he later affirms to be the case, a duplicate of them. 'Harnessing' strongly suggests the yoking of two material things. But the alleged relation of mind and body is a unique one and not to be assimilated at all to the relations of physical things to one another. I think this is what Professor Ryle most overlooks when, in pursuance of the policy of 'deliberate abusiveness', he lampoons Descartes' theory as the doctrine of 'the ghost in the machine' and treats distinct acts of thought or purposing as being, on the view he rejects, duplicates or rehearsals of the visible physical behaviour. In all this he closely resembles Hume. Hume declared, as we have seen, that he could 'never catch himself at any time without a

1. *The Problems of Perception*, p. 181.

perception'; and I suspect that the trouble with Hume, as with his philosophical progeny today, is that he sets out with the assumption that there must be something to be observed sensibly, or in some kindred way, in the mind—or nothing. It does not occur to him to look for anything that is in no way like a perception. Much of the force of Professor Ryle's polemic against the sharp distinction of mind and body turns on presenting alleged distinct mental processes as quasi-physical ones of which there is clearly no manifestation in experience. It is easy to ridicule the notion of shadowy mysterious inner 'transactions' once the idea is implanted that if they exist at all they must be like processes in the world outside us. We can laugh at the notion of my thought and purposes literally going on in my head, and once the Cartesian is manoeuvred into saying something vaguely like this, his case is also easily put to scorn. But Descartes in fact went out of his way to insist that mind is not in space at all. When I sustain my intention to ride a bicycle there is no frantic ghostly inner pedalling to 'rehearse' the physical process, but if my action is willed or conscious there must surely be something going on all the time besides the physical pedalling. This is a *sui generis* mental process.

If the question is asked: 'How do we come to know such processes, since they cannot be observed like external occurrences?', the answer must be that everyone is aware of his own mental processes in having them, it is not a case of looking on at our thoughts or wishes or emotions or of noting them in some way. We may indeed note them if we wish, and much of the work of psychology, especially in introspection, consists in doing just that. But this is made possible because there is the awareness of what these mental states are like in having them. It is not even a case of immediately observing what 'goes on' in our minds, like turning round to watch ourselves, but rather, in the first instance, the awareness of a mental process involved in having it, we might well say indissoluble from having it. For this the philosopher Samuel Alexander, often regarded as the last of the great meta-physicians, coined the phrase[1] 'living through'; and he spoke

1. *Space, Time and Deity*, p. 11.

in the same way of 'enjoying' our mental states. This is the 'experienc*ing*' as distinct from the 'experienc*ed*'.

It is this alleged 'private access' that Professor Ryle is most concerned to deny. He contends that if we had such privileged access to our own thoughts, if we knew ourselves in some way which others could not share, we could not ever be mistaken about ourselves. Neither our friends nor the professional psychologist could ever correct our own impression of ourselves. But it is plain that they often can. This need not however trouble the advocate of 'private access' very much. For he can well allow that we may be mistaken in our way of describing our mental states or in our view of their relations to one another; and above all he can admit errors in our estimate of what we are likely to think or do on some future occasion—and that we may forget what we were like in the past. The privileged access and the knowledge which in essentials cannot be mistaken concern some states of mind while we have them.

Professor Ryle also supposes that to have privileged access to our own minds would be tantamount to being imprisoned in unrelieved solitude. 'Absolute solitude', he declares, 'is on this showing the ineluctable destiny of the soul. Only our bodies can meet.' A theory which had this consequence, for which the technical name 'solipsism' is sometimes used[1], would obviously be absurd. But 'private access' involves nothing of the kind. It is our own thoughts that we know strictly at first hand. But this does not preclude us from having very full and intimate knowledge of the thoughts of others in indirect ways. As has been stressed earlier I cannot know your thoughts as I know my own, but in other ways I can know them very well indeed.

A further common ploy of Professor Ryle's is to accuse the traditionalist or the sponsor of the official view of falling into linguistic confusions, most of all in the form of 'category mistakes'. This happens when we fail to note the very different ways in which certain expressions are used. We have seen instances of that earlier. Professor Ryle adds some entertaining

1. The term is also used for the dogmatic denial of the existence of anything other than myself.

ones. He refers for example to the 'lady who arrived in a sedan chair and a flood of tears', and it is plain how ridiculous it would be to suppose that we meant the same sort of thing in the two descriptions of the lady's arrival. More seriously he warns us not to overlook the difference between saying that the tide is *rising* and saying that hopes are *rising*. And following on this he accuses his opponents of supposing that when we say that mental events *occur* we mean the same as when we say that physical processes *occur*. Now we can make mistakes of confusing different uses of language, and we would do so if anyone supposed that hopes could rise in the same way as the tide. But we are not bound to fall into such mistakes, and it does not seem to me that there is anything out of place, but on the contrary all good sense, in supposing that thoughts occur no less truly than outward events — we have certain thoughts, or they go on as we say, for a certain time, they are real happenings — I have certain thoughts about Professor Ryle's work while writing this passage. Such thoughts obviously occur. Suggestions of linguistic lapses cannot do duty for explicit refutation.

Professor Ryle also gives much prominence to a distinction between 'knowing that' and 'knowing how'. I know *that* it is raining, I know *how* to play cricket. I am not recalling certain truths to mind, or enunciating rules or giving myself instructions when I know how to play. This is certainly true. But it does not follow that there is no on-going mental process of any kind beyond the physical movements while I play. The surgeon's skill does not, indeed, 'function in his tongue uttering medical truths', but does it follow, as Professor Ryle concludes, that it consists '*only* in his hands making the correct movement'? The surgeon is continuously purposing these movements, although not of course in the way of a shadowy 'rehearsal'.

Closely connected with this preceding argument, and very indicative of Professor Ryle's position as a whole, is the proneness to suppose that mental processes, if they occurred at all, would be easily datable and that they must be thought to monopolize our history while they do so and that they alternate with the physical processes they influence: as if in digging the garden I took some time off my physical digging to do the necessary volition, then dug a while and then again, as the impetus died down, reverted to the mental activity and gave my physical movements a further jolt by another volition, acts of will being to the physical movements of digging what a shunting engine is to the trucks. This is obviously the crudest parody, and it ignores altogether the many-sided character and varieties of our mental processes at any time and the fact that they continue during the physical processes they direct.

On its positive side Professor Ryle's position turns much on his account of dispositions. Having dispensed with the 'inner man' altogether, he induces certain dispositions to take his place. A disposition is not unlike certain qualities of material things. We say, for example, that the glass is brittle. This does not mean that the glass has been, or ever will in fact, be shattered; it only means that it will be shattered in certain conditions, if a stone is thrown at it for example. In the same way I may be generous or I may have a bad temper; I may not be making a gift now, perhaps I have little to give, but I am prone to give at need when I can, and, while I may not be angry at the moment, I am very easily made angry. Dispositional traits of this kind make us the sort of persons we are, and among our dispositions are many beliefs about things which are not in our thoughts at a particular time. I believed this morning, and have believed all day, that Paris is in France, but I have not had this thought in mind, or any other thought about Paris, at any time during the day before this moment. In addition, if I can be said to know certain things (in distinction from merely believing them) there are various things which I must be able to do, like giving the right answer to certain questions. Our dispositions and abilities are in these ways very important, and careful heed of them, and of the many varieties of them (like the ones we are aware of and the unconscious ones), is very necessary in a proper study of man and his nature. Professor Ryle is justified in giving them prominence.

It is another matter, however, to reduce all that we normally regard as ongoing mental processes to dispositional tendencies and abilities. Take the sensation of pain, to choose an example which Professor Ryle himself admits to be a difficult one for him. If I am in pain I certainly tend to do certain things, to clasp or massage the place which hurts, to shout aloud, to seek help, to run to the doctor, and so on. But none of this is what I mean by 'being in pain'. The pain is what I directly feel and which accounts for my proneness to do these various things. A tickle was once said by Professor Ryle to be an 'inhibited disposition to scratch'.[1] This seems to me about as false as anything can be. The tickle itself is a sensation which I feel and which makes me liable to scratch. Anyone can observe the scratching or hear my cries of pain, and my friends can discover how readily I cry out if I am hurt, but no one can have my pain in the sense in which I have it. They may sympathize and share my pain in that way, and this may even induce a like pain for them. But no one can strictly feel my pain for me. It is mine alone and I know it as no one else can.

If Professor Ryle's position collapses at this point it is put in peril at once on the entire front. I have little doubt that there are mental processes quite distinct from observable behaviour and that each individual has an access to his own experiences in having them which is not possible for the most favoured observer.

Many have tried to mend the breach made in Professor Ryle's position or to provide an alternative to the 'official doctrine' less severely at odds with our normal impression. Mr. Peter Strawson, for example, in a well-known book,

1. But he has modified this a little since. In his article "Feelings", in the *Philosophical Quarterly* for April 1951 he wrote: "Having or feeling the tickle, I have an impulse to scratch or rub the part of my cheek that was brushed by the cobweb. But feeling the tickle is surely not the cause of which the impulse to scratch is an effect . . . I have elsewhere argued for the idea that a tickle just *is* a thwarted impulse to scratch. . . . But I do not think now that this will do. . . . There is a close parallel between feeling a tickle and feeling like writing to the "*Times*". Both are bound up with not-yet-satisfied inclinations to do certain things." The main point seems to be an alleged existence of a logical relation between feeling tickled and wanting to scratch or laugh, "to feel tickled seems logically and not merely causally to involve having an impulse to laugh. . . My feeling tickled was, more nearly, an effect of the existence of an impediment to laughing. It was amusement under duress."

Individuals, allows that we must distinguish between mental characteristics and physical characteristics, but he is also convinced that we cannot 'drive a wedge' between them; for they belong, not to a composite entity but literally to the same thing. 'The very same thing' is tall, so many stones in weight, etc., and brave, angry, thinking about philosophy and so forth. Much of the argument in support of this position turns on the way we talk, in effect on the appeal to ordinary language. We say 'I am tall' and we say 'I am angry'. This is of course quite correct. I am sitting at the table and I am thinking about mind and body now. But this is after all a very rough description of the facts. It is quite adequate for ordinary purposes and it serves these better by being very simple. It would be wastefully clumsy to be always saying 'My mind is pondering a problem and my body is sitting at the table'. Indeed 'sitting' implies something that is willed or intended. But important distinctions, including distinctions which are very evident to us, need not be reflected in what we normally say. If they are very general distinctions it would not be relevant to mention them all the time. We thus cannot allow philosophical questions to be settled by what we normally find it most convenient to say.

One of Mr. Strawson's other main arguments turns on the assumption that we can only know one sort of thing in one sort of way, a variation on the theme that meaning depends on method of verification. If this principle holds we can only know mental characteristics in one way. But it is evident that when we know other people's minds their bodies are involved, and it seems thus to follow that the body must be involved in any knowledge we have of our own minds. But neither Mr. Strawson nor any who proceed in like fashion have shown what justification there is for the initial assumption that one sort of thing can only be known in one sort of way—it seems to be just a piece of positivistic dogmatism.

The same attitude is reflected in the contention that we see certain bodily movements, like coiling a rope, as actions, that is we see a movement which is also a purpose. But it would be more correct to say that what we strictly *see* is the physical movement and that we infer from the nature of this that there is a certain purpose behind it. At this point Mr. Strawson's position comes fairly close to the views of Professor Stuart Hampshire in a very difficult book, *Thought and Action*. It would be very hard to reproduce the substance of Professor Hampshire's intricate arguments within a short space. But the drift of them can perhaps be seen in statements like the following:

The 'mistake has always been not to acknowledge that the standpoint of the observer is one physical fact among others, and that the observer is always a self-moving body among other bodies which he observes and intentionally manipulates'.[1] 'I do not know how I would identify myself as a disembodied being, and I do not know what this hypothesis means.'[2] 'We are in the world as bodies among bodies, not only as observers but as active experimenters.'[3]

There are many variations on this and kindred themes in recent philosophy, and many extensive critical discussions of those. It is hoped that the reader will sample such writings for himself and consider them more closely than is possible here. They lie at the heart of recent philosophical controversy.

But these are not the only features of the mind-body controversy to have prominence today. The subject has also been debated much in terms that turn less on prevailing philosophical fashions. This has led to impressive restatement of more traditional, and to my mind more weighty, arguments against the sharp distinction of mind and body — a position to which the word 'dualism' is often applied, although, as we have seen, the words 'monism' and 'dualism' have other uses in quite different contexts. Samples of such arguments may be found in Chapter Seven of the book by Professor R. J. Hirst from which I have quoted already, namely *The Problems of Perception*. Here we are reminded of the difficulty which many have felt of acknowledging the influence on one another of entities so essentially different from one another as mind and body are alleged to be on the interactionist thesis. Does not causal efficacy require some common nature? To this

1. *Thought and Action*, p. 50.
2. op. cit., p. 50.
3. op. cit., p. 53.

other writers have replied, very properly in my view, that we only learn about specific causal relations from experience of them, this being something which empiricists like Hume have themselves helped us to realize. We cannot on dogmatic *a priori* grounds rule out causal relations, however peculiar, if we find in fact that they do occur. Another difficulty is the obviously close dependence of mind on body—the slightest damage to my brain and my mind is deranged, a stuffy atmosphere and I am dull. No one can deny these facts. But they do not tell directly against the interactionist thesis as such, as Professor Hirst tends to think. They only accentuate the difficulty of expecting the mind to survive the body and function on its own. But even here, the difficulty, although serious, is not fatal. The facts show a very close dependence of mind on body in the conditions we normally find, they do not show that the mind could not function at least independently of my present body under some other conditions or in some other kind of existence.

Professor Hirst's own position is that thinking and other experiences are the inner aspects of process of which the outer aspect is brain activity. The distinction to be drawn is not between two separate (but connected) processes, but between different ways in which the one process is disclosed. This is sometimes called 'The Identity Hypothesis' and at other times 'The Double Aspect Theory'. It implies, in the words of the author himself, that our experiences are 'the same events or activities as neurologists may observe from without'. My own objection to this position is a basic one, namely that we know from the very nature of what thoughts are like that they cannot be the same as the brain or any other part of my body. The neurologist may examine my brain but he certainly does not observe my thoughts, however close the dependence of my thoughts on what can be observed. The Identity Hypothesis gets into serious difficulties also over the question of freedom. It certainly could not allow genuine libertarian choice between truly open possibilities; but it is hard to see how it could even admit that thoughts and purposes have any course of their own or any efficacy. If a process of thought is another aspect of changes in the brain, it would seem possible in principle, however difficult in fact, to anticipate what I shall do in the future on the basis of adequate knowledge of the state of my body (in particular my brain) and my material environment. It could be known in this way, for instance, that I shall shortly get up and open the door. But in that case is it not an illusion that my mind, my thoughts and intentions and so on, have anything to do with it? My opening the door would be a foregone conclusion whatever I thought about it — or is it that I am bound to think as I do because of the physical movement? Both views seem quite out of accord with experience.

Some try to cope with this problem through what is known as 'the principle of complementarity'. This means, to reduce it to very simple terms, that we could give two very different, but complementary accounts of the same thing — or, in the current jargon, tell two different stories. We could describe the same process in material object terms and also in terms of purpose and choice — much as print on a page may be considered as ink on paper and also as meaningful statements. But the latter is a very questionable analogy, and it is hard to see how the 'two stories' could be told without implying two very different things or processes to be described. The principle of complementarity has in any case been very much blown upon of late.[1]

My own conclusion is that no recent discussions of the mind-body problem have succeeded in showing that we can dispense with an absolute distinction between mind and body, and I much urge the student, when he has taken a good look at criticisms of 'the official doctrine', like the ones noted in this chapter, to consider equally carefully some of the impressive restatements of the dualistic or interactionist position, like those of Dr. A. C. Ewing and Professor C. A. Campbell. I have made little mention of these and kindred writers in this chapter, mainly because I have been myself following the sort of course they take. But study of them will be very rewarding.

It should also be borne carefully in mind that, while

1. See P. Alexander's 'Mackay on Complementary Descriptions', *Mind*, Vol. LXVII.

empiricism has been having its day in the philosophy of the English speaking world and reflecting much that we find in contemporary thoughts and attitudes, in other countries, and especially in France and Germany, the picture has been very different. In particular, existentialist thinkers have made the problems of personality central to their thought and have laid much stress on freedom and responsible decision. Much of their thought is impressionistic and lacks the clarity and coherence of good philosophy. But it has also much penetration and a shrewd, almost prophetic, sense of where the cruces and growing points are found in contemporary thought and culture. It can summon much literary power to its service; and even in the accents of a harsh, almost morbid, secularism, it betrays a profound concern for the fate and dignity of man as a spiritual being. Much of this kind of existentialism centres on the 'interiority' of what is deepest in man's nature, and few have given finer expression to this than the French thinker whom many professional English philosophers consider to be the figure of most philosophical consequence among the existentialists, namely Merleau-Ponty. It is the interiority of consciousness that he made the theme of an inaugural lecture which he delivered at Paris shortly before his untimely death, at the age of fifty-three, ended his tenure of a professorship which he would have made very influential and distinguished.

It is this interiority, rightly understood, that I would also stress. My stand is thus at the opposite pole to the denial of 'private access' that has been so much the fashion. A proper defence of it would require much space and consideration of issues beyond the scope of this kind of book. But I shall attempt, in the next chapter, to give an indication of some of the main ways in which the present feature of human existence bears upon some of the central concerns of religion and on major theological questions. I shall only manage to raise the curtain on the scene as I see it.

FURTHER READING

The student would do well at this stage to ponder closely the very different views of the self to be found in the work of Descartes (see specially 'Second Meditation' in the selections by Anscombe and Geach, pp. 66–75) and Hume (*Treatise of Human Nature*, Part IV) and then go on to Kant's reply to Hume as it is expounded in A. C. Ewing's 'A Short Commentary on Kant's Critique of Pure Reason' and in H. J. Patons' 'Self Identity' in his *In Defence of Reason* (Hutchinson). Attention could then be given to those who write today in the tradition of Hume, e.g. Gilbert Ryle in *The Concept of Mind* — Chapters I and II and Chapters VI and IX especially (Hutchinson) and Peter Strawson in Chapter III of his *Individuals* and Stuart Hampshire in *Thought and Action* (Chatto and Windus). Papers in criticism of these views will be found in *Clarity is not Enough* (as above) and in the first part of C. A. Campbell's *Selfhood and Godhood*. A classical defence of the notion of the self as a non-material entity will be found in James Ward's *Psychological Principles* (Cambridge) and there is a celebrated criticism of materialism in G. F. Stout's *Mind and Matter*, Chapters IV, V, VI and VII — Stout thinks however that mind and matter involve one another and thus speaks of 'the embodied self'. A notable treatment of the problems of self identity is found in C. D. Broad's *The Mind and its Place in Nature* (Kegan Paul) — see especially Chapter III. In Chapter VII of *The Problems of Perception* (Allen and Unwin) R. J. Hirst criticizes the interactionist view of mind and body and defends the view that both are aspects of the same reality. Much of the physiological information relevant to this problem is found in *Man on his Nature* by Charles Sherrington (Cambridge). Helpful suggestions for the study of the mind–body problem appear in Nicolai Hartmann's *Ethics*, Volume III (Allen and Unwin), especially the notion of 'plus of determination'. A key to existentialist accounts of personality will be found in *Six Existentialist Thinkers* (Kegan Paul), by H. J. Blackham, and the reader who wishes to go deeper into the subject is urged to study Mearleau-Ponty's *In Praise of Philosophy*, translated by John Wild and James M. Edie (Northwestern University Press, 1963).

CHAPTER TWENTY-FIVE

SALVATION

This chapter will have an unusual course. It will consist almost entirely of passages reproduced from what I have written elsewhere. This will make it a rather personal chapter. But this seems to me the best way for me to open up the subject further at this point. Consider first then the following passage:

'There is a very profound and important sense in which it is impossible for us to know what it is to be another person. This is a very difficult point to explain, and I am not at all sure that I ought to do more here than note it. We can quite clearly know what other persons are like in one sense, the sense that is relevant in ordinary discourse. We may know that X is pleased or angry, or that he is disposed to be pleased or angry, or whatever it may be, on certain occasions. We have a wealth of knowledge of this sort of each other; human life would not be possible without it, however incomplete and uncertain our understanding of others may also be. Moreover, for X to be pleased means the same as for me to be pleased. There is no great mystery here, whatever the view offered of the way we come to have this knowledge. And yet there is a sense in which I can never know what it is to be another person having these experiences. There is an ultimacy and mystery about self-identity and the distinctness of persons which we cannot reduce at all. It is not that there are some things about other persons which we do not in fact know, nor that we can never be quite certain of our opinions about one another. Both these things are true, and it may in practice be very hard to know some things about other persons or to eliminate the possibility of error and misunderstanding here. But there seems to be no regard in which the kind of knowledge we already appear to have in some respects about other persons is inherently incapable of extension. The difficulty I have in mind now is not that of completing or consolidating our knowledge of one another in the ordinary sense, but the much more radical one of knowing what it would be like to be another person having my present experiences or others similar to them.'[1]

I do not know what the reader will make of this passage as it stands. But I would like to suggest to him to consider how far it makes sense to say that we are mysteries to one another in the way indicated. I shall not go further here into the implications of this contention, but even if the point I have just been making is questioned, it could still be maintained that there is a certain inwardness in all experience in the way implied in the last chapter in criticizing views like those of Professor Ryle. This is not the only point of importance about the soul, nor the only reason for speaking of a soul and not merely of a self or person. But it is the point that matters most in a philosophical context and in the bearing of that on religion. This is what I attempt to bring out in the passages from another paper[2] which will take us to the end of this chapter. I begin at the point where, in the paper mentioned, I am drawing attention to two ways in which we may be said to inhabit a private world. After noting the way in which each one must be aware of his experiences in having them I continue:

'It is sometimes thought that there is a further sense in which experience is private, namely that whereby the "real" or genuinely physical world is mediated for us by sensations or impressions private to each. The truth here seems to me rather complicated. I believe we are confined, in the first instance, to impressions of our senses, although these are not, as has been thought, modifications of our minds; and I have maintained elsewhere that the modes in which we have such impressions, even in their initial extendedness,[3] may vary radically from one case to another. But I much doubt whether this mediates for us an objective world that is not to be understood in terms of correlations within our own experi-

1. *Prospect for Metaphysics*, Ed. I. T. Ramsey, p. 211.
2. 'The Idea of Creation and Conceptions of Salvation' printed in *The Saviour God* (Ed. S. G. F. Brandon).
3. See my 'Public and Private Space'. *Proceedings of the Aristotelian Society*, 1952.

ences and as between those and the experiences of others. But this alternative to Representative Perception, and the account of the communication with others to be given in terms of it, is too large a subject to be embarked upon here. At the moment my concern is to distinguish between the senses of private world involved in the present contexts and the more complete and immediate privacy by which each of us is aware of his own experience in having it but can have no such direct access, not even in paranormal cognition, to the experiences of other persons.

'The latter privacy is not without kinship with the initial privacy of our sense impressions, important though it may be to distinguish the two. But the main point at the moment is that, in both these respects and in the first in particular, man is essentially a solitary being. He is also of course an essentially social being. The life that we know could not be conceived without relations with others, mediated though they must be. The mediation is so unobtrusive that we are not usually aware of it and only sophisticated people reflect upon it. We can therefore have extremely close and intimate relationships, and the solitary aspect of human experience is thus not always obtrusive. But it is never absent. Nothing can eliminate it, for it is an essential characteristic of finite experience as such. This is what ultimately lies behind such expressions as "the light of the alone to the alone", or the oft-quoted, and rarely understood, definition of religion as "what a man does with his solitariness".

'Aloneness in this sense is apt to be made obtrusive by loneliness in the ordinary sense. When relations with others are slight or have been cut off, a person is thrown much on his own resources and apt to be driven in on himself. He becomes in this way more conscious also of the special inwardness which characterizes all finite experience as such and which is made more explicit for us in some situations, very often the situations which impress on us also the irrevocable character of external events and those features of our environment which most resist moulding to our own desires. Realism and proper subjectivity go together more often, and more naturally, than is usually appreciated.

'These are matters for which much evidence may be found in recent and contemporary literature. As has often been observed, there is much in the life of today to induce loneliness and to sharpen the sting of it. The organization which improves our amenities and makes for greater mobility is apt also to make our relationships more impersonal and remote even in the very process of throwing people more closely together. The social surroundings, often very homely ones in which we grow easily and naturally into ripe relationship with one another are disrupted and give place to more contrived and unstable situations in which the individual finds it harder to feel that he is at home and belongs. The paradoxes of this situation, the manifest distress of many whose life seems also to be the gayest, the outright complaints of loneliness where life appears also to be most gregarious, the herding of peoples in impersonal artificial communities where outward prosperity leaves them more and more frustrated—all this has been told often enough in literature and public pronouncements which also show how much these conditions have been accentuated in our time. It is not surprising therefore that loneliness and its problems have become at various levels, from the simplest to the most sophisticated, a subject for much discussion and concern. Nor is it surprising that in the probings of more shrewd and sensitive writers, there should be intimations not merely of the isolation and aloofness specifically induced by certain social situations and modifiable in various ways, but also of the deeper and inescapable sense in which an individual is bound to be a world to himself.

'It is not expected that fiction and general literature should discriminate neatly between these different sorts of solitude and their ramifications in the complicated web of human affairs, least of all when they affect one another so much. But it is not an accident that those writers of creative literature who are also given to general reflection and philosophical thinking for example existentialists, should give so much prominence to the sense of isolation and destitution in a very profound and disturbing form as a feature of human experience as such and, as many suppose, beyond remedy. These writers may often be muddled philosophers but that would not preclude them from stumbling, in ways which amateur and uncertain philosophizing may have helped, on profound truths of great importance for their time.

'I was much impressed recently to read the closing words of a collection of stories[1] which have deservedly been widely praised for their literary excellence and penetration. They belong to the tough-minded variety of modern fiction, but their realism is the genuine one of a skilled and sensitive artist. The last story ends with the words: "What really, can any of us know about any of us, and why must we make such a thing of loneliness when it is the final condition of us all. And where would love be without it?"

'The secularist copes with this situation by acceptance and as much charity as one can muster. Religions offer more positive remedies. In monistic religions the aim is to eliminate the isolation of the individual by absorbing him entirely into the whole. He is no longer a world to himself but as completely at one with others and with God as it is possible to be. There are no barriers but the total flow of one life into another. This seems however to release the individual by totally destroying him as such, and there are in fact many other difficulties, on which I cannot dwell now, in the notion of our total absorption into the life of the whole. In the non-monistic religions the ultimacy of our finite status is accepted and the ills attendant upon this, in the various ways in which these are felt and understood, present a situation for which a remedy is sought. There is no attempt to supersede or eliminate our finite state. Nor is there mere stoical acceptance of the inevitable. But acceptance has none the less an important part to play in the solutions that have most understanding of the situation to be met.

'This will be acceptance of the essential conditions under which we find that we exist, but acceptance based on the recognition of our status as a dependent one and involving an acknowledgement of the Unconditioned or Supreme Reality in relation to which all else has its place and significance. Acceptance, in humility and gratitude, is part of the

1. *Sermons and Soda-Water*, by John O'Hara.

worship we give to God, and in recognizing His glory and transcendent claims we submit ourselves to the fulfilment of ourselves appropriate to our place in relation to God and in this way find rest in Him.

'This is especially prominent in the religions where the idea of creation sets its seal most explicitly on the distinctness of the finite individual. There is here no inducement for the individual to seek to transcend himself. He is not in rebellion against being the sort of creature he is or having the mode of experience which he finds that he does have. And if we find, as I maintain we do, that a certain inwardness is an incident of all finite experience and that fellowship with others, both man and God, has for this reason an essential element of mediation, we do not set ourselves in hopeless rebellion against these conditions or attempt the futile and inhibiting task of bursting the bonds of our finite nature and raising ourselves to the level of God. We acknowledge the mystery of God and find in this acknowledgement an enhancement of the mediated knowledge of God which is possible for us within the modes of the experience we do have.

'In the same way we accommodate ourselves to the sort of knowledge we have of one another. We do not seek to know as God knows and we recognize that we can never have direct or immediate knowledge of other persons similar to that which we have of ourselves. In duly acknowledging God as our Creator we are helped also to appreciate that aspect of the sanctity of persons by which they too are, in a more limited way, mysteries we must not seek to reduce; the mystery of their creation is written into the distinctness of persons and is not suspended even in the most intimate fellowship we may have with one another. On the contrary, fellowship is deepened and enriched when we come into it with due understanding of what it means for us all to be, in Biblical language, the children of God and severally the objects of the loving concern which begins with our creation.

'The more we appreciate this the better equipped we shall be to cope with ills which seem to have been much aggravated in recent times. We read much, in fiction as in social studies, of unnatural passions and perversions, of violence and sex in most unruly forms. One reason for this, I submit, is that, with our growing sophistication, we have a great urge to break into the inner recesses of the lives of others, to find them off their guard and without disguise in extremes of fear or passion, and this is one form of the desire to know others wholly from within, to know as we know ourselves and as God knows us, to pass beyond irremovable barriers of our finitude which religious humility teaches us to understand and accept. Sartre and other existentialists, in their strange way, have taught us much of this.

'But it is not merely in these general ways that the recognition of our created status, and of the inwardness, ultimacy and sanctity of personal experience which this involves, affects our conception of salvation and the needs from which it springs. There are further, more specific, applications of the same principle apprehended in varying degrees of adequacy in different religions and their theologies.

'We find, for example, that in virtue of being confined, in one way which I maintain is a very fundamental one, to a world of our own, we are very prone to allow this to impose itself unduly on our conspectus of the public world as each one apprehends it. This is one of the main reasons for the distorted pictures we often present to ourselves of our environment, the lack of realism or the superficial romanticism for which artists and prophets have often to supply the corrective. But the more we appreciate that all things do not in this way revolve around ourselves and that the whole of the reality encountered in experience is God's creation, the more, that is, that we think of ourselves and of all things in relation to God, the less shall we be tempted to view them through artificial and misleading perspectives of our own. The ultimate cure for romanticism, and the false moral impressions which this involves, is in understanding the basic source of it and the essentially religious character of its ultimate corrective.

'But it is when we consider the specifically ethical aspects of experience that the main importance of our recognition of the distinctness of persons appears. On monistic views there can be no proper place for the final moral responsibility of persons. Nor has the sense of sin and guilt been very prominent in the cultures most affected by monistic views of the world. It is not that ethical ideas are absent in these cultures and the religions which inspire them. No one conversant at all with Hinduism and Buddhism could maintain that. The compassion we find, for example, in the thought and practice of the highest forms of Buddhism is extremely impressive. So are ethical features of the Gita and of parts of the Upanishads. All the same, the moral life presents itself here in the main as a discipline, not as a categorical demand which the agent is totally free to accept or reject and which leaves him, in the event of failure, with a burden of guilt. Even where the ideas of guilt and accountability appear in their proper form, and not in the travesties of mere pollution or spiritual disease, this is not easily accommodated to a view of the individual which regards him as an element in one Whole of Being where everything takes its place inevitably by the necessity of the Whole. If man is really a part of God what room is there for sin?

'This is not the place in which to discuss closely the nature of freedom and responsibility. I have attempted to do that elsewhere and must be content now with a statement of my own belief that the choice required by moral accountability is of an absolute kind, not determined by character or environment or even by God, and that the proper appreciation of this is of quite fundamental importance for our understanding of the main problems of human life and its worth. I cannot expand this principle here, but it will be evident that, if I am right in subscribing to this libertarian view, there is here a quite radical feature of human experience for which no place can be found in monistic conceptions of the world. It was this, as I have noted, which troubled many Hegelian idealists, and it is interesting that thinkers like Sri Aurobindo show the same concern today about Oriental monisms.

'But wrongful choice is not only evil in itself, it is the cause of other evils. It tends to infect the whole of life and poison all our attitudes and relationships. We are, moreover, in our closest social relationships especially, the heirs to the accumulated evil effects of wrongful deeds in the past. This is one element of truth, but one that is largely misrepresented, in the traditional doctrine of original sin.

'The most grievous and lasting effect of sin is to slacken our hold on the world around us and distort our impressions of it. In more religious terms, it alienates us from our neighbour and from God. The state of the sinner has its analogue in that of sick persons in conditions of extreme debility. They have lost their hold on life and the world around them, and the sinner in the same way has not the concern for himself and others which he would normally have. In some religions a condition not very dissimilar to this is part of the goal of life or a feature of the final release; in others a sounder instinct presents the state of isolation, privation and debility as the appalling penalty of sin, the death which is the renunciation of life. In this living death, in the sense of unreality and the dissolution of the world around us, the individual is driven more and more into himself, and the inwardness inevitably attendant upon his experience and having a function in the economy of his relations with others, becomes the dominant feature of experience unrelieved by a properly objective grasp of the world and healthy relationships with other persons. His own world becomes the centre and discloses itself, in this isolation, as a bleak unsustaining one.

'This is the deeper dimension of the loneliness which, as a pervasive malaise of present society, is presented in more general terms, and linked more exclusively to features of contemporary life, in fiction and other works of art today. The ultimate understanding of it is, I submit, religious; and this begins with due appreciation of the relation of created beings to their Creator. It is not insignificant that much of the literature to which I allude has profound religious undertones, however remote it may seem from conventional religion.

'It is the sense of desolation and destitution engendered by sin and guilt which constitutes, in the non-monistic religions, the need to which salvation and redemption are specially addressed. The issue is no longer that of coping with limitations and ills inevitably attendant on a finite state, but of cleansing the individual and his society of the evil which individuals first bring on themselves and which imprisons the individual in a frightening world of his own unrelieved by a proper sense of God and our neighbour within it.

'Of the ramifications of this in a social context and of the variety of ways in which religions claim to meet it, little can be added here. Nor can I go into the distortion of the truth in various doctrines and creeds in which these ideas of salvation and redemption are often enshrined. Space likewise precludes speculation about the appearance in cultures that are mainly monistic of ingredients, like certain notions of cleansing and redeeming, which only take their place properly in non-monistic cultures. We have at all times to remember the varieties and complexities of religion and the many deviations of live religion from its more sophisticated expression. But there seem to me to be few more valuable guides to the varieties of religious thought and practice, as the scholar makes these more fully and reliably available to us today, than that of considering them in terms of their appreciation of the significance of creaturely status and the implications of this for ideas of sin and salvation. Professor R. C. Zaehner, in a celebrated lecture,[1] has reminded us sharply of the considerable difference of substance there may be in religious notions, like the doctrines of release or incarnation in various religions, which may appear superficially very similar. If the thesis of the present paper is sound it offers one way in which the points of affinity and of differences in the leading notions of various religions may be discriminated better.

'In the Christian religion the idea of salvation is directed especially to the alleged bondage of sin and the alienation of man from God. The Christian doctrines of Reconciliation and Atonement, and of the work of the Holy Spirit within this scheme, do not require us to suppose that the influence of the Holy Spirit is such as to deprive us of our own freedom and responsibility in moral choice, although this has often been supposed in Christian theology. Reconciliation is directed to the situation of estrangement consequent upon sin, and the operation of grace in this process does not remove all possibility of genuine temptation. We shall understand this and other main features of Christianity better when we link

1. *Foolishness to the Greeks.* Inaugural Lecture at Oxford.

he Christian doctrine of the Incarnation, and especially its
once for all character, closely to the Judaeo-Christian understanding of the creaturely nature of man and the consequent
imprisonment of each in a forlorn unsustaining world of his
own by which the wages of sin are collected. This is the world
into which God enters in Christ and whose bonds He breaks
by the completeness of His penetration of it. The proper
elaboration of this theme would require a closer scrutiny of
Christian doctrines and traditions than can be attempted here.
But we may do well to reflect how significant a feature of the
work of Christ is disclosed to us when, at the climax of His
passion, he uttered the cry of extreme destitution: "My God,
my God, why hast thou forsaken me?"

'The significance of this cry is only properly plain to us
when we have a sound conception of man as well as of God,
and while this has ramifications too wide to be considered
further now I cannot forbear to quote, for the point they
give to this theme, the well-known and beautiful lines of one
of the most percipient of our poets, Walter de la Mare:

> Though I should sit
> By some tarn in thy hills
> Using its ink
> As the spirit wills
> To write Earth's wonders,
> Its live, willed things,
> Flit would the ages
> On soundless wings
> Ere unto Z
> My pen drew nigh;
> Leviathan told,
> And the honey-fly:
> And still would remain
> My wit to try—
> My worn reeds broken
> The dark tarn dry,
> All words forgotten—
> Thou, Lord, and I.

The limited mystery of man is bound up with the absolute
mystery of God.'

FURTHER READING

The volume in which the passages just reproduced appear, namely *The Saviour God* (Ed. S. G. F. Brandon), contains many valuable studies of various forms of the idea of salvation. The reader should consult also:—

The Bible Doctrine of Salvation by C. Ryder Smith (Epworth Press)

Early Christian Doctrines by J. N. D. Kelly, chapter xiv (A. and C. Black)

Grace and Personality by John Oman (Cambridge)

Theology of Salvation by U. Simon (MacMillan, N.Y.)

CHAPTER TWENTY-SIX

SOME OUTSTANDING PROBLEMS

There are many problems of religion which have not yet been discussed in this book. I can do little now to repair the omission. But I shall attempt, in the present chapter, to indicate the shape which these problems take, and the way they may be approached, in the light of what has already been said about the relation of God to man. These further problems could well form the subject of another volume in the Teach Yourself Series, and it would be possible in that way also to go more thoroughly into the relations of ethics and religion than has been possible in the present work.

Miracle

Few will doubt that the idea of a miracle presents many problems. The main way in which philosophy comes into these appears when we ask what could be meant by a 'miracle' or how would anyone recognize a miracle if one were to happen. How is a miracle different from some other event? A common reply which is made to this question (and I think it is not very far off the mark) is that a miracle must involve, as one condition, a total break in the normal or natural continuity of events. It would, in that case, defy all normal explanation. It would not happen in accordance with any law or regularity in the course of things. It would supersede or suspend such laws. That, above all, is what makes it a miracle.

To this the reply may however be made that it is not so easy as it looks to know what is meant by a break in the continuity of things. Events may be very odd or out of accord with the laws of nature as we understand them in some limited way or in some restricted field of their application. But they may still fall into a continuity or intelligible pattern of events when our knowledge is made more comprehensive; it is only through severe restrictions that they defy explanation. Many of the things we do today might thus seem altogether miraculous to a primitive man – or indeed to some of our near ancestors. Flying or making ourselves heard or seen across continents would be obvious examples. To become weightless would be even better. We all know, it might be said, that unsupported bodies fall to the ground, that is the clear law of gravity, it has kept wingless creatures chained to the earth through all their history. To hang in space or move about would defy all that. Yet we know that this happens and that it is not at all beyond explanation, it does not 'defy' the law of gravity but happens in accordance with what a sound understanding of gravity would lead us to expect.

If I were to stumble by chance on some substance containing penicillin and apply it to somebody's wound I might bring about a cure in unexpected and speedy ways. No one could perhaps account for it. But it is not hard for a scientist to give the explanation today. Accordingly, some would maintain, we have no reason for supposing that anything is in principle beyond explanation. We may never find the explanation, but that only shows how limited we are. If only we knew more or understood things a little better the explanation would be forthcoming. There are odd events but none that are inherently unaccountable. There must be some explanation for everything.

This is a natural line to take. It is also rather hasty. Those who adopt it are often influenced in one of two ways. They may take their start from an idealist position in philosophy or move in an intellectual atmosphere much affected by idealism, as was the case with much liberal theology earlier in this century. This would set up an initial presumption that there is an ultimate rational explanation of everything. We have seen earlier how this should be. Others have been affected more by recent philosophy and led to the view that explanations depend on the map or grid through which we view the facts and that the suitable map would have some way of taking care of everything. Neither of these positions seems to me sound, and my reasons for thinking so will be evident by now. Evident also will be my view of an attitude of mind which lies behind the first, and in a odd way the second, of these philosophical positions and which is also likely to have most to do with the way the layman, sophisticated or simple, feels certain that all things have some explanation.

This is the conviction or insight that nothing could ultimately just happen to be. But we have also seen that what this really amounts to is that there is some self-subsistent transcendent Reality behind all there is and in this way accounting for all things. This goes beyond even the most exhaustive rational explanation, and, while it is involved in and guarantees the rationality we properly count on, it gives us also the sort of dependence on an ultimate Source which would be consistent with occasional variability which fits into no intelligible pattern. A world created by God, if we understood the notion of creation aright, has room for miracle in it.

But this does not quite get us out of the wood. The fact that explanations are in due course forthcoming for events which were wholly bewildering once remains disconcerting. For even if we are prepared to say that miracles, as involving some break in the natural continuity of things, could happen, it is another thing to be assured that in fact they do. Will there not always lurk in our thought the suspicion that, in fact, the most inexplicable happenings will eventually fit into place in 'the scheme of things'? Miracles may be possible, but have there ever been any?

Many who are impressed by this difficulty, or who are perhaps reluctant, for reasons like those indicated earlier, to admit any ultimate lack of continuity, will be apt to take refuge in some different notion of miracle. It will be held that an event could be miraculous although it is capable of a normal or scientific explanation. It will be a miracle because it has religious significance. This suggestion, as it stands, seems however to have much too wide a coverage. It could extend to all there is, and indeed some writers have boldly accepted that consequence. For the sun to rise each day is as much a miracle as it would be for it to stand, as alleged 'upon Gibeon'. 'Every bush is a burning bush'—as it was once eloquently put. But this will hardly do, for it seems pointless to speak of miracle if everything is a miracle; why not just say that the world is God's world and so on? The word 'miracle' becomes otiose here. But it seems also otiose on modifications of the present suggestion, such as the view very ably presented by thinkers like F. R. Tennant and H. H. Farmer, namely that a miracle is a very rare combination of events that have some distinctive significance for individuals or peoples — the crossing of the Red Sea in the Biblical account, for example, if ascribed to unusual combinations of winds and tide. My own impression, after examining many variations on the theme that there can be miracles within an exhaustively rational scheme of things, is that it is much better to dispense with the term — or to deny that there are miracles — than to attempt to save the notion in a meaning so divorced from the one we normally give it as to be extremely misleading and confusing. Without the requisite 'break' there seems to be nothing which could not be properly treated in the terms we normally use in religion without recourse to the special notion of miracle.

We have seen in any case that we have to postulate the requisite break of continuity to allow of the free choice which responsibility requires. Such choices are not however miracles. They are acts we perform in the normal course of things. What more does a miracle require? It requires that the variation be ascribable to divine intervention or, at the very least, to some supernatural factor in which God should be especially involved, like the devoutness of some saintly person — and in the latter case we have to be very careful if we are not to be found invoking nothing more than an unusual mode of the general continuity, as in paranormal phenomena; the latter are not themselves tantamount to miracles, they are unusual gifts or powers which some people sometimes have, but no more miraculous than speaking or lifting one's arm; they do supersede certain natural processes, but even moving my arm involves what Nicolai Hartmann has aptly called 'a plus of determination' which uses physical processes without wholly suspending them.

But here again the problem becomes acute of how could we ever know that miracles happen. Could we ever know that there is more than some rare or super-normal event? Does God, to put it in the sharpest and bluntest form, ever intervene? I think we could reply, if what has been maintained about religious experience is sound, that God does intervene in the normal course of things to shape such experiences—that is what divine disclosure involves. But again it will not do to treat this as miracle. For that would also give the word too wide and unusual a meaning. What we wish to know is whether God intervenes (or whatever approximation to this we may allow) beyond the disclosure in experience, and how is that established.

There are two difficulties in our path here. One I have elsewhere called a theological one—for lack of a better term. It is, very simply, this. Is it in keeping with the nature of God and with what we learn about Him that he should disrupt the order of things as He has ordained it? Do not shifts of that sort imply some imperfection? More particularly, is it in accord with the dignity and wisdom of God that He should act in that way at our behest in prayer? If there is strict 'petitionary prayer' that is what seems to be involved. But does that make religious sense? The Greeks would certainly not have thought so. God affects things, as in the case of Aristotle's 'unmoved mover', for them in ways that do not involve taking a special interest in the world. But a view like the Christian one—it is the obvious and pre-eminent example here—stresses the close and intimate fellowship of God with man, and in this context it becomes less strange that God's activity in the world could vary in peculiar ways according to the requirements of His personal dealings with us. The Fatherhood of God has for the Christian much to do with belief in miracles.

But miracles are claimed by others—and in very different contexts. Should all these be ruled out? By no means on the present score. I suggest that, so far as the present difficulty is concerned, we should take the Christian understanding as our norm, and where, in other ways, a claim seems plausible deal with the theological or kindred religious difficulty in the way marked out in the Christian conception of God's relations with men and with Christian sensitivity to its implications.

But even with such difficulties out of the way, the question of fact remains. Granted that miracles are not on religious grounds out of place and that we may even reasonably expect them in some circumstances, can we ever know that they do happen? Could we recognize one? The root difficulty here has already been made plain. Strange things happen but for all we know they may admit of some natural explanation. 'But,' someone will say, 'in the case I wish to instance, the end which came about had been prayed for—I was ill beyond all hope of recovery, but I prayed and behold I am well.' The difficulty with this is that many have prayed, devoutly and sincerely it would seem, and not been made well. The force of this objection can indeed be reduced — for some prayers are not worthy ones, it may not be God's will to grant all that we ask, our faith may be too weak. This would make it sensible to believe in petitionary prayer while allowing that many prayers are not granted. But it would not make it plausible to appeal to apparent instances of answer to prayer as a way of proving, in the first place, that God acts in this way. The reference to prayer does none the less give us our clue. For what we plainly need is some concomitance of events which seem to defy explanation in the ordinary way and of some religious factor. I have elsewhere suggested that this may be found in a heightening of religious awareness and its accompaniments in those instances where in other ways there appears to be an initially good case for a miracle. I think much might be learnt by investigating the subject afresh in this way. In the case of Jesus, as the Christian thinks of Him, the closeness to God would be peculiar and sustained, and here we would therefore expect to find the substantiation *par excellence* of the claims for miraculous performances.

But Jesus, by His own example and teaching, also helps us to keep this subject in the right perspective. It is not a peripheral question, but neither is it a crucial one. The essential Christian claims, for example, are not jeopardized if the miracles are questioned. These are not the decisive indications of the divinity of Jesus. It is especially misleading to attempt, as alas many do, to establish the miracles in some secular way (by normal historical evidence for example) and then prove from this the doctrines of 'the Person of Christ'. That is to go to work crudely and in quite the wrong way. It puts entirely the wrong interpretation on the prominence of miracles in the

Gospel narratives and much over-simplifies the issue. I think we shall find the position not radically different in the cases of other charismatic personalities or central figures of the great religions. Few topics have in fact been more misunderstood or mishandled than miracles; and this has often brought discredit on religion and made the way of its defenders hard.

Evil

Evil is only a problem, in the proper intellectual sense, for a religious view or for some form of metaphysics which finds supreme goodness at the heart of things. It is, of course, a problem for everyone, believer and agnostic alike, in the practical sense that we have to cope with evil or overcome it. But as a problem in the strict sense it arises when we have to reconcile evil with the goodness of God — or whatever takes His place. In its simplest terms it is this. God is alleged to be all-good and also all-powerful; how then does there come to be any evil in the world — or, as it is more popularly put, why does God allow it? This is not just a problem for speculative thought or detached reflection. It is for many a major obstacle to faith, and it is a constant source of strain and tension in the life of the believer; indeed there are few more testing experiences for saintly and sensitive persons than to be the witness of sustained and heart-breaking evil in one of its many forms. This, as the Psalms testify well, is where the worshipper is most moved to devout, and sometimes even bold and reproachful, expostulation.

One way of dealing with the problem of evil is to think of God as a finite or limited Being. The notion of a 'finite God' has been mentioned already. It is found as a rule in philosophical and sophisticated contexts more than at the live centre of religion. The suggestion is that while God is good in all He intends there are some things He cannot encompass; He is in the van of the struggle against evil, and He calls us to co-operate with Him, but His triumph is not complete. This doctrine has the merit of making us very genuinely co-workers with God. It encourages and stimulates the good man, he feels that he is on the side of God but that something substantial is still left to him. The weakness of the doctrine, and in my eyes it is a fatal one, is that the way we are forced to think of there being God rules out the possibility of His being anything but transcendent and thus utterly supreme. This has been shown at some length. Nor does the doctrine accord well with religious experience and attitudes. Here, in spite of dismay and bewilderment, the worshipper continues to proclaim his trust in God and looks to casting all his burdens upon Him. There may be much for us to do and many trials to endure but beyond this lies the unquestioning confidence, the 'peace that passes all understanding', the 'sure mercies', the strength of 'the everlasting arms'.

This holds also of the notion to be found in some religions, mainly Persian ones like Zoroastrianism, that the universe is the scene of a struggle between two great forces of good and evil. These religions have affected men's attitudes in other cultures but have not on the whole disturbed the ultimate serenity of the religious outlook as we normally find it. Even Zoroastrianism tended to rest in the ultimate triumph of good, the assured subjection of all evil powers.

In sharp opposition to the notion of a finite God, motivated as this is by a keen sense of the starkness of evil, we have those approaches to the problem which question the reality or ultimacy of evil. Evil becomes now an appearance or illusion. We have already seen how this comes about in various monistic systems, and we can also see what makes it plausible in a Christian understanding of the ultimate union of being and perfection to conclude that there can be no evil which is not just a privation of goodness. These views seem to me none the less vastly mistaken. Evil is genuine and positive, and I have indicated already some of the main defects in systems which question its reality. The practical effects of treating evil as mere illusion have also been noted. But it must be added, in fairness to the religions and cultures which tend to give evil, in the last event, no proper place in the universe, that much in the initial stages of the attitudes they represent involves a profound, almost obsessive, preoccupation with evil. It is the unendurable spectacle of evil in its most distressing and insidious forms that prompts the desperate search for release or oblivion by which mind and heart are alike averted from the reality of evil.

This kind of escapism cannot, in my view, be good for either the individual or his society. It involves an elaborate suppression, the effects of which on the balance and sanity of our outlook we should be well placed to dread today in the light of all that modern psychology has taught us about it.

Evil then is real, and we must burke no issues by questioning this. But I must now note one way in which there is considerable easement of the problem if what has been earlier maintained is sound. It is that the worst form of evil is not the one which occasions the most difficulty. I refer of course to moral evil. The view, in which most people I believe would concur, that moral evil is the worst form of evil—in a class by itself as it were—is not indeed without its own difficulties. These centre on what is technically known as 'the commensurability of values'. Can we really compare such things as moral evil and suffering? I should be disposed to say that we must in as much as we could hardly deny that at some point the extent and gravity of suffering would compel us in practice to choose the mitigation of the latter in preference to the discouragement of moral wickedness—our own wickedness not being involved, as we would not be wicked if we choose to act for what we thought eventually the best. But whatever we say of this and kindred tricky questions, there seems little real doubt of the unusual gravity of moral evil. This has, however, little part, if any, in the religious problem of evil.

That is because we are ourselves accountable for moral evil—we incur it by wrongful choice. We cannot therefore put it also at God's door. If God was to create us free and enable us thereby to have the maturity and dignity of responsible beings, He had to allow us to sin. It is no part of His omnipotence to encompass the contradictory. In His wisdom He gave us freedom, and if we sin then that is unavoidable. The suggestion that God could have made us free and also guaranteed that we never misuse this freedom seems to me blatantly false, and it is very starkly so if freedom is taken here, as I maintain that it should be, in a libertarian sense. The facts of moral evil as such, then, are reconcilable with the goodness and power of God; and the more we understand our status as distinct created beings the more is this evident.

This explanation of evil covers also, in large measure at least, the harmful consequences of our evil choices, the hurt we do to ourselves and to others. For there could be no serious responsible choice if the bad consequences of wrongful choice were always averted. It could of course be argued that we could have been made incapable of inflicting certain forms of harm on one another. But some grievous harm we must be allowed to perpetrate if we are to be in any way arbiters of our own destiny and have the social and cultural experience we have as truly human beings. What falls outside this, if anything does, can go into the reckoning, for the purpose of our problem, as part of the much more intractable problem created by the evidence of evils we have not brought on ourselves and on one another, evils which are not expressly involved in our being accountable creatures.

It is certain that much of the evil in the world is due to the wickedness of men. But much is also due to folly and ignorance; and much is not expressly due to human action at all. It comes as we say 'by evil chance' which we are also apt sometimes to describe, significantly for our problem, as an 'act of God'. The most obvious examples are many forms of suffering. Unenlightened religious teaching has sometimes ascribed all these to sin. Jesus expressly corrected this harsh and mischievous assumption—when He said for example of a man He healed that 'neither this man nor his parents have sinned that he should be born blind'. There must have been much suffering among sub-human beings before man came on the scene and it is certainly not by his coming that nature is so often 'red in tooth and claw' and the denizens of field and forest so often afflicted in other ways. It is not by 'what man has done to man', grievous though that is, alone that there is appalling mental and physical suffering and all the deformity and ailment of body and spirit that man is heir to. There are thus extensive non-moral evils that are not in any way due to our own 'grievous faults'. Why then does God allow these? Where in the world He made and sustains is there place for agonizing incurable illnesses, for famine, flood and fire, for the torment of the parent who has to look helplessly on the agony of his babe?

To these questions many answers have been given. It has been maintained, for example, there cannot be a sum of suffering, it does not consist of units that can be added up. This seems hardly relevant, for whatever we say of strict multiplication, there can certainly be more and less suffering, more and less stupidity and error. Others have urged that there is a point beyond which we do not suffer. When pain reaches a certain intensity unconsciousness mercifully supervenes. I do not know how far this is true, but even if it were invariably the rule the ceiling, as Professor C. A. Campbell has pointed out, is distressingly high before insensibility comes. Nor do other ills admit the same relief. The extent and acuteness of non-moral ills is made little less disturbing by somewhat artificial and remote considerations of the kind just noted. What these show for the most part is the insensitivity and lack of imagination of their authors. I think this must also be said of religious folk who remind us how small our 'present light affliction' is by comparison with eternity. The ills of this world are real enough while they last; and even if they are, in a long view, of short duration it is a strange indication of loving-kindness to allow them on that score. A human parent could not be excused in the same way for tormenting or neglecting his child.

There are however much more weighty considerations offered in solution of our problem. It is pointed out, for instance, that certain ills and inconveniences are incidental to the continuity and system of the order of nature. Without such a system, without the dependability of a proper causal order, we could not manipulate things and live as we do in the world. This is quite true and it need not be laboured now. No one can reasonably complain that everything in nature is not immediately bent to his will. But then there could be an order of nature that did not involve the more appalling sorts of ills, including acute physical pain to which we are prone now. Our nervous system might be different, and surely, it will be said, an omnipotent Being could be expected to have arranged things better in that respect.

As a further attack on the problem we shall be told that suffering ennobles character and gives a new depth to experience. Some who have endured grave physical ill or sorrow have even said that they would not have been without it, they have gained so much in the fires of their tribulations; and there is no doubt substance in such claims, they may well reflect genuine experience more often than affectation or morbid self-mortification. The trouble with this answer is that there is much suffering which it does not cover, suffering which degrades more than it ennobles, distress or debility which reduces men to a state akin to that of brutes and does little to deepen the character and sensitivity of those who witness it. The same applies to another answer that has much truth in it, namely that suffering and need bring out charity and sympathy. It would certainly be a poor world in which men never had the opportunity to bear one another's burdens, but again there is a surd which cannot be brought under this explanation; there is a wide range of ills which seem out of proportion to any benevolence they help to display or elicit. There are situations of sudden catastrophe and bereavement where it is perverse and provoking to proffer such consolation. Nor are we much aided here by the thought of compensation in after-life. Many have indeed lived in the hope of this—and not without reason. It is a firm Christian hope and it is one aspect of the notion of Karma so basic to Hindu religion. But unless we understand in principle how such compensation may operate, it seems again hard to see how the blessings we may enjoy hereafter could not be obtained without the cost of some of our present ills. The random character of much that men suffer also makes it hard to bring all non-moral evil under some principle, or a combination of principles, which establishes a plausible pattern of compensation or a clear working for good in all that befalls us. It is not merely that we fail to see all the detailed application of such principles, but that there is a considerable surd which does not begin to come under them.

In short, then, it comes to this. There are many explanations of evil, and it is well to have them in mind for support in distress and for sound understanding of our purpose in the world. A life that is made to run no risks or ever be put to the test is a poor thing. But this does not provide for an exhaustive rationalization of evil; and there is a point where even the more plausible and impressive explanations serve only to aggravate and caricature the ills they are thought to allay or redress. Facile solutions are particularly harmful to the cause of true religion.

What then shall we say? The religious apologist, if he knows his business, will not put his trust in further refinements of the arguments just noted—even the most plausible. Nor will he seek variations on the same general theme. The student of religion should of course make himself much more familiar with the substance of such arguments than the slight reference to them here will have made him. They constitute an important part of religious thought and they help to indicate and induce the proper attitude for the religious person to adopt in the face of adversity or in the encounter with grievous calamity, in his own life or that of others. But this is not where he will find his ultimate source of strength. On the contrary, he will remind himself that his knowledge of God is not obtained in the first place from reflection on the way things go in the world or any nice balancing of good or ill turns of fortune. He will know that God is involved in the being of all things and that in this way a transcendent power and perfection lies at the heart of all there is, the most untoward as much as the most pleasing. He will likewise have found this transcendent Reality yet closer to him in a variety of ways through its disclosure of itself in experience and history and in the assimilation of that into the changes and varieties of his individual experience which gives him the sense of the presence of God in his own life. This assurance is not blind, but based on due appreciation of appropriate evidence, however little there may be of formal reflection on the manner of it. The believer will know what God is like and what He does, and he will know this in a way that is not dependent on what he finds in other ways in the world. His faith will have this firm foundation of its own. It will not be a desperate wish to believe or a clinging to vain hopes against the facts. It will have its own warrant and will thus give the religious person a source of strength and insight which the spectacle of evil cannot properly upset. That will certainly not justify a lighthearted view of evil in any of its forms; there will still be dismay and bewilderment and strain, and the most devout will find himself echoing that recurrent theme of the psalms, the taunt of the ungodly—'where is now your God?' He will be wholly at a loss on occasion to justify the ways of God to man. But in this he will never be quite 'cast down'. He knows that answer there must be somewhere; it may not be an answer that we can even in principle begin to grasp. For we have to do here with a mysterious and transcendent Reality which we cannot wholly understand. The ways of God are not our ways, and how His purposes come to fruition we cannot always know. But we can know with ever deepening insight and loving response what God is like and how unlimited is His concern for us and for the fulfilment of our fellowship with Him. The more profoundly this is apprehended the more the disquiet of the soul is stilled and the more it rejoices in the necessity, nay even the privilege, of resting content in the infinite and most amazing love of God.

This is what Job came to learn in his many tribulations, and few have written with a finer understanding of the proper religious attitude to evil than the author of the remarkable book which bears his name in the Bible. But it is, for the Christian, in the fulfilment of God's purpose in the events the Gospels describe that the insights of Job and the Psalmists and the prophets come to their ultimate depth and refinement. For here is given the ultimate assurance, the final disclosure of what God is like and what He intends in thus coming Himself to the very heart of what man is and does. I have been at pains to indicate, albeit in outline, how this assurance comes, and I must hasten to admit that it is often faltering and flickering. It needs all the cultivation and refinement we can give it in all religious discipline and committed religious living. The way of faith is not lightly or easily trod; it is beset with constant perils—as Bunyan so magnificently showed. There are times when the pilgrim is faint indeed, and not least when he is forced to consider the frailty of his present existence and its not so distant and inevitable end. But there is, all the same, like an unfailing glow to light the path, the triumphant assurance of the nearness and care of God as seen in Jesus and ever renewed in the experience of all who come to Him, and set themselves to serve Him, with their whole mind and heart.

They are the ones who can say with St. Paul—and few, as it is well for us to remember, knew more than he of the trials and disorders of this world at first hand:

Nay, in all these things we are more than conquerors, through him that loved us. For I am persuaded that neither death nor life, nor angels, nor principalities, nor powers, nor things present, nor things to come, nor height nor depth, nor any other creature, shall be able to separate us from the love of God, which is in Christ Jesus our Lord.

Death and Immortality

Of all the ills to which men are subject none, on the whole, is more dreaded than death. There are indeed persons who view their own imminent death with great equanimity and even with lightness of heart, though they have no sort of faith to support them. The case of David Hume was mentioned earlier. Others regard the approach of death very differently, and unless it hastens upon them too speedily for them to contemplate it, in the heat of battle or in sudden disasters or collapse, it spells the utmost distress or terror. In its wake are joylessness and gloom, and unutterable grief. Terror is augmented for those who hold grim views of punishment to be visited on the guilty when this life is ended. But quite apart from this sort of fear of doom and damnation, the thought of the total eclipse of one's own existence, the end for ever of all that we have become and attained, is apt to fill the stoutest heart with foreboding. The usual pictures of death are grim, and it may well be that those who are able today, aided by the distractions and rush of life in our time, to thrust all thought of death out of their mind have the dread of it affecting them in graver measure than they imagine at more subtle and unconscious levels of experience.

It is not surprising, therefore, that men have cast about them for reasons for believing that death is not after all the end. The prospect of survival is not of course in all ways an agreeable one. It has its very sombre side. But it none the less affords joyous release from the grim anticipation of the total eclipse of one's being. That is how it normally presents itself, and most persons, I believe, would dearly welcome any assurance that the blow which death deals to everyone is not final.

The hopes and aspirations prompted in these ways are many. For some, at the present day especially, they are very obscure. We are told by some of our linguistic friends that survival in the proper sense is unthinkable. To speak of 'after-life' is a confusion of religious language and secular language. But we must, it is argued, none the less speak of resurrection and the hope of glory. Such language is not the language of life 'going on and on' but of some radically different religious assurance. I find this very difficult to follow. Admittedly any existence we may have beyond the present one will be peculiar by our standards now; it will come after the dissolution of our present bodies, and it may well involve the annulment of the temporal order of events as we find it now. There may be much in 'after-life' which we cannot comprehend at all at present. But it must be thought of all the same as some kind of existence. Otherwise the expectation of it is empty; it must, to put the matter bluntly, be something and not nothing. For the same reason we must not think of after-life or of 'eternal life' as just a quality of our life now—as some are apt to do. The 'hope of glory' surely means more than a peculiar 'existentialist' way of bringing out something outstanding and distinctive in the present life. If we have life eternal we must *be* in *some* way 'after' death.

Such existence will for some mean absorption into some One Whole of Being, not our continuance as distinct entities, but I shall not discuss this notion further now as I have said enough earlier to indicate the ways in which I consider it radically absurd and unsatisfactory. The doctrine of creation, rightly understood, gives shape to the hope of triumph over death as involving some perpetuation of distinct entities. This is the kind of hope which the Hebrew-Christian tradition specially requires.

Such a view is not affected by any conclusion we draw about

the extent of the belief in immortality among the Jews in pre-Christian times. The view to which Biblical scholars generally incline is that the Hebrews had not initially much expectation of personal immortality. They looked forward more to the prosperity of the nation—the good man would be blessed in his seed and so be compensated for all the ills that befall him now. It was only in apocalyptic literature (starting about 250 B.C. and well represented in the Book of Daniel) that the idea of life after death properly took shape, and even then its acceptance was uncertain and faltering. This is the view commonly taken by Hebrew and Biblical scholars, but some allowance has at least to be made for the references to Sheol as some shadowy place of the dead; and I have many further misgivings, shared by some Biblical scholars, about the accepted view. Even where the more explicit emphasis is on the eventual destiny of the nation in this world, I find it hard to account for all the expressions of hope and of divine concern for man in the Bible without reference to an expectation, throughout the history which the Bible reflects, of personal as well as collective salvation. That is certainly what accords best with the centrality of the notion of 'Creation' with which the Bible formally opens. It is an idea which enhances distinctly the significance of individual persons, and in the ripening of it there seems to be an increasingly sharp appreciation of the responsibility and dignity of man as a being destined to pass beyond death into closer union with God.

Such is undoubtedly the Christian view—and that is some norm for the processes that went before and found their fulfilment in it. The soul of the individual is here unmistakably of inestimable worth, the one lost sheep must be saved at all cost, there is joy in heaven over one repentant sinner; and the ultimate hope is of a life beyond death in which the soul is not diminished but fulfilled and in which there is the most complete union of individual souls with each other through the completeness of their fellowship with God. How this becomes possible, what further is involved in redemption and salvation, how far salvation is 'conditional', what is the fate of those who are not redeemed, what is the true meaning of doom and damnation in a Christian context?—all these are extremely important and difficult questions. We should much deepen our understanding of religion if we examined them. But that is hardly possible here. It must suffice to note the concern of the Christian religion with the individual and the firmness of the hope held out to him of a life beyond death. The form of this is not certain—'it has not yet been disclosed what we shall be', but of the hope itself there is no doubt—on a Christian view. To my understanding, there is no proper form of Christianity without a hope of 'after-life'.

Those who cling to such a hope, in a Christian or any other form, are sometimes tempted to seek general or metaphysical proofs of it. Many such proofs have been attempted from time to time. Among the most famous are those of Plato. He sometimes contends that the process of learning and understanding is essentially a process of recollection—anamnesis—which implies that we have all had a previous existence and will presumably pass on to some other state at the end of this life. It is never quite clear how strictly this argument must be taken in Plato's works, but in some form he plainly attaches importance to it—it is understandable that the idea of pre-existence should have prominence where, as in Plato's case, there is no notion of creation in the Christian sense. Plato contends also that the soul has more affinity with invisible 'forms' of being than with material reality and that this determines our proper destiny. The soul is, again, said to be self-moved and thus to be in some way eternal. The soul we are also told could only be destroyed by some evil peculiar to itself, namely its own injustice; and since this is not a material reality the soul is at least not to be destroyed by material things and is not subject to them. Others have followed Plato in contending that the soul is by its nature indestructible, the most famous of such attempts in recent times being those of J. E. McTaggart. But there are others who have argued in very different ways. They have not tried to show that the soul is inherently indestructible but have contended instead that, while life beyond the present one is not inevitable, there is good reason to hope for it.

One of the best known of such arguments is that of Kant. He maintained that moral obligation sets before us a demand which could never be completely fulfilled short of eternal life; in the sort of universe which the facts of moral obligation require such a condition would always be guaranteed. There are grave objections to this argument, and it is specially hard to see in what sense any proper moral demands upon us cannot be fulfilled where they fairly present themselves. Many of Kant's followers would agree, and there are few who would accept his argument as it stands, even allowing for the character given it by its place in Kant's system of thought as a whole. But it has been thought to have set us on the right lines by linking the thought of immortality with moral conceptions.

In our own day much has been made of the alleged findings of psychical research. This is also a vast subject in itself. It is significant that some keenly critical thinkers, like H. H. Price or C. D. Broad, take the subject very seriously and consider some of its claims to have an impressive weight of evidence for them. If survival after death could be proved in this way, that would undoubtedly break through a barrier of doubt and enlist our interest more profoundly in the fuller religious implication of the facts. In a materialistic age this could be exceptionally important. Nor shall we be much daunted by the apparent triviality of alleged communications from the dead. As H. H. Price has shown there could be many explanations of that.

It is not, however, to these considerations, or to any other forms of general argument for immortality, that the religious person turns in the last analysis. I have not myself been much impressed by the metaphysical arguments for immortality; those of Plato are thought to be particularly unsuccessful, although it is not unimpressive that a mind of such range and profundity should have held so firmly that the destiny of the soul is 'beyond'. But I am certain, and so must anyone be who thinks of finite beings as created beings in the Christian sense, that there is nothing in our nature that is inherently indestructible. Our existence could come to a total end, just as it is possible, on a sound view of mind and body, for us also to survive. Whether we do survive depends wholly, in my view, on God.

But the Christian claims that he knows the 'mind of God' towards us, that this has been made known 'at sundry times and in diverse manners in times past' and that God has 'in these last days spoken to us by His Son'. This leaves it very open what mode of being we shall have after death. Nothing is lost, but much gained, by speculating on this, by asking what a disembodied state would be like and whether there are degrees of disembodied existence—and so on? But the subject is bound to remain bewildering in many ways and will present us with some mysteries we cannot, in our present state, reduce. That does not daunt the Christian. His faith rests in what he knows of God and of the general purport of what God has meant us to be and to become. It is certain that this involves eternal fellowship with God, and where we do not hinder the work of God our salvation, and with it the removal of any ultimate sting of death, is assured. In the due appreciation of this hope there will be many reflections and processes of thought such as have been indicated already. But it is essentially a religious hope and not the conclusion of any independent philosophical arguments adequate on their own account. The Christian faced with death or bereavement finds his strength in the renewal of his essentially Christian hope and understanding, and when he falters it is to the original source of his faith in the experience of God in Christ that he turns. He does not claim that 'all things are put under him', infirmity and death will affright and strain him as they do others. But he will meet the 'last enemy' as he meets every other, he will put on the whole armour of God, and having made firm his faith, he will be able 'having done all to stand'. He will stand, not with stubborn determination of his own but in the strength of God.

FURTHER READING

On **Miracle.** A good general account of what has been thought on this subject may be found in *Miracle in History and Modern Thought* by C. J. Wright (Constable) and in the article on miracle in Hastings' *Encyclopedia of Religion and Ethics*. A good way of coming to grips with the subject is to examine Hume's famous treatment of it in *An Enquiry Concerning Human Understanding*, Section X, and consider it in relation to some recent discussion of Hume's arguments like those found in *Hume's Philosophy of Belief*, by Antony Flew, Chapter VIII (Routledge). This should be undertaken along with study of the position of Alan Richardson (*in Christian Apologetics*, Chapter VII, S.C.M.) as discussed by Ronald Hepburn (in *Christianity and Paradox*, Chapter VII), for the figure of Hume is much in the background of the sharply contrasted views of these writers.

Attempts to reconcile miracles with an unbroken continuity in the order of nature are found in H. H. Farmers' *The World and God* (Nisbet) Chapters VII, VIII, IX and X, and in F. R. Tennant's *Miracles* (Cambridge).

An approach along the lines of the position discussed in Chapter Ten of this book is found in I. T. Ramsey's *Miracles* (Oxford).

On **Evil.** A classical treatment of the problem of evil is that of Leibniz in his *Theodicy* (see English version, edited by Austin Farrer, Routledge). References to solutions in terms of the notion of 'a finite God' were given at the end of Chapter Thirteen. A sample of the views of F. R. Tennant on evil is found in Chapter XXIV of Ninian Smart's *Historical Selections in the Philosophy of Religion*, and the position of Tennant is discussed by Smart in Chapter VI of his *Philosophers and Religious Truth*. There is a section on 'The Mystery of Evil' in *Readings in Religious Philosophy*, edited by MacGregor/ Robb, and in Part VII of Geddes MacGregor's *Introduction to Religious Philosophy* (Macmillan). I particularly commend the chapters on 'Suffering' in C. A. Campbell's *Selfhood and Godhood* already mentioned.

On **Immortality.** For Plato's view see the *Phaedo* and the *Phaedrus*. For an indication of the attitude to death appropriate to the sceptic see *Immortal Longings*, by Stephen Findlay (Victor Gollancz).

Impressive critical discussion of the arguments for survival is found in C. D. Broad's *The Mind and its Place in Nature*, Section D.

A helpful presentation of the Christian view is that of William Temple in *Nature, Man and God*, Chapter XIX (Macmillan) and *Religious Experience*, pp. 112–23 (James Clarke). *Immortality*, by Pringle-Pattison is suggestive and informative, and I much commend the Address given by H. H. Price to the Society for Psychical Research in 1952. (*Proceedings* of the Society, Volume 50.) In this lecture Price offers some surmises as to what it would be like to survive.

CHAPTER TWENTY-SEVEN

OTHER RELIGIONS

A student of religion ought to take good account of religions
other than the one in which he is most at home, his own
religion or the religion of the culture and community to which
he belongs. Indication has already been given of the varied
significance which certain religious issues have in different
situations and contexts, as the same basic strains may have
very different embodiments in various modes of animate
existence. We learn much for this reason about religion from
inspection of the many varieties of it to be found at different
times and places. Much is gained by contact with unfamiliar
religious phenomena. On the other hand, no one is well
placed to understand such phenomena unless he brings to
them a sympathetic understanding from within a religious life
of his own. This does not mean that nothing at all may be
gained by the purely external study of religion. There are
many questions of fact that can be settled in that way, the
occurrence of certain events important for religion or the
formal nature of some religious performances. But the true
significance of factual matters of this kind, the inner meaning,
is not apprehended without proper sensitivity to what
religion is like obtained through our own involvement in it.

This has often been overlooked in the past, and there are
many scholars of today who aspire to bring the same sort of
exactitude to the study of religions as we require in the
physical sciences—and the same sort of objectivity. The result
of this is to restrict the scope of the subject severely. We can
bring strictly scientific methods to the study of some features
of religion, whether we think of religions of our own times
or of the remote past. We can conduct statistical investigations
of people's church-going habits, for example, or of the rise
and fall in the membership of various denominations. Not
that these matters are always as straightforward as might

appear at first. Church attendance means different things in different contexts, and it is well known that there are different ways of looking at figures. But there is no doubt that socio-logical studies of religion can be conducted in these and other ways, and that they can often be very revealing. It is no doubt of interest to know how membership of churches comes out in relation to various age-groups in a community, and how it is affected by economic changes. In the same way, it is of con-siderable interest, and sometimes of great value to general scholarship as well as to the study of religion, to have exact determination of the time ancient temples were built or of the period when instruments of worship, or other relics of early religions, were in use. Chemical analysis of the soil in which these were deposited can yield very precise results today, and we can sometimes date manuscripts or other copies of sacred writings with much exactitude by scientific methods. Of the value of these and kindred studies there can be no doubt. But they are also far from exhausting the subject, indeed I would say that they do not bring us to the core of the subject at all. For the vital thing about religions must surely be the aims and beliefs which people have in the observance of outward practice; and these we can only study by the exercise of much discrimination and judgement to interpret the evidence as plausibly and wisely as we can. The atheist will of course interpret much of it differently from the believer. But if, as I am convinced, the believer is right, he must, in a cautious way bring his understanding of what he finds religion gener-ally to be like to his interpretation of religious data remote from his own religion and culture.

This, as was noted earlier, commits us to various hazards, among them that of forcing the evidence too uncritically into the grooves with which we are most familiar ourselves. This is a risk we must take—and also a temptation we must resist. But there is nothing viciously subjective in examining the evidence available in the study of religions from within the understanding of religion we have in the practice of our own religion.

A distortion of this principle is the objectionable subjectiv-ity which overlooks the radical differences between religions and assumes too lightheartedly that there is a very close identity of substance or meaning in practices which are outwardly similar. At the other extreme we have the danger, into which many have fallen, of failing to recognize extensive similarities of substance when the outward forms and practices are different. It is because these perils beset us constantly that the subject of the study of religions calls for particular effort; although in some ways deceptively easy, it is in fact a difficult subject, but also an extremely rewarding and exciting one.

It is at an unusually exciting stage at present. To appreciate this we must cast our minds back over the development of the subject. It is, as the student will do well to remember, a subject of fairly recent origin. There have in the more distant past been sporadic attempts to collate information about religion and reflect upon it. Examples from antiquity may be found in the writings of Herodotus, Aristotle, Cicero and Plutarch. A study more in line with modern notions of the subject, and one of much interest still, is that of Lord Herbert of Cherbury. Speculations similar to those of Herbert, but not based on any systematic investigation, appear in the writings of Locke, and from the pen of David Hume there came a classical statement of the very 'naturalistic' account of the origin of religion which became the established approach to the subject for a period in the nineteenth century. This was *The Natural History of Religion* to which attention has already been drawn. I consider this book to be mistaken in all its main contentions, but I much admire the skill and clarity with which it presents one view of the origins of religion which is attractive in many respects and has been widely held. But in spite of these gifted sporadic attacks on the subject, it was not before the nineteenth century that the systematic study of the origins and development of religions began to take a clearly recognizable form.

This came about through the advance of science and the general acceptance of the idea of evolution. The notion of man's ascent from inferior modes of life naturally focused much attention on the question of origins, ethics being traced for example to animal sympathy and sometimes discredited for that reason. Notable archaeological discoveries stimulated anthropological studies in various parts of the world and many theories were formed about pre-historic times and about important stages on the way to civilized existence. The religious side of this study was much influenced at first by the conditions which prompted it, including the belief, given expression in the writings of Herbert Spencer and some followers of Hegel, that history showed a continuous and inevitable progress from simpler to more elaborate modes of being. A tendency to read back our own ideas and purposes into the practices of other peoples, and thus to 'rationalize' these practices unduly, was also evident.

This resulted in the view of religion known as animism, according to which religion began with personifications of natural objects and worship of the spirits of the departed. It was thought that this led at later stages to various forms of monotheism resulting from the craving for system and unity. Notable exponents of this view were E. B. Tyler whose treatise *Primitive Culture* was published in 1871 and Sir James Frazer, author of the renowned and widely read work *The Golden Bough*. Both writers, but especially Tyler, owed much to Comte. Comte wrote before the publication of Darwin's *Origin of Species* and propounded the view of religion as passing through the following stages: firstly, there was the worship of many gods leading to the worship of one God, secondly, the latter gave way to metaphysical notions and the belief in abstract essences, and finally we have the dissolution of religion before the scientific explanation of phenomena. The proneness to make man himself 'the measure of all things' has thus been clearly at work in 'The Study of Religions' as a systematic study and is still very marked in much of the course which it takes today.

A rude blow was struck at these notions of early religion as man's attempt to read his own experiences into the world around him by the discovery, made known especially by Andrew Lang in his important book *The Making of Religion*, of High Gods among very early peoples, the High God being a Supreme Being who created Himself and the earth and was sometimes thought to have dwelt at one time on the earth, for example the All-Father of the Australian aborigines.

The High God appears to have been too remote from men's ordinary concerns to have had a permanent hold on their interest, but it is very significant that there should be this evidence of the acknowledgement of a Being totally different from ourselves among our primitive ancestors. R. R. Marett and J. H. King are also notable scholars who exposed the artificiality of Tyler's animism. J. H. King, in his *The Supernatural, its Origins, Nature and Evolution*, stresses the presence of the element of mystery in all religious experience, while Marett coined the term 'Animatism' for the view that the savage responds to the discovery of life and power in nature by treating it as a supernatural occurrence. The French anthropologist Lévy-Bruhl drew attention also to evidence of what he called 'prelogical' factors in primitive mentality. But much the most important name here is Rudolf Otto. He completely reversed the naturalism of his predecessors in the field of comparative religion by finding in the earliest forms of religion some of the most important evidence for his view of religion as man's response to a Supreme Reality wholly other than man himself, the *mysterium tremendum et fascinans*.

The course which the Study of Religions takes today is much influenced by two factors. The first of these is the importance ascribed by many influential theologians to the idea of the transcendence of God. The most important name here is that of Karl Barth, but ideas very similar to his in substance are found in the writings of persons whose names are often bracketed with his, namely Emil Brunner and Reinhold Niebuhr. A like emphasis on the transcendence of God is found in the work of writers known as the Neo-Thomists, and, if I am correct in what I have maintained earlier, they have a shrewder grasp of the true significance of God's transcendence and the way it is forced upon us. It is this that has enabled them to exhibit to us the genuine importance of the traditional arguments for the existence of God, which was the subject of discussion earlier in this book. The position of these writers leaves room for natural theology and a grasp of certain truths about God independently of God's particular disclosure of Himself in Hebrew-Christian experience. For Barth, however, and for many of his followers, the 'otherness' of God is understood in such a way as to exclude the possibility of His being known at all outside one distinctive revelation. This attitude is much conditioned by a notion of the corruption of man's faculties through his sinful state which is bound up with the very inadequate way in which Barthians have grasped the idea of God's transcendence to which they are so genuinely and profoundly sensitive. The upshot of it is that they tend to deny, and sometimes do firmly deny, that there can be any significant and reliable truth about God outside the Christian revelation, and they affirm, for this reason, that there is no truth in non-Christian religions.

This view does not encourage patient study of other religions, and it certainly does not conduce to a good understanding of them. They tend to be studied as merely natural phenomena, as modes of human interest and activity which have nothing to do with religion in the proper sense. In this respect, as in many others, the Barthian theologian is apt to join forces with the humanist and offer some entirely sociological or psychological account of 'other religions'; these come to be interpreted in terms of fear or the desire for security, and they are sometimes ascribed to crude superstitions. There is no doubt much crudity and superstition in most religions, and no religion can claim to be entirely free of corruptions of this kind. Christians have often lapsed into idolatry and superstition, and they have often thought of God as a Being before whom we stand in abject terror and not One to be approached in a spirit of worshipful awe. It may also happen that God is not a reality genuinely experienced by all professing Christians; God may be for them, as for others, a figment of the imagination set up for our comfort. There are no doubt bogus forms of Christianity, and there are likewise genuine forms of other religions. If the Christian is right, no other religion has the whole truth as he has it; and there are aspects of other religions which he must reject, as members of other religions must reject much which he holds. But the Christian is in no way bound to deny that there is genuine awareness of God in other faiths or to suppose that God has not been at work in any way in other religions.

The notion that we must have a sharp dichotomy between

Christianity and other faiths, in the sense that Christianity must claim a monopoly of all truth about God, goes along, as I have said, with much which the humanist says about world religions; and here we come to the other main influence on the study of religions which I wish to note, namely the empiricism of which closer account was taken earlier in this book. The spread of empiricism has given a new impetus to accounts of religion entirely in terms of man and his hopes and fears in this world. Much in the anthropological study of religion today has taken this course. But we have also seen that, if the challenge of recent empiricism is properly faced, it gives us a new and subtle understanding of religion; and the most exciting feature of the study of world religions today is found, in my opinion, when we bring to bear upon the problems they present the insights obtained in seeking to discover how precisely to answer the empiricist and the demands associated with his approach to the problem of truth. It has often been taken for granted, for example, that Buddhism is a 'religion without God', and there is much in some of the main sources of our information about Buddhism,[1] like the Pali Canon, to support this view. A more subtle analysis of the relevant texts, however, will disclose that Buddha seems to have been anxious, not to dispense with God in the true sense, but to get rid of crude notions of God and come to a very subtle understanding of what it is really like to encounter God in the way set out by those who stress the elusiveness and mystery of God today. There are similar ways in which some of the major problems of Confucianism or of Islam are set in a new and most revealing light by the advances in our understanding of what religion is like today. We acquire, in the same fashion, a much profounder grasp of the origins of religion and of what is altogether involved in what we sometimes describe as 'primitive religions'.

This is not the place to follow out these suggestions further. They would need a book to themselves, and the present work is already somewhat long for the series in which it appears. As I hinted at the outset, one of the constant and most trying problems of the philosopher is to limit the scope of his

[1]. See my 'Buddha and God', *The Monist*, 1963.

investigations, since major philosophical problems run into one another, and this is true of the 'study of religions' in its relation to the philosophy of religion. One must, however, set oneself a reasonable limit, and the most that I can do now is to urge the student of religion to consider the problems raised in this book, and the solutions suggested for them, in relation to other religions than his own and to seek to inform himself as fully as he can about the main features of such religions and their history. There are available now many instructive popular books on the subject, and scholars are, I believe, gaining a better understanding of the true nature of the problems presented by the study of religions. The near future should see some exciting developments in the conduct of the subject, and there are also new and colourful discoveries about various religions made possible by new techniques and more exhaustive knowledge of the appropriate languages and their history. If the historical scholar and the philosopher can overcome some natural suspicion they still have of one another and pool their resources, the study of religions could become one of the most illuminating features of contemporary culture, and it will have no mean place in the attempts of people all over the world today to solve urgent practical problems and learn to work for the good of all with mutual respect and understanding. The philosophy of religion, in its vigorous renewal today, has its part to play in this wide context as well as in the more strictly academic one, but it must not be debased in the process. It can best serve the aims of general culture and the needs of society at large by being altogether true to itself as a patient search for truth and understanding. Nowhere is the lure of the 'short way' to be more firmly resisted than in the philosophy of religion and the studies with which it is most closely allied, like the history of religions. In urging the reader, as I earnestly do, to conduct his philosophical study of religion in close association with the more historical study of various religions, and perhaps to make a particularly close examination of one or two religions other than his own, I must also impress upon him the need to extend his own knowledge of the philosophical problems of religion far beyond the very limited view of them by which, one hopes, his appetite for the study of religion has been whetted in this elementary work.

FURTHER READING

The following books will be found a useful addition to the books mentioned in the preceding chapter.

Comparative Religion. Geoffrey Parrinder (George Allen and Unwin Limited).

Comparative Religion. E. O. James.

The Ancient Gods. E. O. James (Weidenfeld and Nicolson).

At Sundry Times. R. C. Zaehner.

A Dialogue of Religions. Ninian Smart (S.C.M.).

World Religions and World Community. R. L. Slater (Columbia).

The first of the books listed here, namely Parrinder's *Comparative Religion* provides a very valuable survey of the present state of the subject. In Professor Slater's book the place of various religions in the general life of society is given prominence. Outlines of the main beliefs and other features of the great religions are provided in a series of books on the great religions in Hutchinson's University Library and in the corresponding books in the Penguin series.

INDEX OF NAMES

INDEX OF SUBJECTS

OTHER BOOKS by H. D. LEWIS

Morals and Revelation

'Professor H. D. Lewis is an academic philosopher with the courage to be unfashionable. Not only does he challenge some of the presuppositions of both the main schools in ethics; he even goes so far as to discuss at length and with a conviction of its first-rate importance the connexions between ethics and religion.'

'The whole book is closely reasoned and trenchantly expressed: it demands and rewards close and con-concentrated study.' *Guardian*

Freedom and History

'Discussions of the nature of history, of objectivity in history, of religion and history, and of responsibility in law and morality which express deep concern about freedom and the way it is imperilled by misunderstandings and abuses.'

'Sensitive and intelligent, this delightfully reasoned book by a scholar of deep Christian devotion is most welcome.' *Cork Examiner*

Clarity is Not Enough

'Should be of keen interest to the Christian who has any interest at all in the philosophy of religion ... a volume of real significance and should be read by all who are interested in what the thinking world is saying today.' *Christian*

Our Experience of God

'In many ways this book is a model of what philosophical writing about religion should be like.'
Ethics

'A consistent Christian shows over a wide area of reflections what thoughtful belief can be like.'
Philosophy

'One is carried along as though in a rigorously logical channel ... we can do no more than call attention to the inestimable service he has rendered by the scholarly and liberal spirit in which he has treated some of the leading problems in the philosophy of religion.' *Times Literary Supplement*

'The present study in the philosophy of religion is an admirable example of the vitality and richness of this broader, non-linguistic current of English philosophical thought and its relevance to the contemporary world ... There is an extraordinary amount of intelligent, sensitive, and eminently quotable wisdom contained in the author's reflections on the relation between religion and art, symbolism, morality, etc.'
The International Philosophical Quarterly

Published by Allen & Unwin

40 MUSEUM STREET LONDON W.C.1.